Searching For My Identity

Volume 1

The Chronological Evolution Of A Troubled Adolescent To Outlaw Biker

---

Edward Winterhalder

Blockhead City
Jenison, Michigan

Published by Blockhead City, PO Box 145, Jenison, MI 49429

Publisher's Cataloging-in-Publication data

Names: Winterhalder, Edward, 1955-, author.
Title: Searching for my identity : The chronological evolution of a troubled adolescent to outlaw biker / Edward Winterhalder.
Description: Jenison, MI: Blockhead City, 2022.
Identifiers: LCCN: 2022934220 | ISBN: 979-8-9858817-0-7 (print) | 979-8-9858817-2-1 (ebook)
Subjects: LCSH Winterhalder, Edward, 1955-. | Biker clubs-USE-Motorcycle clubs-Biography. | Bikers-USE-Motorcyclists-Biography. | Criminal behavior-BT-Criminal psychology-Biography. | Criminal behavior-BT-Deviant behavior-Biography. | Criminals-RT-Criminology-Biography. | Criminals-NT-Outlaws-Biography. | Criminals-Psychology-USE-Criminal psychology-Biography. | Criminals-Rehabilitation-UF-Reform of criminals-Biography. | Ethnology-UF-Ethnography-Biography. | Ethnology-UF-Social anthropology-Biography. | Ethnology-NT-Outcasts-Biography. | Motorcycle clubs-UF-Biker clubs-Biography. | Motorcycle clubs-BT-Motorcycles—Societies, etc.-Biography. | Motorcycle gangs-UF-Gangs, Motorcycle-Biography. | Motorcycle gangs-BT-Motorcycles—Societies, etc.-Biography. | Outlaws-BT-Criminals-Biography. | Outlaws in popular culture-BT-Popular culture-Biography. | Popular culture-UF-Pop culture-Biography. | Popular culture-NT-Anthropology in popular culture-Biography. | Popular culture-NT-Outlaws in popular culture-Biography. | BISAC BIOGRAPHY & AUTOBIOGRAPHY / Criminals & Outlaws | BIOGRAPHY & AUTOBIOGRAPHY / Personal Memoir
Classification: LCC HS101-330.7 .W56 2022 | HM811-821 .W56 2022 | GN301-674 .W56 2022

Paperback: July 2023   1st Edition

To my brothers Joe John Edwards, Bruce "Fuzz" Terreson and Stanley Lynde, who are gone but not forgotten

EDWARD WINTERHALDER BOOKS

IN DUTCH:

De Assimilatie: Rock Machine Wordt Bandidos – Bikers Verenigd Tegen De Hells Angels by Edward Winterhalder & Wil De Clercq (2023)

IN ENGLISH:

A Wild Ride In The Fast Lane: A Collection Of True Stories And Tall Tales From My Life As An Outlaw Biker by Edward Winterhalder (2025)

Real Bikers Of North America: Men Who Rode With An Outlaw Motorcycle Club by Edward Winterhalder (2025)

Searching For My Identity (Vol 1): The Chronological Evolution Of A Troubled Adolescent To Outlaw Biker by Edward Winterhalder (2022)

Searching For My Identity (Vol 2): The Chronological Evolution Of An Outlaw Biker On The Road To Redemption by Edward Winterhalder (2022)

The Blue and Silver Shark: A Biker's Story (Book 5 in the Series) by Edward Winterhalder & Marc Teatum (2015)

Biker Chicz: The Attraction of Women To Motorcycles And Outlaw Bikers by Edward Winterhalder & Wil De Clercq (2014)

The Ultimate Biker Anthology: An Introduction to Books About Motorcycle Clubs And Outlaw Bikers by Edward Winterhalder & Iain Parke (2013)

The Moon Upstairs: A Biker's Story (Book 4 in the Series) by Edward Winterhalder & Marc Teatum (2012). Based on an original concept by Wil De Clercq

One Light Coming: A Biker's Story (Book 3 in the Series) by Edward Winterhalder & Marc Teatum (2011)

Biker Chicz of North America by Edward Winterhalder & Wil De Clercq (2010)

The Mirror: A Biker's Story (Book 2 in the Series) by Edward Winterhalder & James Richard Larson (2010)

Biker Chicks: The Magnetic Attraction of Women to Bad Boys and Motorbikes by Edward Winterhalder, Wil De Clercq & Arthur Veno (2009)

All Roads Lead to Sturgis: A Biker's Story (Book 1 in the Series) by Edward Winterhalder & James Richard Larson (2009)

The Assimilation: Rock Machine Become Bandidos – Bikers United Against the Hells Angels by Edward Winterhalder & Wil De Clercq (2008)

Out in Bad Standings: Inside the Bandidos Motorcycle Club – The Making of a Worldwide Dynasty by Edward Winterhalder (2005)

IN FRENCH:

Une Course Folle Sur La Voie Rapide: Recueil Histoires Vraies Et Récits Fantastiques Tirées De Ma Vie De Motard Hors-La-Loi by Edward Winterhalder (2025)

Vrais Motards D'Amérique Du Nord: Les Hommes Qui Ont Roulé Avec Un Club De Motards Hors-La-Loi by Edward Winterhalder (2025)

Tous Les Chemins Menent A Sturgis: Une Histoire De Motard (Livre 1 de la Serie) by Edward Winterhalder & James Richard Larson (2023)

Le Miroir: Une Histoire De Motard (Livre 2 De La Serie) by Edward Winterhalder & James Richard Larson (2023)

Un Lumière Venant: Une Histoire De Motard (Livre 3 De La Serie) by Edward Winterhalder & Marc Teatum (2023)

La Lune À L'étage: Une Histoire De Motard (Livre 4 De La Serie) by Edward Winterhalder & Marc Teatum (2023)

Le Requin Bleu Et Argent: Une Histoire De Motard (Livre 5 De La Serie) by Edward Winterhalder & Marc Teatum (2023)

Recherche De Mon Identité (Vol 1): L'évolution Chronologique D'un Adolescent Troublé Au Motard Hors-la-loi by Edward Winterhalder (2022)

Recherche De Mon Identité (Vol 2): L'évolution Chronologique D'un Motard Hors-la-loi Sur La Route De La Rédemption by Edward Winterhalder (2022)

L'Assimilation: Rock Machine Devient Bandidos - Bikers United Contre Les Hells Angels by Edward Winterhalder & Wil De Clercq (2021)

Motarde Femmes: L'Attirance Des Femmes Pour Les Motos Et Les Motards Hors-La-Loi by Edward Winterhalder & Wil De Clercq (2021)

L'Ultime Anthologie Biker: Une Introduction Aux Livres Sur Les Clubs De Motards Et Les Motards Hors-La-Loi by Edward Winterhalder & Iain Parke (2021)

Biker Chicz D'Amérique Du Nord by Edward Winterhalder & Wil De Clercq (2021)

L'Assimilation: Rock Machine & Bandidos Contre Hells Angels by Edward Winterhalder & Wil De Clercq (2009)

IN GERMAN:

Eine Wilde Fahrt Auf Der Überholspur: Eine Sammlung Wahrer Geschichten Und Fabeln Aus Meinem Leben Als Outlaw-Biker by Edward Winterhalder (2025)

Echte Biker Von Nordamerika: Männer Die Mit Einem Outlaw-Motorradclub Fuhren by Edward Winterhalder (2025)

Alle Wege Führen Nach Sturgis: Die Geschichte Eines Bikers (Buch 1 Der Reihe) by Edward Winterhalder & James Richard Larson (2023)

Der Spiegel: Die Geschichte Eines Bikers (Buch 2 Der Reihe) by Edward Winterhalder & James Richard Larson (2023)

Ein Licht Kommt: Die Geschichte Eines Bikers (Buch 3 Der Reihe) by Edward Winterhalder & Marc Teatum (2023)

Der Mond Nach Oben: Die Geschichte Eines Bikers (Buch 4 Der Reihe) by Edward Winterhalder & Marc Teatum (2023)

Der Blau Und Silber Hai: Die Geschichte Eines Bikers (Buch 5 Der Reihe) by Edward Winterhalder & Marc Teatum (2023)

Auf Der Suche Nach Meiner Identität (Band 1): Die Chronologische Entwicklung Eines Schwierigen Jugendlichen Zum Outlaw Biker by Edward Winterhalder (2022)

Auf Der Suche Nach Meiner Identität (Band 2): Die Chronologische Entwicklung Eines Outlaw Biker Auf Dem Weg Zur Vergebung by Edward Winterhalder (2022)

Die Übernahme: Von Der Rock Machine Zu Den Bandidos Der Bikerkrieg In Kanada by Edward Winterhalder & Wil De Clercq (2021)

Biker Frauen: Die Anziehungskraft Von Frauen Auf Motorräder Und Outlaw-Bikers by Edward Winterhalder & Wil De Clercq (2021)

Die Ultimativ Biker-Anthologie: Eine Einführung in Bücher über Motorradclubs & Outlaw Biker by Edward Winterhalder & Iain Parke (2021)

Biker Chicz Von Nordamerika by Edward Winterhalder & Wil De Clercq (2021)

Die Ubernahme: Von Der Rock Machine Zu Den Bandidos – Der Bikerkrieg In Kanada by Edward Winterhalder & Wil De Clercq (2010)

IN JAPANESE:

自分の正体を求めて(第1巻)：悩み多き青少年からアウトロー・バイカーへの経時的進化 by Edward Winterhalder (2024)

自分の正体を求めて (第2巻)：贖罪への道を歩むアウトロー・バイカーの経時的進化 by Edward Winterhalder (2024)

IN SPANISH:

Un Viaje Salvaje Por El Carril Rápido: Una Recopilación De Historias Reales Y Cuentos Fantásticos De Mi Vida Como Motero Fuera De La Ley by Edward Winterhalder (2025)

Auténticos Motoristas De Norteamérica: Hombres Que Cabalgaron Con Un Club De Moteros Fuera De La Ley by Edward Winterhalder (2025)

Buscando Mi Identidad (Vol 1): La Evolución Cronológica De Un Adolescente Con Problemas A Un Motociclista Fuera De La Ley by Edward Winterhalder (2022)

Buscando Mi Identidad (Vol 2): La Evolución Cronológica De Un Motociclista Fuera De La Ley En El Camino Hacia La Redención by Edward Winterhalder (2022)

Todos Los Caminos Llevan A Sturgis: La Historia De Un Motorista (Libro 1 de la Serie) by Edward Winterhalder & James Richard Larson (2023)

El Espejo: La Historia De Un Motorista (Libro 2 de la Serie) by Edward Winterhalder & James Richard Larson (2023)

Uno Ligero Que Viene: La Historia De Un Motorista (Libro 3 de la Serie) by Edward Winterhalder & Marc Teatum (2023)

La Luna Arriba: La Historia De Un Motorista (Libro 4 de la Serie) by Edward Winterhalder & Marc Teatum (2023)

El Tiburón Azul Y Plata: La Historia De Un Motorista (Libro 5 de la Serie) by Edward Winterhalder & Marc Teatum (2023)

La Asimilación: Rock Machine Volverse Bandidos – Motociclistas Unidos Contra Los Hells Angels by Edward Winterhalder & Wil De Clercq (2021)

Mujeres Motociclistas: La Atracción De Las Mujeres Por Las Motocicletas Y Los Motociclistas Fuera De La Ley by Edward Winterhalder & Wil De Clercq (2021)

El Último Antologia Biker: Introducción A Los Libros Sobre Clubes De Motociclistas Y Motociclistas Fuera De La Ley by Edward Winterhalder & Iain Parke (2021)

Biker Chicz De América Del Norte by Edward Winterhalder & Wil De Clercq (2021)

EDWARD WINTERHALDER WEBSITE & SOCIAL MEDIA

Website:

http://www.blockheadcity.com

Wikipedia:

http://en.wikipedia.org/wiki/Edward_Winterhalder

IMDB:

http://www.imdb.com/name/nm3034980

YouTube:

http://www.youtube.com/c/BlockheadCity

LinkedIn:

http://www.linkedin.com/in/edwardwinterhalder

Instagram:

https://www.instagram.com/blockheadcity

Twitter:

https://twitter.com/BlockheadCity

Edward Winterhalder Music

AT LONG LAST
Warren Winters Band
Vinyl LP Record (1980)

AS I WAS
Warren Winters Band
Vinyl LP Record (1984)

CROSSBAR HOTEL
Warren Winters Band
Vinyl LP Record/Cassette (1988)

THE BEST OF WARREN WINTERS
Warren Winters Band
CD (1995)

THEN & NOW
Warren Winters Band
Digital Album (2020)

THE NAME OF THE GAME
Warren Winters Band
Music Video/Digital Song (2020)

Searching For My Identity: The Chronological Evolution Of A Troubled Adolescent To Outlaw Biker

Table Of Contents

Searching For My Identity: The Chronological Evolution
Of A Troubled Adolescent To Outlaw Biker

Searching For My Identity: The Chronological Evolution
Of A Troubled Adolescent To Outlaw Biker

Introduction

Looking back on my life now that I'm in my mid-sixties, it's easy to see the good, the bad, and the ugly. Some of the choices I made were good, some were bad, and some downright reckless. Some of my decisions had consequences, while others didn't. Part of my behavior was inherited and part of my behavior was learned. I realize and accept I'm psychologically skewed, and the primary reason is deeply rooted in my dysfunctional childhood.

Raised by my adopted mother and father—an alcoholic who didn't have the capability to love or care for a child—in an environment devoid of nurturing, the situations I experienced in my developmental years impacted me throughout my entire life and left me constantly searching for my identity.

The lack of affection I experienced during childhood was compounded by the constant arguing that occurred between my adopted parents on a daily basis, as well as my adopted father's increasing lack of interest as I got older.

The heavy burden of childhood I carried was hidden away for decades and never discussed with family or close friends. During my journey from troubled adolescent to outlaw biker the signs of dysfunctionality were plain to see as I traveled the road of life, but I was deliberately oblivious.

After I met my biological father in 1994 and got to know him well, I realized he was also psychologically skewed from a dysfunctional childhood. His emotional capabilities were also compromised, leaving him self-centered and unable to love or care for another human being.

Over the years I've often wondered about the origins of my dysfunctionality. Is the primary cause of my psychologically skewed mind the result of inherited behavior, learned behavior, or a combination of both?

Another unusual aspect of my life—until I was 44 years old—was the type of women I was attracted to and enjoyed being with, for almost all of them had a common trait. They suffered some type of abuse during their childhood and/or had low self-esteem. Because I was around strip joints on a daily basis, as well as involved in the management and ownership of the dance halls, a lot of these women were strippers.

I never realized this characteristic until my daughter's therapist pointed it out one day in 1998. She said, *"It's obvious that you have dated the same type of female over and over again your entire life. You must change the selection pool from which you choose your women, or you'll never have a healthy relationship."*

Although it took a few days for that conversation to sink in I soon realized she was correct. It was a revelation that caused me to reconsider the appealing attributes of the females I dated in the future.

Did I date strippers, women who had suffered childhood abuse, and women that had low self-esteem because of my psychologically skewed mind? And if so, was it the result of inherited behavior, learned behavior, or a combination of both?

The primary reason I've sought acceptance my entire life has eluded me. Have I sought acceptance because I never had a positive male role model during childhood and my adopted father repeatedly told me I'd never amount to anything, or maybe it was the result of being abandoned by my birth mother the day I was born and spending the first six months of my life in an orphanage?

You are about to embark on a strange trip into a world you couldn't possibly imagine, but before you dive in to my chronicles please be advised that it's my intention to provide you with a more accurate portrayal of a typical motorcycle club member than what you're accustomed to. I hope my life experiences will bring you a much clearer perception as to what an outlaw biker really is, and why he—or she—is an outlaw biker.

The majority of the world's motorcycle club members are legitimate hardworking men that rarely cause anyone problems. Contrary to the meth-addicted violence prone image regularly portrayed by the media, most of today's outlaw bikers are productive contributing members of society that love motorcycles and the lifestyle, and the only thing they're guilty of is having too much fun on the weekends.

While exploring my tumultuous world, you'll take an extraordinary journey into the hostile environment where I lived for almost thirty years as a member of—or closely associated with—major outlaw motorcycle clubs worldwide. The majority of the time I was gainfully employed, but simultaneously lived most days as if every day was a holiday—living that way was mandatory in the traditional biker lifestyle I maintained.

As a full patched member and national officer first with the Rogues motorcycle club and then with the Bandidos motorcycle club, I regularly traveled the world. Along the way I authored books about the outlaw biker lifestyle; produced television shows that have been seen all over the world; spent time in prison; and bought, sold, built and repaired hundreds of Harleys.

During my life I also managed a rock band; owned a construction management company; produced, recorded and manufactured four record albums of songs I wrote; bought, sold and flipped residential real estate properties; raised a beautiful daughter; and married the most beautiful woman I've ever known, my Conquistadora.

This is my story, written in my own words over the last eighteen years. I apologize in advance if you find the writing style crude or immature, but please understand I'm an outlaw biker, not a literary master who has benefited from creative writing or journalism classes at university.

I truly hope that you enjoy the journey while you read both volumes of *Searching For My Identity.* Volume 1 of my memoir— from the sixties to January of 2001—is *The Chronological Evolution Of A Troubled Adolescent To Outlaw Biker.* Volume 2—

Searching For My Identity: The Chronological Evolution
Of A Troubled Adolescent To Outlaw Biker

from January of 2001 to December of 2020—is *The Chronological Evolution Of An Outlaw Biker On The Road To Redemption.*

Don't ever forget you're the master of your destiny, always believe in yourself and ride safe!

Edward "Connecticut Ed" Winterhalder

January 2022

Chapter 1

The Very Beginning

June 1955 To September 1967

The day after I was born in the summer of 1955 my birth mother gave me up for adoption and I was sent to a foster home. At the time my biological father had no idea what was going on—my mother was in the process of getting divorced from him, and they had no contact with each other. As soon as he became aware of my fate my father petitioned the court in Hartford for custody but was unsuccessful. I've often wondered if this inauspicious beginning contributed to the path I took in life—adventure, recalcitrance, and misadventure—which eventually led to the world of outlaw bikers.

Six months later I was adopted by Warren and Helen (Dolly) Winterhalder. The childless couple resided in Hamden, a quiet suburb of New Haven, Connecticut. Warren was a World War II veteran and business forms salesman, and his wife a homemaker. I spent the first few years of my life playing in the backyard of our Gorham Avenue home, and attended kindergarten nearby.

Not long after I turned six we moved to a brand-new house in the center of a middle-class neighborhood in Northford, a town of less than one-thousand residents. A thirty-minute drive from Hamden, our new home was a three-bedroom, split-level house on Carlen Drive, which was a cul-de-sac. On the north side of the

1

turnaround area at the end of the street was a pond, on the south side a large field where the neighborhood kids played baseball and football, and between the pond and field was a basketball hoop. The pond had a man-made dam, and there was a narrow bridge over the dam just wide enough for a human or bicycle to cross.

My earliest memory of the neighborhood was my mom allowing me to walk our dog, Skeeter, for the first time. I had to work hard to convince her that I could handle the canine, which weighed about as much as I did. Not long after Dolly handed me the leash Skeeter must have seen a cat, and the chase was on. I must have looked like a flag on a flagpole as the dog dragged me across the cul-de-sac. By the time she got Skeeter to stop running, I had suffered my first case of serious road rash. My pants and shirt were ripped open and I was a mess, bleeding all over the place.

In September of 1961 I started first grade at the William Douglas elementary school in Northford. I was nothing special, just another new kid on the block, but I did manage to get run over by a bunch of fifth graders playing football at recess time, causing my left leg to fracture below the knee.

When I was eight-years old I transferred to another school in Northford, along with every other student who had completed second grade. My only memory of the Stanley T. Williams elementary school is when president John F. Kennedy was assassinated on November 22nd of 1963. All the teachers were crying and the children were dismissed an hour early—school was even closed for the next few days. Everyone I knew was excited to be out of school until we found out that every TV channel had nothing on except news about the murder.

One day I was exploring the woods on the other side of the pond and discovered a yellow jacket hornet's nest in a hollow at the base of a tree. I was fascinated with the little creatures, but not knowing a thing about them, I put my hand into the tree to see what would happen. It didn't take long to find out, and as a result of my stupidity I was stung more than fifty times. It took my mom an hour to pull out the stingers and apply baking soda to my wounds.

By the time fourth grade rolled around I had figured out that I was smarter than most of the other kids. I was basically a straight A student, and spent a lot of time reading. Although I liked to read, I also loved watching television. Among my favorite shows growing up were *Bonanza, Wagon Train, Route 66*, and *Mission Impossible*. I found out years later that my biological father was an actor on *Wagon Train*—there I was glued to the television set, unknowingly watching my real father acting in one of my favorite westerns.

I soon developed a fascination with Myron Floren, who played accordion on the Lawrence Welk show, and as a result convinced my parents to let me take accordion lessons at the Betty Revegno music studio in Wallingford. Eighteen months later I was lucky enough to win first place in a state competition for ten-year old accordion players, but soon discovered the instrument wasn't very hip—I decided the guitar was a much better choice.

My mom and dad wouldn't let me have a guitar or take guitar lessons, so I continued my accordion lessons just so I could learn from a guitar teacher at the studio. I would go there early, and she would let me sit in the room and watch the sessions. After my accordion lesson I was able to borrow a school-owned guitar and practice what I had learned. It would be years before I could put all those guitar lessons to work, but I eventually did.

Until September of 1966 my life was fairly normal, with the exception that most of the neighborhood kids ostracized me for being intelligent. Like most kids my age I wasn't good at sports, and failed miserably when given the opportunity. Despite the fact, I joined an organized Little League baseball team for a year and got to warm the bench, play outfield and second base. At an early age it was obvious playing sports was clearly not my forte and I moved on to bigger and better things.

When I was ten my entrepreneurial spirit began manifesting itself—I started shoveling snow, mowing lawns, and helping out at a dairy farm that bordered the neighborhood. The work didn't pay much, but provided enough money to purchase vinyl LP records from my favorite musical artists at the local discount store.

A favorite pastime of mine was watching new houses get built in the neighborhood. This was the era of urban sprawl, and houses were going up left and right. For reasons unknown to me at the time I was fascinated with the construction process—it was as if building was ingrained in my soul. Thirty years later I learned that my biological father, grandfather, and great-grandfather were all master builders and carpenters. The apple definitely doesn't fall far from the tree, and I eventually followed in their footsteps.

It was around this time that my parents told me I was adopted—this revelation changed my perspective on life in general. Although initially I was a little surprised when I heard the news, the stark reality of the situation explained a lot of things. Although the thought had crossed my mind, now I knew for sure why I was so different from my adopted parents in appearance, mentality and character.

The constant bickering that had been occurring in my home on a daily basis for as long as I could remember also had a profound impact on my childhood, and still does today. Warren would start drinking as soon as he got home from work, and then start arguing with Dolly shortly thereafter. My adopted parents would quarrel about everything, even mundane issues like the location of ornaments on the Christmas tree. They argued before dinner, during dinner, and after dinner—it never stopped. In the summer of 1966 I started avoiding the situation by not coming home after school, and eating dinner at a friend's house whenever I could.

Searching For My Identity: The Chronological Evolution
Of A Troubled Adolescent To Outlaw Biker

My adopted father was an average man who carried a lot of emotional baggage from the sudden death of his father when he was twelve. In hindsight I suppose it's likely that Warren was self-medicating, but I was too young to understand the concept. Although my mom was proud of my high intellect, my dad resented it. One time he got very upset when I managed to put together a Christmas present I received—Warren had been unable to assemble the toy and must have been embarrassed, because he never bought me another present that required assembly.

Until this time I didn't have any close friends, and loneliness was my constant companion. Music was an escape mechanism that allowed me to avoid the reality of my home life, but that was no longer keeping me pacified. I was beginning the search for my identity, but didn't know it.

I was transferred to the junior high school in North Branford for the start of sixth grade in September of 1966. Northford was part of North Branford, and I had to travel about five miles on the bus to get to school, which I thought was a long way to travel!

The sixth graders from North Branford were different, and I soon fell into what some would say was the wrong crowd. These kids didn't mock me for being smart, or condemn me for my lack of talent on the sports field. They accepted me as one of their own, and soon I was one of the group's leaders and main instigators. My new friends were from the 'other side of the tracks', but I felt at home with them for reasons I didn't understand. Since I had been raised as an only child all my life, it's quite possible that for the first time I felt what it was like to have brothers.

During my sixth-grade year I went through a massive amount of change. Until then I had been a model student and diligent son, but now I was starting to question all types of authority and developed new friendships that would have a monumental impact on me. The first and foremost was Peter "Pete" Hansen. Pete was the sixth of seven sons, and he was my age. He had two older brothers that I knew of then, Walter "Walt" Hansen and Harry "Skip" Hansen. They were all big, tough kids with serious reputations for not taking shit from anyone.

Pete and I did a lot of stupid things together the next few years, none of which made our parents proud. We found it easier to skip school and get in trouble, than to do our homework. We became the best of friends and were almost inseparable. After sixth grade ended in June of 1967 Pete ran away from home. I hid him in the woods, about two miles from my house, in an abandoned campground near a train track. Our immature plan was for him to hop the train, which was supposed to take him to a land of pleasure somewhere, but he overslept and missed the train.

When I caught up to Pete the next morning his big brother Walt was closing in. As we were crossing a huge sand pit going to who knows where, we saw his brother driving toward us from a mile away. Pete and I hid in the bushes at the side of a creek while

Walt stopped the car on the other side, less than fifty feet away. Not realizing the two of us were nearby, Walt started hollering for Pete and then shouted, *"If you can hear me, you better go home now!"* If Walt had caught him, I'm sure Pete's ass would have been grass.

By this time I was totally disgusted with the accordion, and to my parents' dismay had quit taking lessons as well as practicing. Making money had become one of the most important things in my life, for I had figured out that having money made the world go around. The summer before, when I was eleven, I had worked hard mowing about twenty lawns every week using my dad's older Simplicity riding lawn mower. The Simplicity was a novelty and I felt like the king of the hill racing around on the machine, but at the end of the season the engine gave up and died from my abuse. The fact that I drove the mower like a hotrod no doubt helped it along to its final resting place on the scrap heap.

Wanting to teach me a lesson I'd never forget (which he did), Warren went out and bought himself a brand-new riding lawn mower at my expense. To my horror he spent every dime I had saved from mowing lawns, so I had basically worked all summer for free. I was upset, and vowed to find another source of income.

Although I still cut one or two lawns on my day off, the summer of 1967 I went to work at a local dairy farm. Two things happened at the dairy farm that summer that made me much smarter—two things I've never forgotten. There was a cow on the

8

milking line that I was never supposed to milk. The foremen called her Linda, and he had warned me to never to go anywhere near her, for the cow had an attitude. One day while the foreman was gone, I worked my way down the line as I always did with the automated milking machine until I got to Linda. But this time, since I had worked there for a while, I thought that I had enough experience and confidence to take on the bovine.

When I hooked the suction tube to one of her teats, Linda kicked me in the chest so hard that it knocked the wind out of me and cracked a rib. I landed in a fresh pile of shit in the trough behind her, and because the cow had knocked the wind out of me, I was unable to move. To complicate matters Linda then pissed all over me. I almost lost it there that day, but fortunately the foreman came back just in time—he saved my life, but not my dignity.

The second lesson I learned later that summer involved feeding the newborn cows. It was my job to feed them every morning when I got to work, and every evening just before I went home. The most important aspect was to never feed them too much food, for calves are capable of eating continuously and have no way of knowing when to stop.

In a natural setting the mother controls their eating limits by refusing the calf any more milk. One evening I forgot to remove the source of nourishment at the allotted time, and the next morning one of the calves was dead. Although I was only making fifty cents an hour at the time, I had to pay fifty dollars for the calf that died. My oversight cost me two weeks of pay, and I promptly quit as soon as the debt was paid in full. Once again I was upset at myself, and vowed to never be that stupid again.

I immediately found employment at a vegetable farm owned by the father of a friend. The job was a lot easier because migrant workers handled the majority of the dirty work. I learned to drive an old six-cylinder flatbed truck which was used to collect boxes of harvested vegetables. Even though the Chevy had a standard transmission and required clutching to shift gears, I soon found that driving came naturally. The money I made there enabled me to buy everything I wanted until school started.

Chapter 2

The Very Beginning

September 1967 To September 1971

Seventh grade was the beginning of the end for me. School was a breeze and I was bored to no end. I had firmly established myself in the crowd of troublemakers that ran the school, not through brawn but with intelligence. In the fall of 1967 Pete and I skipped school and went walking aimlessly, looking for trouble. We ended up at a Forte's Market grocery store where we intended to purchase some cigarettes, but instead my eyes caught the welcome sight of a car that had been left with the keys dangling in the ignition. I wasted no time climbing into the car, starting it up and taking off down the street. Pete, making a wise decision, refused to join me for the joyride.

It was the adventure of a lifetime for a twelve-year old, and eventually found myself back in Hamden, about three miles from my old home on Gorham Avenue. I was barely tall enough to see over the steering wheel, so it wasn't a surprise when an observant police officer noticed me driving at a school crossing. After being transported to the Westbrook barracks of the Connecticut state police, my embarrassed father came to get me. Although I endured the long ride home that day, from then on it was all downhill, and things at home got worse every day.

Searching For My Identity: The Chronological Evolution
Of A Troubled Adolescent To Outlaw Biker

Somehow or other I made it through the seventh grade in spite of all the trouble the stolen car had gotten me into. There was a constant need to satisfy an itch, and the itch needed to be scratched. I was always in search of a challenge and something to stimulate my intelligence. Stealing cars became the answer, and a habit that was impossible to quit. The adrenaline rush was intoxicating, almost like a fresh breath of air, and the aura of invincibility was almost as powerful as the crime. As a bonus, the parameters of my playing field had grown twenty-fold; I could now travel easily more than twenty miles from my home.

I turned thirteen in June of 1968 while Pete's older brother Skip was in Vietnam fighting the war. Pete and I had the whole world by the balls—we had discovered girls, and I was fascinated with one in particular who was my neighbor. Marcia and I were experimenting with sex on a regular basis, and having her next door was no less than convenient. Pete and I used to laugh when the guys our age talked about sex, because we were having sex regularly while our friends were only dreaming about it.

It was the time of bad ass muscle cars, and by now I was an expert when it came to stealing them. Almost every weekend Pete and I enjoyed some type of Chevrolet hotrod that I had stolen, but sometimes I went after mundane vehicles when nothing else was available. On rare occasions we dismantled the cars and sold some of the parts to a local salvage yard. Every once in a while we would beat the car up with sledgehammers, and sell what was left for scrap. I was also regularly sneaking my dad's car out after my parents went to sleep, and then sneaking it back in the garage before they woke up in the morning.

Eighth grade went by real fast. I passed all of my subjects with flying colors, and before I knew it, the summer of 1969 was upon us. There was a huge music festival in Woodstock, New York that was about peace and love, which I didn't attend, and an American astronaut landed on the moon, which everyone watched on television.

At the annual carnival in North Branford that year a monumental event occurred that would alter my life forever. While hanging out watching girls with a few of my friends, I heard this loud, unusual sound, which can only be described as a rumble. A pack of Harley choppers pulled up and parked close to where I was standing. The bikers were members of the local motorcycle club from New Haven, but they had two Hells Angels with them.

I had never seen or heard of the Hells Angels and was completely taken in by the outlaw bikers, who represented the epitome of coolness and attitude. The way they parked their bikes, the way they dismounted, and the way they walked projected sheer confidence with a message attached that said 'don't fuck with me'. The winged death's head emblem the two Angels wore on the back of their sleeveless blue jean jackets—I didn't know they were called patches or colors at the time—made them look like harbingers of trouble.

Searching For My Identity: The Chronological Evolution
Of A Troubled Adolescent To Outlaw Biker

I was mesmerized by the aura of power and intimidation the outlaw bikers projected, and noticed how everybody stepped aside as if they were celebrities. In awe of their beautiful Harleys, I vowed silently that I would someday have a motorcycle just like the choppers I was looking at. I had just discovered a reason for living, and knew that I was going to become an outlaw biker some day!

One night later that summer I took my dad's 1967 Pontiac Lemans for a final ride to freedom—I was tired of all the arguing at home and determined to find greener pastures. Pete and I broke into an Elk's Lodge to finance a trip to Florida, and with two girls and a friend along for the ride, we headed south on Interstate 95. The five of us made it all the way to South Carolina, almost one-thousand miles from home, before we ran out of money and gas.

While siphoning fuel from a car in a rural neighborhood we were noticed by a police officer and arrested. All of us were incarcerated at the Orangeburg County Jail in Orangeburg, South Carolina, while we waited for Pete's father, my father, and the father of one of the girls to come get us. I can assure you that the twenty-mile ride home from the Westbrook State Police barracks two years before paled in comparison to this nine-hundred mile ride home; this journey was a nightmare! When we finally got home I was read the riot act and grounded for a year—that, however, only lasted a few days before I just ignored the mandate and snuck out as usual by jumping out of my bedroom window.

Searching For My Identity: The Chronological Evolution
Of A Troubled Adolescent To Outlaw Biker

It was September of 1969 when I started ninth grade at North Branford High School. I was now fourteen-years old and extremely intelligent for my age, but channeled all that brilliance into the wrong things. On one of the first days of school Pete and I were walking down the hall when some smart aleck senior made a negative comment about the Hansen family and asked Pete if he was related. Pete responded the only way he knew—he proudly told the senior that he was Skip and Walt's little brother, and then proceeded to kick the shit out of him. Somehow or other we avoided the teachers who came running to investigate the commotion, and made it to class without getting in trouble.

It was during the ninth grade that things went from bad to worse. My history class was held on the second floor and the teacher's name was Haskell—everyone hated him. Every day after entering the classroom, weather permitting, he opened the windows. One day Pete and I unscrewed the hinges on one of the windows and carefully placed the window back into its locked position. When the teacher opened the window, the window and frame fell out. The window hit the ground below with a thundering explosion, and it was all we could do to keep from laughing.

On the first really warm day in the spring of 1970 the queues at the drinking fountains in the school were backed up forever. There was no way Pete and I could get a drink, and we definitely weren't willing to wait in line. We did the next best thing—we turned off the water to the entire school. In the process of hanging out on the hillside before and after school each day, we had discovered the main water shutoff for the entire school located in an underground concrete box.

All we had to do was open the door to the concrete box, and turn a giant gate valve about twelve inches across. Since we had previously broken the lock on the door in the process of determining what the lock prevented us from accessing, turning off the water was a piece of cake. When we went back inside the school Pete and I were quite amused—there wasn't enough water pressure to power the drinking fountains, and the thirsty students were complaining to anyone who would listen.

Although my reputation as a car thief was well-known in the area by the time I turned fifteen, I was also becoming quite an accomplished auto mechanic. I seemed to have a natural ability when it came to things mechanical, and loved tinkering with cars. Some of my older friends let me work on their vehicles, and I learned a lot in the process. I knew that as soon as I was old enough, I would seek out some kind of mechanic's job, preferably at a Chevrolet dealership. Later in life I found out why—my biological grandfather on my mother's side had been a mechanical engineer—apparently the mechanical aptitude was in my genes.

My tenth-grade year was my last full year in high school. I was bored out of my mind with the drivel that was being taught in my classes. Although I had already completed geometry and algebra, and was starting to learn trigonometry, I was uninterested.

For the first time in my life I had fallen in love, and my new girlfriend was all I could think about. I had met Cathy at a church-sponsored dance—she was a year younger than me, cute as could be, and a freshman at my high school.

I spent many an evening hitchhiking across town just to be with her for an hour or two. Cathy lived right across the street from the Bondo factory, and I still think of her after all these years every time I'm in a body shop, because Bondo is a trade name for a compound used to smooth out damaged auto body panels. I dated Cathy for the better part of two years, and like every other kid that age, thought that we would be together for the rest of our lives. I stretched our relationship to the breaking point by abusing her emotionally and mentally, and my youthful dream to be with her until the end of time was shattered.

Just before Thanksgiving I got caught in a stolen car again. I had borrowed a Mercury station wagon from the owner, but kept it way too long and had started to believe the car was mine. I liked the station wagon because it didn't stick out like a sore thumb like the muscle cars did, but time wasn't on my side.

When a police officer recognized the car as belonging to the local pharmacy owner, I was busted. Inside the car, to complicate my situation, was a plethora of stolen items taken in a slew of residential burglaries. My goose was cooked and I knew it. Off to jail I went, but this time I kept going. I wound up at the juvenile detention center on Orange Street in New Haven, where I

17

stayed until just after the new year. When I promised I would stay out of trouble and never return, the judge released me to the custody of my parents after spending more than a month in a real prison environment.

The promise I made to get out of jail only lasted a few months. Late in my sophomore year in high school, with my grades failing and my attention who knows where, I sealed my fate one day before math class. One of the guys I hung out with had a M-80 firecracker that was supposed to be the equivalent of a small piece of dynamite, and he dared me to light it and put it in the toilet in the boy's lavatory. Not being a chicken, but obviously lacking common sense, I lit the M-80 and tossed it in, flushing the toilet simultaneously. I figured the water would snuff out the fuse, and the flush would wash away the evidence.

This time I wasn't as smart as I thought I was—before I negotiated the bathroom door a huge explosion rocked the school, and pieces of porcelain showered me as I bolted through the doorway. I went to my next class hoping for the best and expecting the worst, but it didn't take long for the consequences of my actions to materialize. Five minutes after class started the phone rang, and I was on my way to the office. By this time the principal was sick of me, and was looking for any excuse to expel me from school. This was the opportunity he had dreamed of, and he spared no time in suspending me for the rest of the school year.

Searching For My Identity: The Chronological Evolution
Of A Troubled Adolescent To Outlaw Biker

Once again my parents were extremely disappointed in my behavior, but by now had resigned themselves to the fact that I was going to do whatever I wanted. They knew there wasn't much they could do about it—I was definitely out of control.

In danger of going back to the custody of the state of Connecticut for more rest and relaxation, I feverishly worked my butt off to pay for the toilet I had blown up. I still can't believe that the high school failed to press criminal charges, and instead elected to let me study at home and work to pay off the plumbing bill. But work I did, and by the time the school year was over, the repair bill had been paid and my grades were sufficient for me to start the eleventh grade, in spite of the fact that I had missed almost sixty days of school.

I turned sixteen in June of 1971, and a driving inspector at the Connecticut Department of Motor Vehicles issued me a driver's license in spite of all the trouble I'd been in. With four years of driving experience behind me, I passed the exam on my first try with flying colors.

I spent the first part of the summer working at a car wash but hated every minute. When a job opening to pump gas at a local ARCO gas station in Northford came around, I jumped at the opportunity. Back then we called gas Ethyl, and I told everybody I knew sarcastically that I was pumping Ethyl for a living. I saved up enough money to buy my first legitimate car for three-hundred dollars, but promptly blew the engine in it three weeks later.

Later that summer Pete moved up the shore with his family to a small seaside town called Old Saybrook. His mom and dad had a boat not far from there in the town of Westbrook, and I started going there almost every weekend. When Pete's parents were at the boat, we had the house to ourselves—if his parents were at home, then we had the boat to ourselves. Both locations provided us with abundant opportunities to play house with our girlfriends, or a place to hang out with the guys.

In the fall I got talked into going back to school for what would have been my junior year, and the principal allowed me to return. By now I was a legend at school, but knew that the first sign of trouble would be my doom. It only took a few days and some slacker called me out during lunch hour. The fight was on, and an hour later I was history, permanently expelled from high school for the rest of my life. At that point I didn't really care—it felt as if a huge monkey was finally off my back, and I knew that there were bigger and better things waiting for me somewhere down the road.

Chapter 3

Working For A Living & The US Army

October 1971 To March 1973

In spite of all the hell I had put my parents through in the last five years of my life, my adopted dad was the one who came to my rescue when I was permanently expelled from high school. Warren had a friend and business acquaintance who owned a truck body installation company, and my dad talked him into hiring me. As a bonus, Connecticut Truck & Trailer in North Haven was only fifteen minutes from my parent's house. In October of 1971 I started working there as a garage helper, in charge of cleaning up the shop and every other crappy job no one was willing to do. Everybody expected me to last no more than a few weeks, but I did.

Working at Connecticut Truck & Trailer was a riot, and the shop mechanics and welders there loved to have fun. It was not unusual for the shop to come to a grinding halt for a snowball fight. The mechanics would sometimes load their creepers (a board on wheels used by a mechanic to lie on) with snow, then roll the creepers back inside the shop, and the battle was on.

It also wasn't unusual for a welder to have the belt of his pants hooked to the overhead crane from behind while he was welding, and then the crane operator would lift him just inches off the ground, where the welder was left to dangle for ten minutes. A

21

truck hood would often be shut while a mechanic was inside the engine compartment working, without the engine running, and he would be left there for a while banging on the inside of the hood, waiting for someone to let him out.

I loved working there—before long I taught myself how to weld and was allowed to do tasks no one wanted to do, such as repairing the hydraulic cylinders in the back of a garbage truck while it was still loaded with garbage. To facilitate the repair of a hydraulic component, sometimes I had to lay in garbage for hours. Maggots would be crawling all over me and the smell was beyond belief.

I stuck with it, and by spring was installing snowplows and dump truck bodies on brand-new trucks, and quite capable of troubleshooting and repairing every component in a hydraulic system. Because I was single and not afraid to work, I sometimes worked as much as eighty hours per week, and my paychecks were showing the results.

In early spring I screwed up again, but dodged a bullet. I had purchased a black 1963 four-door Pontiac the previous fall for basic transportation back and forth to work. One cold night after partying with my friends and having too much to drink, I ran the car off a small cliff on the way home. I was fortunate to escape without a scratch, but it didn't take long for the neighbors to call the police, and then for the police to find the car. By the time they figured out who owned the car, I had already been given a ride home. Because the policeman couldn't prove that I had been driving, I wasn't charged with drunk driving, but the car was a total wreck and I was back to catching a ride to work with my dad again.

A few months later in early May around 10PM, I left my friend Kurt Newman's house in North Haven on a small motorcycle headed home—it had been raining and I didn't want to walk. Since I was less than two miles from my parent's house I thought I could make the journey without getting stopped by the police for driving an unregistered motorcycle. I only needed to be on the main street for a few minutes, just long enough to make it across the Northford town line. Regrettably a North Haven police officer spotted me, but instead of stopping I took off.

I was sure that I could lose him by cutting up through a school walkway, because it wasn't wide enough for a car, or so I thought. But the squad car followed me right up the walkway, with the fence scraping both sides of the car the entire way. After I showed the policeman my middle finger, he was so mad he knocked me down with the police car, and then arrested me for a myriad of traffic related offenses, as well as resisting arrest. I wound up in jail again, but this time was able to get bonded out in a few hours.

When I showed up in court to face the charges, the judge wasted no time in telling me that I only had two options—go to prison at the Cheshire Reformatory until I was eighteen, or enlist in the United States Army. At the time the Vietnam War was raging, and the Army was looking anywhere it could for recruits. It didn't take long for me to realize I was screwed, and the only option was to enlist. The judge instructed me to make an enlistment appointment with the Army recruiter present in the courtroom, which I did—the judge then placed me on probation.

I didn't want to enlist by myself, so I convinced Kurt to alter his birth certificate to show he was seventeen, and we went to see the Army recruiter together. Kurt wanted to learn a trade for free, and planned to tell the Army his true age after completing school in six months, knowing they would have to let him go because he would still be sixteen. Since the Army was the only way for me to avoid prison, I would have to stay the entire two years. Kurt signed up for an electronics course, and I told the recruiter I liked to work on trucks and knew a lot about hydraulics.

On June 15th of 1972 Kurt and I got up extra early, and before dawn reported to the Army depot in downtown New Haven. From there we traveled by bus one-hundred fifty miles south to Fort Dix, New Jersey, for basic training, where we spent eight weeks in the same unit bunking together, getting physically fit, and learning Army procedures and warfare tactics. From Fort Dix I was sent to the Aberdeen Proving Grounds in Maryland for tank turret mechanic school, and Kurt went off to Fort Belvoir in Virginia to learn electronics.

While at Aberdeen I studied for my GED and passed the test on the first try. When I took the GED test I was a surprised to learn my IQ was 146, and thrilled to have my high school diploma nine months before my classmates at North Branford High School were scheduled to graduate.

By late November Kurt was finished with electronics school and the Army. He had learned all he could, so my friend marched into the commander's office and put his feet up on the desk. When the commanding officer ordered Kurt to remove his feet from the desk, he produced a copy of his real birth certificate which proved he was only sixteen-years old.

Although the commander was angry, there was nothing he could do about my friend's behavior and attitude. A few hours later Kurt walked through the main gate to Fort Belvoir for the last time, and then hitchhiked to Aberdeen so I could drive him back home to Connecticut that weekend in the 1957 Chevy I had recently bought.

I graduated from tank turret mechanic school a few weeks later, and took all the leave time I could get before I was to report back to Fort Dix for my impending departure overseas. I expected to be shipped to Vietnam when I returned from leave, but while I was home the United States government stopped sending new ground troops to Vietnam. It was a stroke of luck, but at the time I had mixed feelings, for I wanted to go. When I reported back after being home on leave, I got sent to Germany.

After a long flight from the United States I arrived in Frankfurt on the 22nd of December. It was cold and overcast, and

25

my new surroundings looked dreary. The first thing we were told at orientation was to leave the German beer alone, for it was supposedly nothing like the beer in the United States. I wasn't much for being told what to do and usually needed to figure things out for myself. That night I got completely snookered on only two mugs of German beer, and by the time the next morning came, I was a firm believer in what I had been told the previous day.

The next day I arrived late in the afternoon at Ayers Kaserne, an Army base that adjoined the town of Kirch-Gons. Thirty kilometers south of Giessen and one-hundred kilometers north of Frankfurt, Kirch-Gons was known as 'The Rock'. I was now a tank turret repairman and a soldier in the 122nd Maintenance Battalion of the 3rd Armored Division, stationed on top of a small mountain in Germany. To complicate matters it was snowing and freezing cold outside, and I hated cold weather.

After checking in with the officer on duty and getting my room assignment, I went upstairs to locate the room. When I looked down the hall I just about had a heart attack, for huge clouds of smoke were coming out from under the doors of some of the rooms. I had heard many stories about rampant drug abuse in Germany, some of those specifically concerning the smoking of hashish. I rapidly deduced that the clouds of smoke were from hash, and hoped I wouldn't end up in one. Although I had abused alcohol on many occasions I was dead set against any type of drug use, and had only tried marijuana once in my entire life.

26

Searching For My Identity: The Chronological Evolution Of A Troubled Adolescent To Outlaw Biker

It was just my luck to end up in front of one of those rooms, so I did the only thing I could think of under the circumstances—I knocked. When the door opened a wall of hash smoke almost knocked me down. The sergeant in the doorway was suspicious, and inquired as to what I wanted. When I told him I was a new guy and was looking for the bed I'd been assigned, he rapidly changed his attitude and welcomed me into the room. So there I was in my dress greens, sitting on my new bed surrounded by a half-dozen soldiers high on hash. Welcome to the Army!

The very first thing one of them asked was whether I had ever smoked any hash before. Doing my best to fake it I told them I had, but not too many times. Before I could get out of my uniform, I smoked some hash and promptly passed out from the experience. I didn't wake up until the next morning when it was time for everyone else to go to work—fortunately I hadn't been assigned a job yet.

While my roommates were getting ready for work they were smoking more hash! In spite of the fact that I still hadn't changed my clothes, my roommates convinced me that I needed to smoke more hash. Once again I passed out from the experience, and didn't wake again until late that afternoon. I had now been there for twenty-four hours, and had spent the entire time sleeping. I hadn't even made it to the mess hall to eat, nor had I changed out of my dress greens!

Searching For My Identity: The Chronological Evolution
Of A Troubled Adolescent To Outlaw Biker

I finally mustered up the courage to take a shower and get changed just before my roommates returned from work. The first thing they did was fire up the hash pipes, but this time I told them the truth—I had enough. As I walked out the door to go eat, the sergeant said they were leaving for Frankfurt in an hour. When he asked if I wanted to join them, I welcomed the opportunity.

I had just enough time to eat before we all caught the train to Frankfurt. On the way to the big city I thought about my first few days in Germany and what I had learned so far—don't drink the beer, and don't smoke the hash; I wondered if this was all I needed to know.

In Frankfurt I got my first taste of LSD. I was eager to experience everything I could and the timing was perfect. Running around town with all my new roommates and their German friends made for an exciting night, but by the time the weekend was over, I was tired of partying and ready to start working. But the Army, in all of its wisdom, had sent three tank turret mechanics to Ayers Kaserne, when the unit only needed one. One of my roommates worked on the night crew in the truck shop, and he volunteered to get me assigned there.

I quickly learned that only the best and brightest mechanics worked the evening shift, but all of them were hash smokers. The evening mechanics would work hard for three or four hours until lunch break—by then had usually accomplished more than the entire day crew, and there were twice as many day mechanics as

28

there were evening mechanics. Not wanting to make the day crew look bad, the evening crew would quit working when it came time to eat. For the remainder of the shift we sat around and partied, smoking hash and listening to music.

The funniest part of this whole deal was that the Military Police (MP's) were housed on the third floor of my barracks. Some of them got high on hash regularly, and those MP's was assigned to guard the truck shop at night. We had it made, for none of us had to endure the daily formation inspections and we could sleep all day. Sometimes we left work a few hours before the end of the shift, and caught an earlier train to Frankfurt.

One night the officer in charge somehow slipped past the MP guarding the truck shop, and caught a bunch of us getting high and goofing off. That was the end of the evening shift for the truck mechanics, and the beginning of mundane duty cleaning up the barracks and yard during the day. None of us were arrested, but we all received some form of extra duty to pay for our insolence.

By the time March rolled around I was getting tired of Germany, and was hoping to get a transfer stateside to receive treatment for a persistent knee problem that had been bothering me since I'd been in basic training. I simultaneously applied for a hardship discharge based on the fact that I was an only child, and that I was needed at home to help my parents out financially.

When I got tired of waiting on the Army to make a decision, I went AWOL—absent without leave. I got a ride to the airport and paid for a one-way ticket on a plane from Frankfurt to New York City. From the airport I took a shuttle bus back to Connecticut where I immediately hooked up with Kurt Newman, Chucky Vanacore, Pete Hansen and Kevin McManus.

Chapter 4

Working For A Living & The US Army

March 1973 To March 1974

I told my parents and everyone else I knew that I was home on leave, and pretty much came and went as I pleased for the next three weeks. I goofed off, worked part-time at Connecticut Truck & Trailer, and went partying with my friends before I got serious about my situation. I knew I would be declared a deserter after thirty days of being AWOL, so I needed to turn myself back into the Army on the twenty-ninth day.

To hopefully add credibility to my medical and hardship claims, I turned myself in at the Pentagon in Washington, DC, but was surprised at how hard it was to do so in spite of all the Army personnel there. I immediately told everyone I came in contact with that I was AWOL and wanted to turn myself in, but kept getting directed from one person to another. When I finally found an officer who was willing to handle the situation, he refused to do so until I got a haircut. A few hours later I received orders to be stationed at Fort Meade in Maryland for temporary observation and medical treatment.

Fort Meade was a dream come true because most of the facility was completely deserted. I landed a job supervising a group of housing units from 6PM to 6AM, but most of the time I watched television or slept. The World War II era buildings I was in charge of were empty, except on the weekends when they were used to house groups of people in transit. I hit pay dirt one weekend when an entire troop of Girl Scouts from Pittsburgh were housed in one of the units under my control. Only seventeen at the time, I felt like a kid in a candy store with all those teenage girls around me, and I was the only Army soldier in sight.

It didn't take long for me to pick out one of the oldest and prettiest—her name was Suzan. Although she was only fourteen, she was drop dead gorgeous, intelligent, and mature beyond her years. I spent as much time with her as I dared without compromising her honor, and we promised to keep in touch after we parted ways. Less than two weeks after I had met her, I went home to take my final week of leave before I shipped off back to my unit at Ayers Kaserne in Germany.

Before I went back to Germany I sold my 1957 Chevy and bought myself a 1968 RS SS Chevy Camaro. The Camaro was black with white stripes, and had an awesome big block 427 L-88 engine under the hood, a four-speed transmission, and 4:88 gears in the rear. The last night I was home I unbolted the headers on the hotrod and drove all over town with Pete, Kurt, and Chucky. When we got stopped by the police for the loud exhaust, I told the cop I was home on leave from the Army. After I told him I was going back overseas the next day, he let me go!

On the morning I was scheduled to fly back to Germany, I got a ride to Kurt's where I planned to say goodbye to Kurt,

Chucky and Kevin. Just before I had to leave at 9AM Kurt chased me all over the house with a garden hose. My good friend soaked me to the bone, which was his deluded version of a goodbye gift. My bags were with my dad, who was going to meet me at the airport limo, so I had no other clothes to change into. I was able to change my underwear, socks and shirt before I got on the plane, and although my dress greens did dry a little on the trip, I was still damp when I landed in Germany eighteen hours later. I thought about Kurt all the way there, and the many different ways I was going to pay him back in the future.

A week after I got back to Germany I made PFC, but lost the rank the next day when I was disciplined for having gone AWOL. I quickly found one of my old buddies from the truck shop, and he got me assigned to a laundry detail. If I thought the truck shop was great, this job was fantastic! We both got up at 4AM and took a loaded truck full of dirty laundry to Frankfurt, where we dropped it off at the central laundry facility. We either went to sleep for four hours or walked around wasting time until the laundry had been processed, and then drove the truck full of clean laundry back to the base.

We soon figured out that only one of us needed to return to Ayers Kaserne, in order to drive the truck back to Frankfurt early the next morning. The other one could stay in Frankfurt all night long, as long as he got to the laundry facility by late morning before the truck had to make the trip back to our base. One of the side benefits was that neither one of us had to get up in the morning to attend the daily formation inspections, so it wasn't long before it was a major chore to keep my long hair under my Army-issued baseball cap.

In July of 1973 my ship finally came in. The Army decided to downsize since the Vietnam War was almost over, and were looking for ways to get rid of anybody who was willing. My application for a hardship discharge was approved, and I was honorably discharged. The master sergeant on duty made me get my haircut three times before he signed the final transfer papers, and I actually went home with less hair than I started with.

I was thrilled to be back home in Connecticut, and even more thrilled to have regained my freedom. I took a few weeks off to get settled in before I started back to work full-time at Connecticut Truck & Trailer. While I had been overseas, Pete had fallen in love with a girl from Old Saybrook whom he had met during his last year in high school—her name was Mary Beth. She had a friend who stopped me dead in my tracks, for she was the prettiest girl I'd ever seen.

Helen was a petite, intelligent, blonde wild child, and I thought we were meant to be with each other forever. Shortly after we met, Pete, Mary Beth, Helen and I were driving around town one night in my Camaro drinking and partying. I stopped by my parents' house for a minute to run in and get something, but while I was in the house, my adopted dad figured out I was drunk.

Searching For My Identity: The Chronological Evolution
Of A Troubled Adolescent To Outlaw Biker

Warren pulled the keys out of the ignition and made all of us come inside the house. There was no way he was going to allow me to drive around with a carload of teenagers drunk. He called Pete's parents, as well as the parents of both girls, and told them what had transpired, then made all of us stay there that night. Helen's parents were very strict, and she was supposed to be home by midnight. There was no way her parents would let her hang out with a bad boy from the wrong side of the tracks, so after that night her father told Helen she could never see me again. Although he made the right decision, I never forgave Warren, for at the time I was madly in love with her.

On the rebound from Helen I renewed my friendship with Suzan. I made plans to drive to Pittsburgh in late August to meet her family, under estimating the amount of fuel the Camaro would require to make the four-hundred mile journey. The cost of gas ate a giant hole in my pocket and almost broke me—the Camaro only got three miles to the gallon! I spent a few days there with Suzan and her family before I realized she needed to stay in school. We knew there was no way our long-distance relationship could survive, and decided to remain friends. With a heavy heart I drove back to Connecticut to explore greener pastures.

A month later Suzan ran away from home and called me on the phone. She wanted to be with me in Connecticut, but I knew it wouldn't work out. I also didn't want her dad to be mad at me, and knew that I could be charged with a crime for harboring an underage girl. In spite of the feelings I had, I convinced Suzie to go back home and stay in school, but that didn't last long. She ran away from home again a year later, got pregnant, and then got married. Over the years I stopped in to visit her and her family, and we remained in contact. More than forty-five years later, we still exchange Christmas cards.

In the fall of 1973 I was back at Connecticut Truck & Trailer working as a shop mechanic and welder. I was doing major jobs now that I had experience, and it was a very happy time for me. I was living at home again, and actually getting along with my parents. It wasn't long before I was reminded of my dream to own a Harley when one of the members from Hole n' The Wall, a New Haven motorcycle club, started working at Connecticut Truck & Trailer. The outlaw biker always rode his Harley to work, and every day I looked at it with a certain type of lust that can only be described as jealousy.

My only problem in the fall of 1973 was that the workload at Connecticut Truck & Trailer was slowing down, and I wanted more hours. I soon found a job at Cooke's Equipment in Wallingford, working on different types of International Harvester construction equipment, as well as some farm tractors. It didn't take me long to settle in there, and soon I was working out of the shop in a company field truck, doing repairs for customers on their construction sites. I discovered that I had a knack for fixing the incredible machines, and realized that I loved doing it.

Searching For My Identity: The Chronological Evolution
Of A Troubled Adolescent To Outlaw Biker

Within a few months I located a second floor apartment on Cherry Street a few blocks from work. It was conveniently located above a liquor store, and my downstairs neighbor was an elderly lady who couldn't hear very well. The apartment soon became party central for all of us. Pete, Chucky, Kurt, Kevin and I spent most every weekend there, partying all night until the sun came up.

Chucky was now working less than a mile from my apartment, building street rods at a car manufacturing company called Total Performance. It wasn't long before I started working there at night part-time, sanding the car bodies to prepare them for paint just to earn a few more dollars. It was there I first met Johnny Cerrone, who was about as crazy as they come—he had a wicked sense of humor that kept us all laughing all day long, every day.

One day at work Johnny cut a hole in the bottom of a small box, which allowed his middle finger to be inserted, protruding through to the inside of the box. He then put cotton all around the part of his finger that was inside the box, and added a mixture of ketchup and water to the cotton and his finger. Johnny then positioned the box just right, carrying it with his other hand, which made it look like his finger had been cut off.

He ran up to the shop foreman screaming that there had been a terrible accident, and that he needed to get to the hospital immediately to have his finger sewn back on. In a panic the shop foreman immediately dropped everything and started driving Johnny to the hospital. About halfway there Johnny's middle finger came up in the box, pointed directly at the shop foreman. Laughing his ass off, Johnny said, *"You stupid asshole!"* The joke was on the shop foreman, but he wasn't very happy about it. We thought it was a riot, because we knew what was going to happen from the start.

I also started rebuilding muscle cars on the weekends utilizing Cooke's shop, and then selling the cars to make a few extra dollars. I would buy them as-is, usually with a bad engine or transmission. After fixing everything that was wrong, I would then drive the hotrods for a while, eventually selling them for a small profit.

It was apparent that I still didn't know everything about diesel engines and heavy equipment when I went out to the yard one cold morning to start a brand-new piece of machinery. I used too much starting fluid, and when the mixture ignited it blew the starter right off the engine. Fortunately it didn't break the engine block, and I was able to repair my screw up without any more problems. But the guys in the shop sure had a good laugh at my expense!

Not long after that, I had a bone-chilling experience with an old bulldozer I was working on that had a diesel engine with an oil bath air cleaner. I was in the process of changing all of its fluids, including the oil in the air cleaner. Apparently I added too much oil to the air cleaner, because when I started it up, the engine rpm started increasing on its own. It throttled up more and more, and there was nothing I could do to stop it. I was scared to death that the engine was going to blow up until another mechanic jumped up on the machine and pulled the top off the air cleaner. He put a board over the air intake pipe terminating the supply of air into the engine, effectively shutting the engine down. The only damage done was to my pride, and once again everyone in the shop had a good laugh.

The next year I seriously set my sights on buying a Harley. It was a major objective, but I was willing to do whatever necessary to make it happen. I just couldn't figure out exactly how I was going to do it, because I didn't know anyone who had a motorcycle. Sometimes strange things happen for strange reasons, and in the spring of 1974 I answered the door to find an irate outlaw biker screaming at me. His home had been broken into and his stereo stolen, and he had been told erroneously that I had committed the burglary and was in possession of the stolen stereo.

I truthfully denied the burglary and allowed him to search my apartment for the missing stereo, which of course he didn't find. Before we parted ways I told him that I was an expert Chevy wrench and that I worked down the street at Cooke's as a heavy equipment mechanic. The last thing the biker told me was that when he found the culprit responsible for the theft, the burglar's ass was grass. A few days later there was another unexpected knock on my door—it was the biker again, but this time he had a case of beer under his arm.

Searching For My Identity: The Chronological Evolution
Of A Troubled Adolescent To Outlaw Biker

Richard "Richie" Doolittle told me he had found the assholes responsible for the burglary of his home, and had recovered the stolen stereo and given the culprits an attitude adjustment in the process. He realized the information given to him about the stereo was a mistake, and to make amends he wanted to drop off the case of beer. I invited him inside, and it didn't take long for us to figure out we needed each other. Richie owned a Corvette that desperately needed a mechanic, and I needed someone to teach me about Harleys. It looked like my appointment with destiny had finally arrived.

Chapter 5

The Birth Of A Biker

June 1974 To November 1976

Richie and I started hanging around together on a regular basis the summer of 1974. We fast became good friends, and while I helped him work on his Corvette he introduced me to the world of Harley-Davidson motorcycles. In the fall I sold my prized midnight blue 1970 Chevy Nova SS to my girlfriend and bought a 1963 Harley Panhead chopper for two-thousand five-hundred dollars from Cecil Pullen, one of Richie's friends.

Cecil was a charismatic outlaw biker who didn't belong to a motorcycle club. He was also one of the best Harley mechanic in Connecticut, so it was an honor to end up with one of his bikes. This particular Harley was very special, for the frame had been altered by Gene the Bean. Gene had added five inches to the down tubes and three inches to the top rail to accommodate an eighteen inch over springer style front end.

Although the chopper was mechanically sound and running, I wanted to take it apart and paint the gas tank, frame and fenders so the bike would be uniquely mine. Because I didn't have a garage at my apartment, I decided that the best place to rebuild the Harley would be at my parents' house. I somehow convinced them that I wouldn't make a mess, and used their garage for disassembly and the basement for parts storage. I planned on using

41

my old bedroom upstairs to store and clean all of the chrome parts, but on the way upstairs with the oil tank I accidentally spilled some oil on the stairway carpet. Warren was livid when he got home— to make peace with him, I paid for the new carpet that was installed a few days later.

I hired a biker from Meriden that Richie recommended to paint the Harley. Gary Parisi was a fantastic body man and painter, and did a great job. He painted the frame pearl ice blue, and the gas tank and fenders dark midnight blue. On the gas tank, Gary air brushed a mural of the tattoo I had on my arm—crossed pistons and a skull, with the words Harley-Davidson and Budweiser on the top and bottom.

As soon as it was assembled and running, the first place I went was my girlfriend's high school to pick her up, in spite of the fact it was too cold to be riding. Much to my embarrassment, I dropped the bike in the parking lot in front of a crowd of teenagers. Fortunately I did the bike no harm, but the incident did take a large chunk out of my pride.

By the end of the year Cooke's Equipment Company was losing work left and right. I was barely getting in forty hours a week, and it looked like I would soon be laid off. I hated the cold New England winters with a passion, and had been thinking about relocating for quite a while. In February of 1975 I decided to move to Tulsa, Oklahoma, and convinced my sixteen-year old girlfriend Toni to join me. My uncle had lived there for ten years in the sixties, and told me that I could easily find work there—Tulsa was also sunny and warm. Pete joined us for the adventure, and volunteered to help me drive and eventually unload the U-Haul trailer that we planned to pull behind Toni's 1970 Chevy Nova SS.

Not long after we left we changed our minds and decided to go to Boise, Idaho. But by the time we got to Detroit, I figured out that we would never have enough money to get to Boise. We turned south at Chicago and then drove southwest to Tulsa as we had originally planned. When we arrived in Oklahoma it was like I had died and gone to heaven, for it was a beautiful sunny day and the temperature was in the mid-seventies. We pulled into a cheap motel at the corner of 11th Street and Memorial for the night, and immediately rolled the chopper out of the trailer and took it for a ride.

Within a day I located an apartment complex that needed a maintenance man and was willing to trade maintenance work for rent. The Orchard Park apartment complex was located just off 64th Street and Peoria Avenue in a nice residential area not far from Oral Roberts University. I was able to negotiate the back-sliding door with the bike, making it possible to park the Harley inside my bedroom where I knew it would be safe. To make ends meet I took a temporary job as a carpenter during the day on a framing crew, until I got a job as a mechanic at one of the local construction equipment dealerships.

Searching For My Identity: The Chronological Evolution
Of A Troubled Adolescent To Outlaw Biker

In early April I started working full-time at the John Deere dealership in Sand Springs, and settled into a routine. I would work during the day repairing heavy equipment, and evenings and weekends around the apartment complex as a maintenance man. Toni refused to work, and spent most of her time running around town getting high however and wherever she could.

I slowly realized over the summer that I had made a big mistake in bringing her to Tulsa. When we did see each other, we fought like cats and dogs—the experience reminded me of my parents, and I hated it. Sometimes she wouldn't come home for days, and other times she would tell me that she was madly in love with me.

What little time I had to myself, I would ride my motorcycle to the local Arby's Restaurant, which at the time was located in the middle of Tulsa's Restless Ribbon. The Ribbon was a two-mile section of Peoria Avenue where all the kids in town hung out every summer night from dusk to dawn. Every business on the Ribbon was the temporary home to a different group.

All the bikers on the Ribbon hung out in the parking lot of Arby's, which is where I got my nickname, Connecticut Ed. Because I never told anyone my last name and my bike had a Connecticut license plate, it was easy for the Oklahoma bikers to call me Connecticut Ed. Within a few weeks the name stuck, and remained my nickname for decades.

Searching For My Identity: The Chronological Evolution
Of A Troubled Adolescent To Outlaw Biker

One night after pulling out of Arby's on my Harley, I got stopped by the police because I didn't have any goggles on. The officer soon discovered that I had a Connecticut license plate, so he decided to impound the bike. I had no idea that he could lawfully do such a thing, and adamantly voiced my disapproval. Because of my protesting the situation soon escalated into a resisting arrest charge—the Harley was impounded, and I was handcuffed and put into the back seat of a squad car.

A few hours later I was in jail—I didn't have the three hundred dollars required to post bail, and there wasn't anyone I could call, because I didn't know the full name or phone number of any of the bikers I hung out with at Arby's. I was confused, and had no idea which way to turn. You can imagine my surprise when I was notified that my bond had been paid, and I was released from jail.

When I walked outside I found some of the bikers I hung out with at Arby's waiting for me. They had seen me get arrested, watched as my bike was impounded, and knew I was in deep shit. They went down to the Tulsa jail, and one of the bikers bailed me out. The others took me over to the impound lot and paid to get my chopper released. Three hours after I had been arrested, I was back at Arby's hanging out again!

Living with Toni became an exercise in insanity, and I knew that I had to get away from her, but didn't know how. When an opportunity presented itself in August, I left her behind (it was

45

what she wanted) and moved to Houston to take a maintenance job at an oil refinery. That was a giant mistake, because in the process of moving one of my toolboxes was stolen from the back of my truck. I also soon realized that I desperately missed the friends I had made in Tulsa, so after getting into an argument with my boss less than a month after I moved there, I packed up and moved back to Tulsa.

This time I bought a house through what is known as a rental purchase contract. It was almost brand-new, and was located in a desolate area between Broken Arrow and Tulsa near the intersection of 61st Street and Garnett Road. I immediately landed a job at the Par-Ex Machine Corporation assembling hydraulic systems for truck mounted oil field rigs. My girlfriend and I were off again, on again—one week we loved each other, the next we wanted to kill each other. Some nights Toni shared my bed, but the majority of the time she was nowhere to be found.

By now Richie had moved to Los Angeles, but it only took him a month to figure out that he hated the area, so I volunteered to drive out there and pick him up. I had always wanted to see California, but when I actually got there, all I saw was smog and miles of cars backed up on the freeway. I drove into Los Angeles, picked him up, and departed. Although I was only in California for ten hours, I couldn't understand why anyone would ever want to live there.

When we got back to Tulsa a few days before Christmas, Richie moved in with me. A few weeks later another friend of his from Vermont, Chris Robison, moved to Tulsa and joined us. Now that there were three of us sharing the three-bedroom house, we split the rent and bills three ways. We used the kitchen as a place to work on our Harleys in spite of the fact that there was a garage attached to the house. Before long Richie fell in love with a young Tulsa dancer, and after she moved in, we had someone to keep the place clean and cook for us.

In February of 1976 I let the house go. I felt that it was just too far from Tulsa and was costing us too much money. Richie and I moved back into Tulsa and split a duplex off of 67th Street & Peoria. It was a nice place in a good area of town and easier on the pocketbook. I got real down on my luck late that spring and sold my 1963 Panhead chopper to pay the bills.

I used some of the money to buy another frame, and most of an engine. This time I wanted to build my own motor, which was going to be a stroker. I went out to the old Harley shop in Sand Springs, and found a set of ULH 80" flywheels and a set of engine cases for little to nothing. I sent all of the engine parts to Truett & Osborn in Wichita, Kansas, and asked them to build me a bad ass stroker motor.

While I was waiting on Truett & Osborn, Toni was actually trying to make our relationship work. She was employed at a bar with Richie's new girlfriend, hustling guys and stripping. One day

Richie, Chris and I were in the bar having a beer, and Toni came to me and told me that a customer was giving her a hard time. I looked over to see an outlaw biker sitting in the corner by himself, so I went over to see what was going on. Before I even said a word, he said, *"I'll fight all three of you guys, if that's the way it's going to be."*

I just laughed, and told him we had no intention of fighting, that all we wanted was for him to come over and join us. His name was Lee McArdle, and he had just ridden to Tulsa from Maine. Lee had been raised in Detroit, but lived in New Mexico for a while before spending a year in Maine. He had worked as a landscaper, an electrician, and as a chef in a fancy restaurant. We got along great, and forged a relationship that afternoon that would last decades. Lee and I rapidly became inseparable, and spent all of our free time together.

I quit my job at the Par-Ex Machine Company in May, and was once again repairing heavy equipment, but this time it was for the local Fiat-Allis dealer. Richie and I said goodbye to the duplex, and moved in with Chris Robinson, who by now had a three-bedroom house on 4th Street near Mingo Road. This place was less expensive than the duplex, and I was able to save more money to put into the new bike. I had a bad habit of spending all my money on the Harley, and cutting myself short on food money. Lee would always come by at the end of the week to make sure I was eating.

One night Lee came by and both of us were completely broke. We walked a few blocks over to the local Shakey's Pizza Parlor, and pooled all of our loose change together to buy a pitcher of beer. While we slowly nursed the beer, we cleaned off everyone's plate after they were done. Almost every customer left some pizza, and by the time we finished the beer, we were both stuffed.

The finished engine from Truett & Osborn arrived from Wichita just in time for my birthday in June. I spent the next few weeks putting the finishing touches on the new bike, trying to get it ready for a ride to Lake Tenkiller on July 4th. At the last moment I realized the front axle was missing, but didn't have enough money to buy one.

Utilizing a piece of threaded rod was a stupid choice for the threaded rod wasn't hardened like an axle would be. By the time Lee and I got to Hulbert, about forty-five miles southeast of Tulsa, my front wheel was about as wobbly as you could get without crashing.

At 1PM in the afternoon the temperature was almost one hundred degrees outside, and I was as stranded as one could be. Lee was forced into going back to Tulsa to get a truck so he could rescue me and the Harley. I waited in the heat all day, and started to worry when he hadn't appeared by 6PM. It was only a one-hour journey to Tulsa each way, and plenty of time had elapsed since his departure. Soon it was dark, no less hot, and still no Lee.

Searching For My Identity: The Chronological Evolution
Of A Troubled Adolescent To Outlaw Biker

By the time midnight rolled around, I had given up and was starting to get mad. At 2AM a truck pulled up alongside of me and there was Lee with a big smile on his face. He had gone to get the truck as planned, but when he got there, he found himself in the middle of a large July 4th party. Lee figured he could have a beer first, but forgot about me until a little after midnight. To this day, I have never forgotten July 4th, 1976!

Later that summer while hanging around at Arby's, I noticed the first member of a motorcycle club that I had ever seen in Tulsa. He was a friend of ours that regularly hung out there, who had recently started prospecting for the Rogues. Johnny Cook was a family man with a bunch of kids, but was a lot older than the rest of us—we affectionately referred to him as the 'old man'.

Not long after that, late one night in the Arby's parking lot, the Old Man stopped by to hang out with us wearing his prospect colors. This time a stranger followed him into the parking lot in a car, and while Johnny was talking to us the stranger approached him. I found out later the stranger was called Shotgun, because he always carried two sawed-off shotguns everywhere he went. The stranger was standing there with a shotgun in each hand, both pointed at the Old Man.

Within a few seconds I figured out that Shotgun was mad at the Rogues, and had no idea who Johnny was. So I did a very stupid thing—I got in between Shotgun and Johnny. With about twenty people watching from ten feet away, I told the stranger to go ahead and shoot me, because I wasn't going to let him shoot the Old Man.

I explained that Johnny was a friend of ours, and that he had a family and a bunch of little kids. I ended the conversation by telling him that he needed to settle his problems with the Rogues, and to leave Johnny alone. To my surprise Shotgun accepted what I said, got back in his car, and drove off into the night.

In late September, as a direct result of the incident at Arby's, the Rogues invited me to attend one of their meetings. They were very appreciative of what I had done for one of their own, and wanted to meet me. One of the other guys that regularly hung around with me at Arby's tagged along.

Rickie "Smoker" Miles was riding a Kawasaki KZ 1000 at the time. At the meeting we were both asked if we wanted to prospect, which meant we would have to do all sorts of things to see if we were worthy of becoming members. They told Smoker that he would have to get a Harley, and we both told them that we would think about it.

During the meeting we found out that there were other Rogue chapters in Oklahoma, as well as chapters in northern Texas and southern Kansas. The Tulsa chapter members present that day were:

Edwin "EJ" Nunn

Roy "Roy" Green

Marvin "Marvin" Brix

Searching For My Identity: The Chronological Evolution
Of A Troubled Adolescent To Outlaw Biker

Robert "Rob" Reynolds

Charles "T-Chuck" Schlegel

Keith "Keith" Vandervoort

Dennis "Rev" Isaacson

Louis "Bill Wolf" Rackley

Johnny "Johnny" Cook

Homer "Spurge" Spurgeon

Michael "Little Mike" Hardison

Calvin "Captain" Dorman

EJ was the president and Bill Wolf had recently transferred from the Oklahoma City chapter. EJ, Roy, Marvin, Rob, T Chuck, Keith and Rev had actually started the Tulsa chapter in 1975 at Halloween, after getting permission from the Oklahoma City Rogues. Johnny, Spurge, Little Mike and Captain were prospects.

It took Smoker and me a few days to make up our minds, but we eventually decided to give it a try. Smoker bought a beat-up old Harley Sportster, and a week later we both started hanging around. I started prospecting a few weeks later, and sewed the prospect rockers on to an old blue jean jacket I had.

I soon figured out that I could no longer make ends meet living in Tulsa, and accepted a job offer over the phone from the International heavy equipment dealer in Richmond, Virginia. It broke my heart, but I quit the Rogues after only prospecting for a few months. After packing up all my belongings again, I moved to Virginia just before Thanksgiving of 1976.

Once again I took Toni with me, which probably wasn't the best idea at the time. It seemed as though we couldn't live without each other, or with each other. At the time we both felt a change in scenery would improve our relationship, but in hindsight there was no way we could have ever made it work—we just weren't meant to be with each other, and that was all there was to it.

Chapter 6

Virginia & Connecticut

December 1976 To October 1978

It didn't take long for the fighting to begin once we arrived in Richmond, and Toni went back to Tulsa. I settled into an apartment on the north side of Richmond and my new job at Rish International. I still hadn't forgotten the skills I learned working at Cooke's, and easily fell back into the groove. Within a few weeks I had worked my way up to a field truck, and that made life easier, for I had my tools with me when I came home each night.

Now that I was making good money and living on the east coast, I started running back and forth to Connecticut, buying and selling Harley parts to pay for the trips. I was seeing a lot more of Cecil Pullen, who had sold me the panhead chopper in 1974. I set my sights on getting a new Harley but knew there was no way I could afford one. I did have an extra Harley rigid frame, a set of engine cases without serial numbers—I had removed them—and an Oklahoma builder's title, so I started looking for a parts bike.

It didn't take long to find a fairly new Superglide. The owner had only ridden it a little more than a hundred miles since it was new, and decided to sell it. The guy was dumb enough to let me take it for a test ride, and I never brought it back. By the time the sun rose on Sunday morning I had taken the bike completely apart in my apartment, and thrown the stolen frame and engine cases off a bridge into a local river.

Packing all the parts up in boxes the following Friday, I set out for Cecil's house in Connecticut. He had a motorcycle shop in the basement of his house, and was willing to let me build the bike there over the next few months. Every other weekend I traveled back and forth to Durham, and in the end wound up with a reliable Harley with a stunning paint job.

The bike was in essence, a brand new Superglide stuffed meticulously into an old Harley rigid frame, electric start and all. Once again I emblazoned the gas tank with a mural depicting the tattoo on my arm—crossed pistons and a skull, but this time left off the words Harley-Davidson and Budweiser. I was on top of the world when I brought the finished bike back to Virginia, and knew it was going to be a great summer. I now had two Harleys in a small one-bedroom apartment, and I thought I had the world by the balls.

The first ride I took on my beautiful new bike was to the local motorcycle shop that I had been in and out of the last few months, buying all sorts of odds and ends and Harley parts, either to sell, or to use on one or both of my bikes. It was still cold outside in March of 1977, but I was so excited I hardly felt it. After showing off the bike, I took a little tour around Richmond, but before I got back to my apartment I was stopped by a Richmond police officer.

Searching For My Identity: The Chronological Evolution Of A Troubled Adolescent To Outlaw Biker

The officer looked at my bike and registration papers, then called the auto theft detectives. Thirty minutes later I watched my beautiful Harley get loaded onto a wrecker and hauled off to the impound yard for investigation. The auto theft detective thought the motorcycle was stolen, but I couldn't imagine why. On my very first ride, the motorcycle had been seized. *What were the odds*? I wondered, on the long, cold walk back to my apartment.

Over the next month I argued with the auto theft detectives about the legality of the parts on the seized motorcycle. I had receipts for all the parts, but there were no serial numbers on the engine cases, and all Harley engine cases were supposed to have serial numbers. I stuck to my story that I had bought the engine cases that way, and eventually the test to locate the hidden serial numbers came back negative.

The auto theft detective in charge of the case was beside himself, for the actual report he received stated that there never had been a serial number on either of the engine case halves. He knew that was impossible, unless the engine cases had been stolen from the Harley factory before the serial numbers had been installed. The detective had even contacted Harley to inquire if they had ever lost blank engine cases, and the Harley-Davidson representative had just laughed.

In the end we made a deal—the auto theft detective would sign a release allowing me to take possession of the entire bike, minus the engine cases. I agreed to disassemble the engine at the impound yard, using my field truck full of tools to do so. He told me that he wanted to use the cases as an exhibit, to show what someone could do with the identification numbers if they had the knowledge. I made that kind of hard for him to do when I took the engine apart, because I smashed the engine cases into about thirty pieces, put them in a large plastic bag, and left the bag at the impound yard for him to pick up. I never heard from him again, but I bet he wasn't too happy when he discovered the bag of destroyed engine cases!

While I pondered what to do with the parts I now had scattered all over my apartment, Pete Hansen arrived for a visit while on leave from the United States Navy. He was excited to find that I still had my other chopper, and he talked me into letting him go for a ride. I figured that he could do no harm to the old bike, and even if he laid it down the paint could be easily repaired—after all, it had been done with a spray can of Krylon paint.

Pete went for a ride, and when he hadn't returned fifteen minutes later I started getting a little worried. When an hour had passed and there was still no sign of him, I became extremely concerned. While searching for him in my truck on the roads that surrounded the apartment complex where I lived, I soon found the motorcycle. It was a bizarre scene—the bike was wrecked, but there was no sign of my friend or any law enforcement authorities on the scene. The chopper was lying on its side in some bushes by the side of the road. I was mystified and couldn't understand why no one had called me. I went back to the complex and got a neighbor to help me load the wreck into my truck, then went back home and tried to find my friend. I called the police and checked all the hospitals to no avail.

Later that night Skip called me from Connecticut and told me his brother was in the VA Hospital, and that he had been operated on for injuries that had occurred during a motorcycle wreck. It had never crossed my mind to check for Pete at the VA Hospital. When he crashed the bike, a concerned passerby had stopped, then taken him straight to the VA hospital as requested.

The next day Skip arrived and we both went to see Pete. We took him to a park outside the hospital where Pete filled us in on the rest of the story. Skip and I thought it was outrageously funny, but Pete didn't think the same. Fortunately my friend soon recovered from his physical injuries, but it took a long time to recover the pride he lost that day.

One good thing came out of Pete wrecking the bike—I now knew exactly what to do with all of my parts. I took the legal engine cases and legal Harley title from the bike Pete wrecked, used all the parts left over from the impounded Superglide, and built a totally legal Superglide in my apartment. The only major difference between the bike that had been seized by the auto theft detectives and this one, was the style of engine cases. Instead of having a set of stolen late-model alternator cases holding the engine together, this one had legal 1958 generator cases. Besides

58

that small detail, the two bikes looked identical—I had learned my lesson and made sure the bike would never be impounded again.

The first thing I did was to take up where I left off by returning to the scene of the crime. I rode back down to the same motorcycle shop I had ridden to a few months earlier, and once again showed off my newest creation. By now everyone at Departure Bike Works knew the story of my impounded motorcycle and the blank set of Harley cases, and they were thrilled to see the bike back on the road. I spent the next few hours hoping that the auto theft detective would see me and pull me over so I could gloat, but I wasn't that lucky.

Shortly after I got the bike rebuilt and back on the road, I was able to change jobs and go to work at another construction equipment dealer across town. It had always been a dream of mine to work for Caterpillar since I started working on heavy equipment at Cooke's, but lacked the required experience. Now that I had enough knowledge, Caterpillar gave me a chance.

The brand was the Cadillac of the construction equipment world, and it was a giant step up in prestige, as well as pay. I was particularly interested in their line of large bulldozers, and quickly developed a good knowledge of the machines.

Shortly after I started working at Caterpillar Toni moved back to Richmond and into my apartment—it seemed as though I'd never get rid of her. We would still fight like cats and dogs on a regular basis, but always made up. She still had no interest in working, and seemed more concerned with spending my money and partying. At this point I was used to her little games, and knew that we had a very unhealthy relationship; it was almost as if we were addicted to each other. She would still disappear for days at a time, but by now I took it with a grain of salt. Rarely did it bother me anymore; I figured that it just came with the territory.

One afternoon that summer I was in the parking lot after work, screwing around on my Harley, showing off for some of my co-workers. I was doing burnouts across the parking lot and ran out of room to stop. I ended up in a line of rose bushes, and the thorns hurt like hell. The bike wasn't hurt, but one side of me was loaded with barbs from the rose bushes. I learned my lesson that day and never showed off again.

Not long after the rose bush incident in the parking lot I was welding a bulldozer blade in the shop when the chain holding the blade broke. This caused the thousand-pound blade to fall on my foot and break some bones, in spite of the steel-toed boot I was wearing and the cribbage under the blade. I was forced to take a few weeks off from work, and spent most of the time off hanging around Departure Bike Works on Hull Street getting to know the employees and customers there who were all outlaw bikers.

Most of them had been involved with a motorcycle club that was known as the Confederate Angels, but the club had disbanded when some of the members decided to become Hells Angels in North Carolina and the rest refused to make the change.

The club disbanded in name only, and the former members maintained the club camaraderie and organizational structure.

It took a while, but by the end of summer they were letting me hang around socially on a regular basis. I attended my first club run with a bunch of them, and in spite of the fact that they didn't wear any club colors, they still functioned as a motorcycle club. It was during this time I heard of the Outlaws motorcycle club for the first time in my life. One of the former Confederate Angels had been killed in a bar fight by a member of the Outlaws in Florida, and I was allowed to attend the funeral which was going to be held in Virginia. It was the first outlaw biker funeral I had ever been to, and was extremely impressed at the way it was handled.

The actual burial was much different than what I had ever experienced up to this point. After the casket was lowered into the ground, his brothers personally shoveled the dirt on top of it until the grave was full. They piled all of the flowers on the grave, and then had a few beers at the gravesite before everyone left. We traveled to the gravesite and back in a pack, and the pack had actually escorted the body from the church to the gravesite.

Because of the injury to my foot, and the amount of time that would be needed for it to completely heal, the Caterpillar dealership cut me loose. I received a small settlement from them for the injury, and we parted on good terms. I took the opportunity to move back to Connecticut, because my on-again off-again girlfriend had decided she was homesick. I had mixed feelings when we loaded up in the fall of 1977 and took everything we owned back to Connecticut, but hoped that the change was for the best.

Within a few days I rented a townhouse on top of a hillside just north of New Haven on the Hamden town line. It was three stories tall, and had a large garage that took up the entire ground floor. It was ideal for the motorcycles, and as an added bonus Pete was willing to rent a room to help pay the bills. He had been discharged from the Navy and had bought his first new Harley, which was a 1978 gray Low Rider. A few weeks later, after we got settled in, I was surprised to find myself happy to be in Connecticut again. It was good to be back home, but once again it didn't take long for Toni and me to start fighting. This time she moved out and took off for California.

Pete and I rang in the new year at the apartment with a small party of old friends, and we both settled into our bachelor routines. During the winter I bought a new Harley motor from the Clinton dealership, took all my leftover Harley parts, and built another bike. I then sold the blue 1958 Pan Shovel, and kept the bike with the new 1978 shovelhead motor for my personal ride.

The first trip of the year in February 1978 was a trip out west back to Oklahoma, to see all my friends there. By now Lee McArdle and Chris Robison had teamed up with Robert "Buffalo" Connaughton to open up a motorcycle shop. The Scooter Shop was located in a small building on North Utica in Tulsa, and I was able to sell some of my Harley parts to them to finance the trip. On the way back I stopped in St. Louis to visit some other Tulsa friends who had moved there, and wound up at a party that lasted all night.

Late that night when I finally got tired, there was nowhere for me to lie down and sleep except outside in a beat-up old van. The van had no heat, and it was below freezing outside. I took a cute little drunk girl with me for heat, and we settled into my sleeping bag for the night. All was well until the girl pissed in her sleep, and soaked the sleeping bag and both of us in the process. I woke up in the van to find my leftover open can of beer frozen, most of me soaked in piss, and the horrible stench from the urine permeating the van.

It was my worst nightmare. All of my dry, clean clothes were in the pickup across the yard. I got out of the sleeping bag half naked, ran to my truck in below zero bone chilling cold, fetched some clean clothes, and went into the house and cleaned up. During this whole ordeal the girl I had slept with never woke up, so I left her and the sleeping bag in the van, and hit the road.

From St. Louis I headed east on I-70 to Reading, Pennsylvania, where I first stopped to see David "Dave" Gruber and then toured the Harley-Davidson factory in York. The tour was fantastic, and I felt like a kid in a candy store! It was amazing to walk beside a new Harley and watch as it was built, then actually see the bike run at the end of the assembly line.

Searching For My Identity: The Chronological Evolution
Of A Troubled Adolescent To Outlaw Biker

As soon as I got back to Connecticut I landed a job about thirty miles away from the townhouse at H. O. Penn in Newington. The Connecticut Caterpillar dealer was a union shop, and I had never worked in a union shop before, but the pay was outstanding. I was assigned to the second shift, and found myself working 3PM to 11PM in the shop.

One weekend morning I awoke to the sound of a motorcycle running in the townhouse parking lot. When I got to my bedroom window, Pete was getting ready to load his bike into the back of his Chevy van. I was about to witness one of the funniest things I had ever seen. To facilitate the loading of the Harley into the van, my roommate had placed a wood plank from the ground to the back of the van, which he intended to use as a ramp.

As he got ready to ride the bike up the ramp, it dawned on me that Pete had probably not anticipated the impact the height of the van's roof would have on the loading process. I quickly calculated that there was only about four inches of room to spare over the top of the handlebars, and realized that my friend would have to stop the loading process at some point because there was absolutely no room for him to fit into the van if he continued riding the bike up the ramp. As predicted, just as Pete almost got the front wheel into the back of the van, he figured out that there was no way he could fit into the van if he remained on the motorcycle.

So he stopped dead in his tracks, forgetting that he was up in the air on the ramp and that there wasn't any way his feet could touch the ground. Pete and the brand-new motorcycle teetered there just for a second, before gravity took over and both of them came crashing to the ground. Then it got funny, because the new Harley was still running in first gear, lying on its left side with the rear wheel spinning. When Pete picked the bike up, the Low Rider took off without him. The Harley made a large circle around the parking lot with my friend chasing it, before falling over on its right side.

The entire incident had happened in about two minutes, and although the motorcycle was less than two months old, it was now smashed up on both sides. I felt bad for Pete, but couldn't keep from laughing. I got dressed and went downstairs to help him get the bike into the van, but there was nothing I could do to repair his pride—it was damaged forever. The experience is a permanent reminder of what not to do when loading a bike into the back of a van.

In May of 1978 my girlfriend came back from California, and once again we fell head over heels in love. Toni swore that she had exhausted her desire to party now that she was almost twenty-years old. We had been together on and off since she was sixteen, and like an idiot I believed her when she told me she had finally grown up. Part of me blamed her attitude and unfaithful actions on the fact that she had been badly injured in a horrible car accident when she was fifteen, and wore a wicked scar across her face as a result.

I dove off into a sea of stupidity when we got married in May. The reception should have been a huge wakeup call for me, but once again I chose to ignore it. Toni got so completely plastered at the reception that she passed out. The combination of pain pills and alcohol kicked her ass, and I spent my wedding night with an intoxicated wife who was unable to perform her customary wedding obligations. The next day the fighting between us was back with a vengeance, and I was forced to face the prospect that she would never change.

Within a few days Toni left for California again, telling me that it had all been a horrible mistake. I took it in stride and went back to life as a bachelor. My wife soon had second thoughts, and after just a few weeks in sunny California she returned to Connecticut and vowed to make a serious attempt at being a wife. I gave her another chance, but this time swore it would be the final time. In July we went to a bluegrass festival for my birthday, and a few weeks later we took off on the bike for a vacation ride to Bowling Green, Kentucky, where there was a major biker rally held every year.

I had made plans to meet the Tulsa crew there, and was glad to see Lee. He had made the journey with some new friends of his who were members of a California motorcycle club called the Mongols. I had never heard of the Mongols before and was surprised to hear that they were living in Tulsa, and more surprised to see them not wearing their colors.

During the rally I ran into the Outlaws for the first time, and it would have an impact on me for decades. I was wandering around minding my own business, but because it was so hot I only had a t-shirt on, and the crossed pistons and skull tattoo on my upper arm could easily be seen. Lee had joked with me earlier in the day about the tattoo being similar to the Outlaws center patch, so I shouldn't have been surprised when I was surrounded by a group of Outlaws looking for trouble. They were pissed off about my tattoo, and their leader Wildman demanded it be removed immediately. I was between a rock and a hard place, with no way out, and found myself praying to the Harley God for a miracle.

I explained to the Outlaw how and where I got the tattoo, and that I'd seen the design displayed on the wall of the tattoo shop in Rhode Island. I told him that I had no idea at the time that the Outlaws even existed. I figured that I might as well go down fighting, so I told Wildman to cut the tattoo off if he thought he needed to, and if not let me go about my business. The look in his eyes told me that I had made a grievous mistake, and just as he whipped out his knife to cut the tattoo off, an outlaw biker appeared from nowhere asking the Outlaws what they thought they were doing.

John "Little Wolf" Killip just happened to be a member of the Rogues from Oklahoma City, and I had met him when I was a prospect in Tulsa. It turned out that he knew most of the Outlaws that had surrounded me, and knew Wildman better than the rest. While I silently thanked the Harley God, the Outlaw explained the situation to the Rogue. Little Wolf told Wildman that he knew me well, and that I was a stand-up guy who regularly crisscrossed the country on my bike.

Little Wolf requested a non-violent resolution, and he complied by telling me to come to the Dayton, Ohio Outlaws clubhouse within thirty days to prove the tattoo had been covered up. I replied that I had no problem with that solution, and told him to expect me at the clubhouse in the near future. The pack of Outlaws dispersed, and I thanked Little Wolf for his interdiction. We talked for a while about our lives, and I learned that he was a frequent visitor to the clubhouse in Dayton. Little Wolf told me the Outlaws were the real deal, and a whole lot more serious about clubbing than the Rogues were. He also told me to not be surprised if he became an Outlaw someday. Before we parted, Little Wolf asked me to come back to Oklahoma and join him as a member of the Rogues, and I told him I would seriously consider it.

I went back to Connecticut where I immediately had my tattoo covered up. As soon as I could arrange some time off from work, I took off in my truck for whirlwind trip to Oklahoma, where I planned to buy a load of Harley parts from Lee's shop for resale in Connecticut. I spent one night in Tulsa, and while I was there I ran into T-Chuck from the Tulsa chapter. I told him all about the

Outlaws and Little Wolf, and that I was thinking about moving back to Oklahoma again. The Rogue told me that he would love to see me come back, and when I did, would be more than welcome to pick up with the club where I had left off.

On the way back from Oklahoma I stopped in to see the Outlaws at their Dayton clubhouse. This time I wasn't unprepared, and I carried with me a .45 caliber Colt firearm for protection. I figured if things didn't go well, I could at least take a few Outlaws with me. When I arrived at the clubhouse, it was almost dark when I knocked on the door. James "Sampson" Marr, a mountain of a man, let me in and then closed the door behind me. I told the Outlaw that I needed to see Wildman but refused to tell him why. Sampson told me that his brother was nowhere to be found, and I would just have to come back some other time.

I told him that I was on the road traveling from Oklahoma, and that I lived in Connecticut. I explained that coming back at another time was not an option, and instead demanded to speak with the chapter president, whoever that was. He laughed at me, then sent one of the other Outlaws upstairs to wake the president up. As I stood there waiting I noticed that there were a half-dozen other Outlaws in the room. I knew there was no way I could shoot them all if things went bad, and resigned myself to the fact that I probably would die in their clubhouse in the next ten minutes.

The president of the Outlaws in Dayton at that time was Kenneth "Hambone" Hammond, and it didn't take long for him to come downstairs. It was obvious he had just gotten out of bed, and I was thinking that this wasn't a good way to meet. He ordered me to sit down at the bar, and asked me if I wanted a drink. I told him about the incident with Wildman at Bowling Green, explained that I was a man of my word, and showed him the covered-up tattoo. I thanked him for his time and got up to leave, telling him I needed to hit the road.

That's when it got tense, for the Dayton president told me there was no way he could allow me to leave. All of the Outlaws in the room were on edge, waiting for the least excuse to beat my brains in, and it looked like it was the end of the line. Then Hambone broke the ice and told me the reason I couldn't go was that he wanted to get to know me. Years later Hambone told me that he was impressed that I had walked into their clubhouse by myself, and he knew right then and there that we were going to be friends for life.

While Hambone and I sat at the bar shooting the shit, he told me that he had talked to both Little Wolf and Wildman, and knew that I would show up at the clubhouse before long. Before we parted he made me promise that every time I passed through Dayton, I would always stop to see him. He promised me that when and if I moved back to Oklahoma, he would visit me whenever he was in the neighborhood.

As I walked out the clubhouse door I took a breath of fresh air and wondered how I had made it out of there alive. I had no idea a permanent bond had been forged or the significance of our meeting, and it would take years to realize that the incident at Bowling Green was a major turning point in my life.

When I got back to Connecticut, after stopping for a few hours to see my old girlfriend Suzan and her family in Pittsburgh, my wife dropped a bomb on me. It turned out that she was pregnant, and had told her father the child was mine. I was convinced it wasn't, and had arrived at that conclusion by calculating the time Toni had been pregnant to determine a probable date of conception—I figured that she had gotten pregnant on her last trip to California. I also thought I was sterile, so I went to see her father. After explaining everything to him, her father arranged for me to go to a local laboratory where I submitted a sperm sample. The test proved beyond all doubt that I couldn't be the father of the child, and Toni soon admitted the truth to her father and me.

He was livid, and his Italian blood boiled at the thought of his daughter being unfaithful to her husband. He literally threw Toni into my truck, and we took her to a local psychiatric hospital for observation. While there she had a quiet abortion and I filed for divorce. There was no way we could ever repair our relationship after this major indiscretion, in spite of all we had been through over the years. In late September of 1978 we were divorced, and I was looking for any reason to get out of Connecticut before it got cold and started snowing.

Searching For My Identity: The Chronological Evolution
Of A Troubled Adolescent To Outlaw Biker

On October 9th the reason came when I learned that T-Chuck had been murdered by his girlfriend during a domestic squabble. There was no way I could attend the funeral on such short notice, but it did propel me to make definitive plans to move back to Oklahoma. I contacted the Caterpillar dealership in Tulsa before I moved, and arranged for a job there as soon as I arrived. It was easy to do because I worked for Caterpillar in Connecticut, and the Tulsa dealership was in need of experienced mechanics. It just happened that the timing was right, or maybe it was my destiny to become a member of an outlaw motorcycle club in Oklahoma. Either way, I moved back to sunny, warm Tulsa just in time to celebrate the third anniversary of the Tulsa chapter with the Rogues on Halloween.

Chapter 7

Back To Tulsa & The Rogues MC

November 1978 To December 1979

As soon as I arrived in Tulsa I moved in with Robert "Buffalo" Connaughton, in a house he was renting off Admiral Place, just east of Highway 169. He and I got along just great—we had the same interests in Harley-Davidson motorcycles and both of us loved the freedom of being bachelors. Within a week I was working at Albert Equipment, the Tulsa Caterpillar dealer. I had my own field truck, and was specializing in the repair of large bulldozers, specifically the D-7, D-8 and D-9 models. By the end of November I was prospecting again for the Rogues, and everything in my life was okay.

In mid-December I hit a snag in the road. As part of my work assignment I was sent to Stigler to troubleshoot the transmission on a customer's D-9. When I got to the jobsite I discovered the transmission had a bad main pressure relief valve, and called the parts department to request a new valve be delivered that night to the drop box in Sallisaw. I rented a local motel room as was customary, and the next morning I stopped by the drop box and picked up the new valve.

It took me a few hours to replace the component, and by noon I had the bulldozer pushing dirt like a new machine. The customer was thrilled, because instead of a forty-four thousand dollar bill for replacing the entire transmission, he would only have to pay two-thousand dollars for the valve replacement. He even bought me a case a beer to thank me, and I headed back to the shop in Tulsa to get my next assignment. When I got there I was immediately called into the office, where the field service manager proceeded to chew me out.

He was so mad I thought his eyes were going to pop out of his head. The manager explained that he had instructed me to replace the transmission, not to test it and fix it! I told him I was a mechanic, and if he wanted someone to replace parts for him, he should have hired a parts replacer. While he continued screaming, threatening to fire me, I figured I just wasn't cut out to be working for somebody else. Since I had never been able to hold down a job for very long, I thought this would be a good time to quit and go to work on my own.

Before I walked out the door, I told the manager to send someone to my house the next day to pick up the field truck after I unloaded it. I slammed the door behind me, and optimistically walked down the hallway to the applause of a few mechanics that had watched the performance. Two years later the manager was arrested for embezzlement—he had been telling customers that their transmission had failed, when in reality the component only needed minor repairs. He then sent the good transmission to a friend's shop for repair, and resold the rebuilt transmission back to

Caterpillar at a tremendous profit. No wonder he was pissed off at me!

To pay the bills I started repairing Harleys, resumed stealing motorcycles, and sold the parts from the stolen motorcycles. In addition, my ability to change identification numbers to facilitate the concealment of stolen motorcycle parts was in demand. I had learned a lot from my experience with the auto theft detective in Virginia, and was putting the knowledge to good use. There were only three bikers in Tulsa capable of changing Harley serial numbers, but my method was by far the best and safest. Prospecting for the Rogues was also a full-time job, but the work complimented my involvement with the club.

A few days before Christmas, Rogues Rickie "Smoker" Miles and Homer "Spurge" Spurgeon took off to Florida with me to visit Hambone at the Outlaws' annual New Year's party in Fort Lauderdale. I had stopped to see the chapter president in Dayton while I was moving to Oklahoma, and told him what I was doing. Hambone had invited me to come to Florida to visit him, and told me to bring some of the Rogues if they had the balls to show up. I told him I would be there as long as my financial situation allowed it.

The three of us drove non-stop to Fort Lauderdale in a pickup truck with a camper shell on it—in the back we had a full-size mattress to sleep on. We rotated drivers every few hours, so one of us was able to sleep in the back while the other two sat in the front. This enabled us to drive all the way there in a little more than twenty-four hours. We planned on being there for Christmas, and then leaving in time to be home for New Year's Eve. While we were at the clubhouse we were treated like visiting royalty, and in spite of the fact that I was a prospect, many Outlaws talked to me as if I was a full patch. I took the time to establish a few new relationships with some of the Florida Outlaws, which eventually proved to be well worth the initial effort. After spending a few days and nights there, the three of us piled into the truck for the long non-stop journey back to Tulsa. We returned home exactly as planned, just in time for New Year's Eve.

I celebrated the arrival of the new year by renting a three-bedroom house in a newer middle-class subdivision on 34th Street, just west of 129th East Avenue. The location was central and the garage twice as large as the one I shared with Buffalo. I was surrounded by young good-looking females who were dancers at the strip joint, but still wasn't emotionally over the relationship with my former wife, so I didn't date any of them for more than a week at a time. I moved two of the strippers into the house to cook, clean, and help pay the bills.

On February 24th of 1979 I was promoted from prospect to full patch. I had fulfilled my promise to T-Chuck, and felt like I had taken his place in the chapter. To celebrate the occasion Smoker and I took off on our Harleys to attend Daytona Bike Week in Florida, and completed the eleven-hundred mile ride in less than thirty-six hours. We had been invited to the annual event by some of the Outlaws from Jacksonville we had met during the party in Fort Lauderdale.

When we got to Jacksonville, Ronald "Arab" Watchmaker introduced me to the chapter bike thief. Edward "Edd" Lackey was a Jacksonville Outlaw from Hogjaw, Alabama. Although he talked with a southern drawl, Edd and I hit it off immediately—we were like two peas in a pod. Since I needed to make some extra money while I was there, it was a no-brainer to steal bikes during Daytona Bike Week and sell them to the Outlaws.

To make it more of a challenge, Edd and I agreed to only steal a Harley if it had less than five-hundred miles on it. We rationalized this game of thievery by calculating that a Harley owner who had less than five-hundred miles on his bike deserved to lose it, for all righteous outlaw bikers rode their bikes everywhere, putting lots of miles on the odometer. We had no problem stealing low mileage Harleys from owners that didn't ride the bikes, and we affectionately called those owners RUBs (rich urban bikers). The RUBs we targeted just owned the bike for show, like someone would wear an expensive gold ring or Rolex watch.

As a further incentive each bike that was stolen would set a new barometer for the amount of mileage on the next one. For example, if Edd stole one with four-hundred ninety miles, I had to get one with less than four-hundred ninety miles on it. I was surprised how easy the pickings were. There seemed to be an abundance of new Harleys around that had less than five-hundred miles on them. Within an hour the new threshold to beat was less than two-hundred fifty miles. A few hours later the threshold was less than one-hundred miles.

The first night we bagged four bikes and delivered them by van to a warehouse for disassembly sixty miles away. The next night, because we had to steal bikes that had less than one-hundred miles on the clock, the selection pool was much smaller and it took us a while to locate acceptable candidates. When each of us had stolen a new Harley with less than one-hundred miles, we loaded the bikes into the back of the transportation van and headed north through Ormond Beach to catch the main highway out of town.

While driving the speed limit on Ridgewood Avenue, an Ormond Beach police officer recognized the driver of the van and stopped us for no reason. The officer soon figured out that something wasn't right with the Harleys in the back of the van. Within a few minutes we were surrounded by a half-dozen police officers, ordered out of the truck, and searched. I was arrested for possession of two stolen motorcycles, and three counts of carrying a concealed firearm. When we had been pulled over, I put all three of our guns in a hidden storage area behind the dash directly in front of me—because the secret compartment was closest to me, I was the one that got charged with possession of the three firearms. The date was March 9th, and I had only been a full patch Rogue for two weeks.

All three of us were taken to the county jail in Deland, but within hours were released on bond. The Outlaws had a full-time bondsman on duty at the county jail, to bail out Outlaws and their associates as fast as possible all week long. Almost every hour during Daytona Bike Week an Outlaw, associate, or ol' lady went to jail. During the next few days the three of us pooled our resources, sold every one of the Harleys we had stolen, and hired the best attorney Florida had to offer, Richard D. Nichols.

Fortunately for us the police officer that initially stopped us was a man of integrity—six months later he admitted under oath at a court hearing that he had recognized the Outlaw driving the van, and in spite of the fact that the outlaw biker or his passengers had done nothing wrong, he stopped the vehicle anyway. It was law that there had to be a valid reason to stop us initially, and to stop us for no reason amounted to an illegal stop. To search the van after making an illegal stop constituted an illegal search, and to impound the bikes after the illegal search constituted an illegal seizure. As a result the presiding judge followed the law and dismissed all of our charges. Because our charges had been dismissed, the police were forced to return the three .45 caliber Colt firearms that had been confiscated.

On the last night of our trip Smoker and I stayed with Edd in his house on Blanding Blvd. The Outlaw talked me into shooting an old black powder rifle outside the window of the bedroom Smoker was sleeping in, to wake him up. But I had been okey-doked—Edd had packed way too much powder into the old gun. When I fired, the antique rifle blew up. The force of the explosion threw me for a loop, knocking me back on my ass. It was so powerful that it blew the window out, and my shoulder was sore for almost two weeks. Surprisingly Smoker slept through the fiasco, and woke up hours later wondering where all the glass in the room had come from.

As a result of my arrest during Daytona Bike Week I had to return to Florida numerous times that spring, summer and fall for court. This turned out to be a blessing in disguise for I soon established myself as a regular with all the Outlaws in Florida. The motorcycle club had four chapters in Florida at the time, one each in Jacksonville, Orlando, Tampa and Fort Lauderdale. Almost every time I was there for court, I stayed for at least two weeks, and made sure I visited each chapter at least once. I rapidly established strong friendships with Outlaws from each chapter. Almost every Outlaw in Florida knew who I was, and many considered me to be a close friend.

In April while I was attending a Rogues party in Prague, Oklahoma, I got into a fistfight with a much larger Rogue from the Oklahoma City chapter. Robert Eugene Harris was six-foot two, two-hundred twenty-five pounds, and had served with the Marine Corps in Vietnam—we called him Rocky. He was drunk, and had noticed that I wore a patch on my vest identifying myself as the Tulsa chapter enforcer. Rocky told me there was no way a little guy like me deserved the enforcer patch, and in fact, he thought I was a punk with no balls. Not wanting to be thought of that way, and certainly not being one, I immediately struck the Oklahoma City Rogue in the face with my fist, giving the punch everything I had.

I actually had to jump up in the air a little to hit him—by luck, the punch caught him unprepared and knocked him over backwards. At that point he was livid, because I had done it in front of a whole bunch of Rogues. When Rocky got up he dared me to try it again, and of course I obliged him. When my fist was about six inches from his face, the outlaw biker grabbed my right arm and jerked me to the ground, where we both wound up in a pile. After figuring out I was badly injured, the brothers took me to the VA Hospital in Muskogee—the diagnosis was an AC (arm & collar) separation that required immediate surgery.

While I was laid up in the hospital recovering from the surgery, my Oklahoma City brother stopped by to see me the next day. He had gotten up that morning and had no memory of the altercation, and when he learned of the incident, Rocky rode his Harley a hundred miles out of his way to visit me. He told me that he had never intended to hurt me this bad, and knew I wasn't a punk. Rocky ended up staying there with me until I was released a few days later, then stayed at my house for another week until I was able to get around by myself. He apparently felt guilty for causing me so much pain, and hanging out with me every day was his way of making things right. As a result we became very close friends, and were together frequently over the next few years.

While I was at home recovering, one of my many lucrative business ventures got busted. I had established an escort agency on the other side of town in a quiet office building near 64th Street South on Peoria Avenue. I hired two straight, non-biker guys to manage it, and was supplying the operation with willing dancers from the local strip joints.

It was a mini gold mine, but the managers I hired soon got too vocal with the advertising. As a result the Tulsa Police Department vice squad determined that the business was a front for an organized prostitution service. The arrests of the managers produced lots of media attention, but in spite of the fact that all the charges would eventually be dropped, I did the smart thing and closed it down.

Around the same time my friend from Pennsylvania, David "Dave" Gruber, moved to Tulsa with the intention of becoming a member of the Rogues. Dave and I had met in Connecticut during the summer of 1978 while he and a friend toured New England on their bikes. I had run into the independent outlaw bikers riding down the highway, and took them to my parents' house for a free meal. After that we stayed in touch, and I had stopped by to see him in Pennsylvania a few times. His home was only a few miles from the main highway I traveled back and forth from Oklahoma to Connecticut on a regular basis.

Searching For My Identity: The Chronological Evolution
Of A Troubled Adolescent To Outlaw Biker

On June 13th of 1979, a bunch of us rode our Harleys to a local rock n' roll bar called Whiskers—we wanted to see the Wednesday night show and have a good time. I was still in my arm brace from the AC surgery, and although I felt well enough to get out of the house, I was far from being fully recovered.

Lyndon Jackson was a bully who hung out at Whiskers regularly terrorizing and assaulting innocent patrons. He normally loved to pick on anyone who was unable to defend themselves, but on this night he was out to prove to the world that he was the toughest kid on the block. Everyone's a tough guy until they actually meet one, but apparently no one had ever told Jackson that it would be suicide to mess with a motorcycle club, since many of the members had served in Vietnam.

The incident started when Jackson's little brother confronted the first Rogue he ran into. In response, the Rogue pissed on the little brother's leg while patiently listening to the threats that his older brother would kill all of them when he arrived. After realizing that the Rogue had pissed all over him, the little brother disappeared into the darkness—the Rogues milling around thought that the altercation was over, but it wasn't.

A few minutes later the little brother returned to the scene with the older brother, and a few of the older brother's friends. Less than five minutes later Lyndon Jackson the tough guy, was Lyndon Jackson the walking dead guy. When Jackson confronted a Rogue with the intent to do the outlaw biker serious bodily harm,

the military veteran did exactly what he had been trained to do—
he defended himself.

After the brawl, which involved more than twenty people,
all of the participants scattered to the four winds. Every Rogue
there, as well as all of their friends and associates, left the parking
lot under their own power. What they left behind was no less than
a scene reminiscent of a Vietnam battlefield, for there was blood
and injured combatants everywhere. Lyndon Jackson was lying in
the parking lot knocking on death's door, and was dead by the time
the ambulance arrived. Only one Rogue required hospitalization—
he suffered a broken nose and two broken cheek bones in the
melee.

Less than thirty minutes after the brawl the Tulsa police
officers apprehended three club members who were thought to
have been involved in the fracas. Rogue Michael "Little Mike"
Hardison was arrested for suspicion of murder, and Rogue Calvin
"Captain" Dorman and prospect Myron Corser were arrested as
material witnesses. We all knew that Little Mike had nothing to do
with the death of Lyndon Jackson, because he was inside the bar
at the time the fight broke out. His only involvement was after the
fight, when he accidentally bumped an innocent bystander with his
motorcycle leaving the establishment.

The charges against Little Mike alleged that he caused
Jackson's death by deliberately running the man over with his
motorcycle, and the actual cause of death was alleged to be the

shifter pedal on the Harley. When the medical examiner testified at a preliminary hearing that Jackson had died from a knife wound likely inflicted by someone with a military background, and not by a shifter pedal from a motorcycle, the judge dismissed all of the charges.

Not long after the incident at Whiskers I decided to spend a few hours being entertained by strippers. As I pulled into the parking lot on the southwest corner of 21st Street and Highway 169, where a half-dozen strip joints were located, I recognized one of the bouncers standing in front of a dance hall. Knowing he would let me in for free, that's the direction I headed.

After my eyes got accustomed to the dim lights inside, I found a seat and waited for the next dancer to get up on the stage. Although the bar had strippers that danced completely naked, I wasn't prepared for what came next—I was immediately attracted to the girl that started dancing. When she got done, I called the stripper over to where I was sitting and asked for her name—she told me it was Jaime.

It wasn't long before Keitha "Jaime" Millis and I started dating. I didn't know it at the time, but this was going to be another on-off, love-hate relationship, identical to the one I had with my first wife. Drawing from the same selection pool always produces the same results, but I didn't know that then.

When I finally recovered from the shoulder surgery and regained full use of my injured arm in mid-August, the Rogues transferred me to the Enid chapter, which was a little more than one-hundred miles west of Tulsa. I established a retail motorcycle shop there as a cover for my illegal enterprises, and rented a residence that doubled as our clubhouse.

In September some of the Tulsa Rogues accepted an offer from the owner of a trucking company—at the time the drivers, all union employees, were on strike, so my brothers agreed to drive the trucks and act as strikebreakers for a lucrative salary. When leaving the truck facility one evening after work a few days later, four Rogues in a car got into an altercation with the strikers at the gate, and a massive riot broke out. The Tulsa police officers present at the time the fight started retreated to the safety of their squad cars until reinforcements arrived.

Rogues Marvin Brix, Arthur "Art" Kohring, Spurge, and Smoker were arrested, and when the dust settled a total of nineteen people went to jail. A myriad of illegal weapons were recovered from the Rogues, and the car they were riding in. As a result of the fight, union representatives from Kansas City, who were associated with the mafia, traveled to Tulsa to meet with chapter president Roy Green. They agreed that the Rogues would be allowed to continue strikebreaking, without the possibility of facing any retribution for what they were doing. The strike ended peacefully three weeks later, and all of the rioting charges were eventually dismissed.

Searching For My Identity: The Chronological Evolution
Of A Troubled Adolescent To Outlaw Biker

In November I took off for another whirlwind trip to Florida. A few days after I got there I was hanging around outside of the clubhouse in Jacksonville while the Outlaws chapter had a meeting inside. When the gathering let out the Outlaws president told me I had been voted in as a member of the chapter—all I had to do was give them my Rogues patch, and move from Oklahoma to the Jacksonville area in the near future. Since I had no intention of moving I declined the offer. Instantly he hit me in the chest as hard as he could with a closed fist, knocking me backwards to the ground and causing the imprint of the Outlaws ring he wore to be indented in my chest.

But this wasn't a fistfight, just his way of letting me know that he was disappointed. The president respected my decision, and as he helped me up off the ground he told me to think about it for the next few days. I felt honored to have been voted into the chapter as a full patch member, and almost changed my mind after thinking about it, but there was just no way I could leave Oklahoma. I felt that the state was my home, and it was my destiny to remain there for a long time.

On December 7th, the anniversary of the invasion of Pearl Harbor, Keitha hitchhiked from Tulsa to Enid late one night with no advance warning or definitive plan in place. I was quite surprised when she called the clubhouse from a payphone at the local truck stop and asked me to pick her up. After spending a few days together, we drove to the apartment she shared with a girlfriend in Tulsa, threw everything she owned into the back of my van, and started living together in Enid—it was the beginning of a tumultuous relationship that scarred me for decades.

Chapter 8

Running With The Bandidos

June 1979 To November 1982

I met my first Bandido in Mobile, Alabama in the summer of 1979. Dwight "Buddy" Boykin was intelligent, ten-years older than me, and a Vice-Presidente in the national chapter under Bandido El Presidente Ronnie Hodge. Arab from the Outlaws chapter in Jacksonville knew the Alabama Bandido well, and since my frequent travels to Florida took me directly through Mobile he thought it would be a good idea for the two of us to meet.

Buddy's house wasn't far from my usual route through Mobile, so it was a perfect stopping place about half way between Tulsa and Jacksonville. I would usually try to get to Mobile by late afternoon, spend the night, and hit the road the next morning. It didn't take long before stopping to see the Bandidos in Mobile was mandatory on every trip, and I went to Florida frequently.

It turned out that Buddy and I got along great, and I looked forward to spending time with him in Mobile. The perception of a motorcycle club is typically based on the first member you meet, as well as what transpires during the time you're together. For example, if it's a violent interaction, then a biker normally wouldn't be friendly with anyone from that organization again. Because Buddy truly believed in the concept of brotherhood, as Rocky and some of the other Rogues did, he introduced me to a different type of motorcycle club that I was extremely interested in. It wasn't long before I started thinking about the possibility of becoming a Bandido and the Bandidos assimilating the Rogues, but had no idea at the time how long a process that would be.

In the spring of 1980 after I had spent the fall and winter rebuilding the Northern Oklahoma chapter of the Rogues in Enid, I was appointed national sergeant-at-arms. Because the organization had more than one-hundred twenty-five members and a dozen chapters spread out over Oklahoma, southern Kansas and northern Texas, there were two national sergeant-at-arms.

My brother Rocky was the other national sergeant-at-arms. Although I was much smaller than him, both of us were well-respected for our ability to take care of business. In a dangerous situation everyone usually noticed the big guy first and forgot about me, which is exactly how we planned it. Rocky and I were a dynamic team, and spent a lot of time on the road together.

At the same time I had been cultivating my relationship with Buddy in Mobile, Rocky had been spending a lot of time with a Bandido from Lubbock, Texas. Judson "Earthquake" McCarter was also a mountain of a man and had a well-deserved reputation for taking care of business, so it was no surprise that the two outlaw bikers hit it off so well. While Buddy had me thinking about becoming a Bandido, Earthquake had Rocky seriously thinking about leaving the Rogues and doing the same.

Searching For My Identity: The Chronological Evolution
Of A Troubled Adolescent To Outlaw Biker

During 1979 and the first half of 1980 I had been working on a life-long dream. I finally realized that vision when I completed my first vinyl LP record in June, which I titled *At Long Last*. The pseudonym I chose was the Connecticut Dust Band; I hoped the name would quietly reflect the fact that there never was a band. In reality the musicians that performed on the album were Kurt Newman, an assortment of studio musicians, and me. In my frequent travels to Connecticut over the years I had established a friendship with a pair of schoolteachers who owned a recording studio in Hamden called Grace Recording Studios, which is where the music was recorded.

For distribution purposes I established a record company, Shovster Records & Music, which was aptly named after a stroked Sportster engine with a Shovelhead top end. Self-taught over the span of a few years, I had learned how to record, produce, manufacture and copyright the songs and music on the record. Although the sound quality wasn't great, and the quality of the songs I had written mediocre, I was quite proud of my accomplishment. For the first few months after it was completed Rocky was so proud of it, he carried the album with him wherever he went.

One day in the summer of 1980 Rocky and I rode together into Oklahoma City from Wichita Falls, where Rocky was living at the time. When we got to the Oklahoma City Rogues clubhouse, everyone present was complaining about the fact that there were

Bandidos in town, and it looked like the Bandidos were setting up a clubhouse and planning to establish a chapter in the middle of Rogues territory. All of my brothers were mad, yet none of them were willing to do anything about it. Rocky and I immediately decided to confront them, and rode our Harleys to the house where the Bandidos were living less than a mile away, ready for World War III.

We both hoped for a peaceful solution but had prepared for the worst—it's always better to be safe than sorry. It only took a moment to get off our bikes and knock on the front door. A Bandido opened the door and asked us to come in, which we did. As my eyes adjusted to the lack of light inside, I noticed a few men relaxing in the living room. Bandidos Tramp, Slyder and Cannon were three of the four men in the room, and they were also ready for World War III.

Although we knew none of them at the time, Rocky and I told them that we both had excellent relationships with Buddy and Earthquake. We explained our concerns about what we had heard, and inquired about their reasons for being in town. The Bandidos told us that they were there to help Bandido Craig set up and run a local strip club, and that there was no reason for concern. They advised us that they had no intention of establishing a chapter in Oklahoma City—they were just there for business purposes. Rocky and I ended the meeting by inviting them over to our clubhouse, and they told us to drop in and see them anytime we wanted to.

After the meeting we stopped to get a bite to eat, and talked about the prospect of changing over the entire Rogues nation to Bandidos. We didn't think it would be possible to change over every member, since some of the Oklahoma City brothers were already heavily involved with the Outlaws, but we did agree that it would be easy to find enough outlaw bikers to start new Bandidos chapters in Tulsa and Oklahoma City. We agreed to sit back and see what the future would bring, and planned to talk to the Bandidos about the possible assimilation. I was going to talk to Buddy, and Rocky would talk to Earthquake.

The planned conversations never materialized—not long after our discussion almost a dozen former members of the Rogues in Oklahoma City completed their one-year probationary period, and opened up the first Outlaws chapter west of the Mississippi River. This new chapter was five-hundred miles from the closest Outlaws chapter in Memphis, and seven-hundred miles from the next closest chapter in Indianapolis. It posed an interesting dilemma, because I had brothers in the Florida and Ohio chapters of the Outlaws—as well as the new Oklahoma chapter—but also had an allegiance to my Rogue brothers to consider. To say the least, it was a certainly a troublesome and tumultuous time for me.

At the same time I was in serious trouble with the law in numerous jurisdictions. It was a navigational nightmare, for I had simultaneous criminal cases ongoing in Oklahoma, Florida and Texas. Each required multiple court appearances, and it seemed as though I had to be in court somewhere in the country every week.

To compound things, during the summer I had been arrested in Jacksonville for possession of another loaded firearm. This time I was standing outside a bar late at night minding my own business, after attending court earlier that day for the Daytona stolen motorcycle and gun possession case. A police officer approached me and asked for identification, then arrested me for drinking in public—he wasn't surprised to find the .45 caliber Colt firearm in my shoulder holster.

In Dallas on March 16th of 1981 I was arrested on a fifth gun charge while sleeping in my van in front of the Scorpions clubhouse. This charge rapidly evolved into a homicide investigation, because the firearm the police officers found—the gun was actually in the back of the van, and belonged to Rocky— had been used in a Kansas murder. After the Kansas detectives arrived at the jail to interview me, my luck changed for the better when they discovered I weighed one-hundred thirty-five pounds and was five-feet eight-inches tall.

It turned out the detectives were looking for a larger man, and it occurred to me that the suspect they were describing was similar to Rocky. The hold on me for the murder investigation was dropped less than an hour later, and I was released from jail on my own recognizance.

I was happy to be released, but the funniest part of the ordeal was still to come. When I was arrested all I had on was a pair of jeans—no shirt, no socks and no shoes, for I had been asleep until I was awakened by the police. At the time I was released from jail I had no clothes with me except the pair of jeans; everything else was in my van, and the police had impounded the van at the time of my arrest.

It was an unusually hot day when I got released. As I hopped from one foot to another to avoid the scalding pavement, I decided to run across the street to avoid burning my feet, instead of going up to the corner and crossing at the light. You can imagine my dismay when I was caught jaywalking by a policeman exiting the building. In spite of my dilemma, the Dallas cop made me go back, walk to the corner, wait for the traffic light, and then cross the street legally.

I barely kept my anger in check, but because I kept hopping from one foot to another, I was able to avoid burning my feet. Things got worse when Rocky came to pick me up. All he owned was his motorcycle, so I was forced to ride as a passenger on the back from the jail to the impound yard. I finally got to my van and clothes, and was so relieved after I put my shoes on.

Between all of my court cases, trying to keep the animosity between some of the Rogues and the new Outlaws in Oklahoma City from turning violent, trying to make a living, and handling our daily business affairs for the club, Rocky and I had our hands full. We spent the rest of the summer balancing our heavy load, and in spite of a few fistfights between members of the two outlaw motorcycle clubs, there were no more major problems that year.

In early August of 1981 I moved back to Tulsa from Enid. My legal problems came to a head shortly thereafter when I went to trial in Tulsa at the federal courthouse. I had been arrested earlier that year for uttering a forged United States obligation and possession of stolen mail—both charges resulted from an attempt to cash a stolen United States treasury check at a Tulsa bank. I had wondered about the authenticity of the check when I received it as payment for a debt, but figured that if it were worthless, the bank wouldn't cash it.

Thinking that getting caught was no big deal, and even if I was caught it would probably only result in a short stay in jail, was a serious blunder. I was using a half-dozen different identities at the time, so I had deposited the treasury check in one of the many accounts I had established under a fictitious name. I figured the fake account would insulate me from getting arrested—but it's amazing how naïve you can be when you're young!

I missed a mandatory Rogues national run in Wyoming over the Labor Day weekend; it was something I had never done since I became a Rogue. I had been convicted in federal court after trial by jury the week before, and was out on bond waiting to be sentenced. I had previously been sentenced to thirty months in state prison after being convicted in Garfield County (Enid) for knowingly concealing stolen property. Two weeks later I was sentenced to an additional seven years in federal court for the crimes I committed concerning the forged treasury check.

Gerb, the Rogues' national president, was pissed off that I had not shown up in Wyoming for the national run, so he ordered the Tulsa chapter president, Marvin Brix, to make me a prospect again. Marvin was upset about the mandate and didn't think it was appropriate, but I was defiant and recalcitrant. I didn't have time to prospect, and needed what little time I had left on the streets to get my affairs in order. So I quit the club, which was my only option at the time—the Rogues concept of brotherhood was nowhere the same as mine.

On October 8th I answered a knock on the door of my house and found more than a dozen cops standing there. They had a warrant for my arrest regarding the Garfield County conviction from 1980—my attorney had forgotten to file the appeal. I was incarcerated at the Tulsa County jail for a day, then transported to the Garfield County jail, where I stayed for four weeks before I entered the Oklahoma state prison system in early November.

I spent nine months in custody on the thirty-month sentence, and paroled out of the state prison system on July 8th of 1982. As I left the Jess Dunn Correctional Center in Taft, I savored my release as I walked down the steps. Two men in suits were waiting there for me—they identified themselves as federal marshals. When they told me that I was under arrest because my attorney had failed to file the appeal for my federal case, I wasn't surprised.

I spent a week in the Tulsa County jail again before I was transported to the federal prison in El Reno, Oklahoma, in the middle of July. It was very hot, in excess of one hundred degrees, and I was put in a third-floor cell. It was like an incinerator in there—whenever I moved, the sweat poured out of me.

I stayed there for two weeks, and then was transferred by bus to the federal penitentiary at Leavenworth, Kansas. It was a wonderful bus ride, one that I'll never forget. Handcuffed and belly chained with leg irons around my ankles, I arrived in early August, spent a night inside the walls at the United States Penitentiary, and then was assigned to the prison camp because my sentence was so short.

While at Leavenworth camp I got interested in the law library. I figured that no one could help me now except myself. If I wanted to get out of prison, I would have to do it on my own, so I learned how to attack my sentence through a provision in the law, and filed a section 2255 motion in the United States District Court in Tulsa just before Halloween. At the same time I was working in the law library, I was also starting to have severe gastrointestinal problems.

As a result of my medical condition I was transferred to the Comprehensive Health Services Unit at the Fort Worth Federal Correctional Institution two days before Thanksgiving. I arrived there in a state of shock, for the facility was coed. To my pleasant

surprise I found males and females hanging out together all over

the place—I thought I had died and gone to heaven!

Chapter 9

Running With The Bandidos

November 1982 To October 1985

There was a massive law library there, twenty times the size of the one I was used to, which was enlightening. At Leavenworth camp all I had to work in was one small cramped room. The law library at Fort Worth was fantastic, and filled to the brim with everything you could ask for. Because I had a pending 2255 motion, I was allowed all the time I needed to study and prepare for my case. I had alleged that I was being held in violation of the Fifth Amendment of the United States Constitution, which guaranteed that a prisoner would receive effective assistance of counsel. This was predicated on the fact that my attorney had failed to file the appeal on the federal conviction for which I was currently incarcerated.

In late January of 1983 an evidentiary hearing was held in Tulsa regarding the 2255 motion, which I handled pro se. I was successful in convincing the judge that I'd been rendered ineffective assistance of counsel, and he agreed with my proposition that the constitutional protection of the Fifth Amendment should apply to appeals. As a result my appeal bond was reinstated immediately, and I was released from custody. Once again I was thrilled to be free, and savored my walk out of the courtroom.

Once again my glee was short lived, for there was a Tulsa auto theft detective waiting for me at the door to arrest me. The warrant Dewayne Smith had in his hand was for crimes I had committed in the spring of 1981, all involving the same stolen Chevy van—the detective needed to arrest me before the statute of limitations prevented him from doing so. The crimes that I was charged with happened so far back, it took me almost a week to remember the van in question.

By the time I bailed out of jail for the stolen van case there were two completely different factions of Rogues in Tulsa—the former members and the current members—most of them didn't like each other. Marvin, the chapter president when I went to prison, had become disillusioned and quit the club. He took half the chapter with him, after some of the other members had been caught stealing my tools, stereo, and business inventory.

Although everything stolen was returned to Marvin's custody a few days later—Lee McArdle and Robert "Candy" McGee had held Smoker at gunpoint with automatic weapons inside his house until all of my possession were returned—Marvin and I weren't on good terms with the Rogues that remained.

Since he had taken care of my affairs while I was locked up, it was a no-brainer for me to move into the small apartment that was attached to Marvin's house in early February. Shortly after I moved in, the Rogues national chapter sent two armed Tulsa members over to Marvin's house to order me to remove my club tattoo—one of them was Smoker, the other Jerry Nelson.

At the exact moment that Smoker and Jerry rode their Harleys into the driveway, Earl Hastings was hiding behind the front door in Marvin's house—he was on the run for shooting a guy in Claremore the day before. The independent outlaw biker, who was a good friend of mine from New England, was all over the television news.

Thinking that the guy he shot was going to die, Earl had decided to shoot it out with the police when he was caught, rather than go to prison for murder. To facilitate the plan he had a fully automatic M-16 machine gun, and a bunch of clips filled with ammunition.

Correctly presuming that Smoker and Jerry were there with the intention to do us all serious bodily harm, Earl volunteered on the spot to kill the two Rogues before they could enter the house and shoot Marvin or me.

I talked Earl out of shooting Smoker and Jerry, although I had a hard time making up my mind for a minute. Leaving Earl behind the door to watch over me, I met Jerry and Smoker in the driveway. When the two Rogues told me they had been sent over to tell me to cover up the tattoo, I told them both that it would never happen, and to go back and tell their national president I said so.

When law enforcement authorities served a drug-related search warrant at his home a few months later, they found the Mac-

10 machine gun and silencer that Smoker had been instructed to use to kill Marvin and me. The Rogue had failed to complete the assignment, and instead served eight years in federal prison for possession of the machine gun.

It wasn't long before the guy that Earl shot recovered from his wounds and was released from the hospital. I convinced Earl to go back to New England, where he avoided capture for two years. When he eventually was extradited back to Claremore to face the charges, Earl lucked out and was sentenced to serve only two years in the Oklahoma prison system.

By the time I was released from prison my roadie and good friend Rogue Robert "Rocky" Harris had sadly been killed in an auto/pedestrian accident in Alaska, and the Rogues membership had shrunk from one-hundred twenty-five plus members in the summer of 1980, to less than fifty. Although most of the Outlaws in Florida had been convicted of federal racketeering charges while I was incarcerated, I was still in contact with Arab, who was locked up in a federal prison near Memphis.

In the summer of 1983 I started traveling to Memphis from Tulsa on a regular basis to visit Arab, and to see another friend of mine that lived there, Thomas "Tattoo Tommy" Williams, who had opened a tattoo shop in a Memphis suburb. Tattoo Tommy had been a tattoo artist in New Orleans for many years, primarily for the Outlaws. As a result of a bomb blast that leveled his tattoo shop in New Orleans the year before, he had relocated to Tennessee.

One day when I was visiting Arab he asked me to locate Bandido Ronnie for him. I had no problem doing this, for I had been in contact with the El Presidente years before when I was a Rogue. Arab hoped to reestablish their friendship and open a direct line of communication, for the two outlaw bikers had been close friends for many years.

I contacted the El Presidente by phone and relayed the message from Arab. While I was talking to him, I mentioned the fact that I was frequently traveling from Tulsa to Memphis to visit the Outlaw. Ronnie asked if I was stopping in Little Rock to see the Bandidos there. I told him I didn't know anyone there. He gave me a phone number for Gary "Wiggs" Wiggs, who was president of the Little Rock chapter, and suggested that I call him the next time I went through Little Rock.

On my next trip east to Memphis, I called Wiggs from a payphone at the I-40 rest stop on the west side of Little Rock. His house was in the city of Little Rock and not far from where I was. I was only there an hour, but spent the majority explaining how I came to be in possession of his phone number and name.

Wiggs wasn't very friendly, and seemed to be extremely suspicious—years later I learned that he wasn't friendly with anyone, and was always suspicious of everyone he met—so I was surprised when he told me to make sure I stopped in to see him on my way back through Little Rock. I decided to stop in one more time before I gave up.

Searching For My Identity: The Chronological Evolution
Of A Troubled Adolescent To Outlaw Biker

A few days later on my return trip from Memphis to Tulsa, I stopped to see Wiggs. I planned on stopping by for just a few minutes, because I told him I would, but expected another unfriendly reception. This time I was quite surprised to find the opposite. Wiggs was just like Buddy had been in Mobile the very first time I had met him, and it was like we had known each other for years. He explained that when I first called, he had no way to contact Ronnie to verify who I was, and if the El Presidente had given me his phone number. While I had been in Memphis, Wiggs had talked to Ronnie and Buddy—both had told the chapter president that they knew me.

From that point on Little Rock was home away from home. Every trip I made to Memphis, I would stop on the way there, and again on the way back. Wiggs eventually introduced me to Robert "Cowboy" Crain, the chapter sergeant-at-arms, and he immediately reminded me of Rocky.

Cowboy and I soon discovered we made an outstanding team. The Little Rock Bandido possessed an impressive knowledge of firearms, torture and violence. I had a successful history of motorcycle and auto theft, knew how to alter serial numbers of stolen motor vehicles, and had an extensive knowledge of criminal law. The collective knowledge we shared allowed us to pursue numerous business ventures, legal and illegal.

One of the most successful endeavors we were involved in was the purchase and sale of LSD. At the time possession of LSD, although criminal, was nowhere as serious as it is now. Simple possession would get you a slap on the wrist, and selling it would usually result in a short prison sentence. The benefits of selling the drug far outweighed the cost if we were caught. As a bonus we could get ourselves, as well as our friends, high for free.

In the summer of 1984 Cowboy decided that he wanted a new Lincoln Towncar, but didn't want to pay for it. We bought a wrecked 1976 model from a local salvage pool for under two-hundred dollars and removed the serial number plate. Cowboy and I then went to Tulsa and spent a few nights shopping for a similar 1976 model at local apartment complexes. We finally settled on a real nice maroon one. It only took me a few minutes to gain entry and start the car, and another few hours to change the serial number and license plates.

During 1983 and 1984 my relationship with the Little Rock Bandidos grew and solidified. By the time the fall of 1984 arrived I had met everyone in the chapter, a few Bandidos from other chapters, and had kept in touch with Buddy. Again I was beginning to think that starting a chapter in Oklahoma was a possibility, and talked to Cowboy about moving there to Tulsa to help me.

While I was out of prison awaiting the results of my court cases during 1983 and 1984, I found the time to record another vinyl LP record. This time I used the name Warren Winters as my stage name, and titled the work *As I Was*. I recorded some of the album at Long Branch Studios in Tulsa, and part of it at Grace

Recording Studio while on one of my trips back to Connecticut. The majority of the songs on the album were about my convoluted relationship with Keitha, who was the daughter of a preacher. Although she had been my girlfriend in 1979 and 1980, Keitha had left me for cocaine and greener pastures in the summer of 1981.

After I was released from prison in the spring of 1983, the federal prosecutors appealed my case to the 10th Circuit Court of Appeals in Denver. They argued that I wasn't entitled to effective assistance of counsel during appeal, and that I should be put back in prison. I argued the appeal again pro se, and was very satisfied when I won and the court upheld my release. The unanimous decision was reported in the law books at 724 F2d 109 (10th Cir. 1983), and the judgment mandated that all criminal defendants in the United States from that day forward were guaranteed effective assistance of counsel on appeal.

As a direct result of the decision, the appeal of my conviction was finally filed by a court appointed attorney. That turned out to be an exercise in futility, for ten months later the Tenth Circuit Court of Appeals in Denver affirmed the conviction, and I found myself back in front of the same federal judge that originally oversaw my trial. Just before Christmas I was resentenced to the exact same term I had received originally, but was allowed me to spend the holidays at home—I was scheduled to report back to the federal prison in Fort Worth on January 4th of 1985.

Searching For My Identity: The Chronological Evolution
Of A Troubled Adolescent To Outlaw Biker

On January 3rd Cowboy and I drove to Fort Worth and spent the night at the home of a Fort Worth Bandido. After a grand tour of every strip joint in Fort Worth that lasted until closing time, we got up early and had breakfast, then drove to the federal prison. I remember my Little Rock brother driving onto the prison property, realizing exactly where he was, and hoping that no one searched the car because the trunk was filled with firearms. I can only imagine what would have happened to us, and what the authorities would have thought, if the car had been searched that day.

On January 4th at 9AM I started serving what was left of the sentence I had started serving in July of 1982. I calculated that I would be released on parole in the middle of October, and had told Cowboy I would see him then. Unfortunately our plans were postponed for more than six years by the events that happened in the following months.

It took me a few weeks to get used to prison life again, and by the middle of January I was back in the law library. Working there kept my mind occupied, and also allowed me to assist other inmates with their legal issues. Some inmates I helped for free, and some I traded for favors like an evening sandwich or personal laundry services. For other inmates that had complicated legal situations, money orders would be deposited in my commissary account.

Searching For My Identity: The Chronological Evolution
Of A Troubled Adolescent To Outlaw Biker

The only good thing about the prison was that it was still coed. There were females and males of all ages wandering around the yard together. We were allowed to eat together, work together, socialize in the common yard area and hold hands, but weren't allowed to sleep together or have sex. As I'm sure you can imagine, there was nothing the guards could do to keep the inmates from having sex.

Almost everyone had what we called a walkie, a member of the opposite sex that we hung out with on a daily basis, and in some cases had sex with. Because the prison was a minimum-security facility, there were a lot of rats (inmates who had testified against their co-defendants to get a reduced sentence). There were only a handful of females I allowed to get close to me, and two of them were from Texas—both were serving time for failing to testify against their husbands in connection with the assassination of a federal judge, so I knew they weren't rats.

Elizabeth "Liz" Chagra, the wife of El Paso attorney Jimmy Chagra, and Jo Ann Harrelson, the mother of famous actor Woody Harrelson and wife of Charles Harrelson, had also known each other when they were on the streets. An independent outlaw biker from Texas always walked with Liz, and I walked with Jo Ann. At forty-four years old she was still a good-looking woman even though Jo Ann was fifteen years older. Although we never had sex or anything close to it, I have to admit that the thought crossed my mind a time or two. Jo Ann and I always had plenty to talk about, and she helped me pass the time. When I left the Fort Worth prison we lost touch, but she remained there for twelve more years until she was released in 1997.

By mid-February I had resumed my regular prison routines—my time was going by fast, and I was keeping busy. I thought that everything would be back to normal in no time. My first indication that all would not be the same when I got out was when I read the February 13th edition of the Oklahoma City newspaper. Almost the entire Outlaws chapter in Oklahoma had been arrested on a myriad of federal charges that included racketeering and drug trafficking charges. Among the members arrested were four former members of the Rogues, including John "Little Wolf" Killip, who had rescued me from the Outlaws in Bowling Green.

After eating dinner on February 21st I sat down in the TV room to watch the national news, as I did every evening. I was shocked to learn that the Bandidos had been the target of a coordinated nationwide crackdown. Almost one-hundred Bandidos and associates had been arrested by state and federal law enforcement agents across the United States. The next morning while reading the Arkansas Gazette I discovered the situation in Little Rock was grim.

Every one of the Bandidos in Arkansas had been indicted on federal charges except one, who had been employed at a tire manufacturing company for years. Along with an assortment of

their friends and a former member, a total of twenty-two people
had been indicted, and the charges were detailed in a forty-four
count federal indictment. Cowboy and Wiggs had both been
charged with running a continuing criminal enterprise, which
carried the possibility of life in prison and guaranteed them a
minimum of ten years.

Cowboy had escaped capture by a stroke of luck and
continued to elude authorities for more than two weeks before he
turned himself in. In addition to allegedly violating the continuing
criminal enterprise statute, he was charged with torturing a federal
witness. I knew my brother would likely spend the rest of his life
in prison if the federal government had its way. In mid-April a
former member of the Little Rock chapter plead guilty after
cooperating with the government to get himself a lighter prison
sentence.

In May Cowboy's girlfriend Sissy came to visit me. It was
the first time I had seen her since late 1984, and it turned out to be
a memorable visit. The guard on duty directed us to sit at a certain
table, which seemed odd to me. Although I didn't get visits often,
I had never been told where to sit. The guard explained that the
other empty tables were reserved for a special family event. We sat
down at the table we were assigned to, and preceded to talk about
all sorts of things. Before long Sissy started asking me some
unusual questions, some of which made the hair on the back of my
neck stand up. She wanted to know all about the illegal activities

Cowboy and I had been involved in, and was most interested in a maroon 1976 Lincoln Towncar.

As I watched her lips move I was thinking that this was a setup. By accident I dropped something on the floor, and when I bent over to pick it up I noticed something strange attached to the underside of the table. When I pried it off I immediately realized that it was a recording device, and presumed that the bug had been planted there by federal agents. It dawned on me that Sissy was likely cooperating, which was no surprise since she was a single mom who would do anything to keep from losing her young daughter. I brought the recording device to the guard on duty, and suggested he call the feds and tell them he found something they had lost.

A few days after my thirtieth birthday in June, I arrived at the Salvation Army halfway house in downtown Tulsa. I worked at a friend's welding shop during the day, and a repossession service at night legally stealing cars. The director of the halfway house was always giving me shit about the companies I was employed at, and the fact that I was able to come and go at any time I wanted for work. On my last day there in October, she told me I needed to sign some papers so I could be officially released, and asked me to be there by 5PM because she wanted to go home.

When I called at 5PM and told her that I was still working and would be there at 6PM, she wasn't happy. When I called her at 6PM and told her that I wouldn't be there until 8PM, she was pissed off. I figured what goes around comes around, so I finally showed up at 10PM and signed the papers. The last thing I told her was that my best friend Lee McArdle was going to be there soon—he was finishing a two-year federal sentence for stolen motor vehicles—and to treat him as well as she had treated me.

Six months later Lee told me that the director had it in for him from the minute he arrived, and he couldn't figure out why. I told Lee that I had been looking out for him when I told the director that he would be arriving soon! After more than nine years, I finally paid Lee back for leaving me with my Harley chopper in Hulbert on July 4th of 1976.

Chapter 10

Waiting On The Bandidos

November 1985 To July 1987

Over the winter I spent a lot of time getting readjusted to life without bars, and moved in with an old female friend. Teresa Williams had a Cherokee Indian house in Glenpool, about twenty miles south of Tulsa. She wanted to start a relationship and I wanted to move away from the north side, where I had resided since late 1981. The house we shared was on a small lot in a subdivision, and although I felt uncomfortable not having some land to roam on, I soon adjusted and went to work buying wrecked cars and fixing them; the damaged vehicles I bought and repaired were commonly referred to as rebuilders.

I returned to the salvage car auction in Little Rock that I had frequented previously, and bid on two hundred rebuilders once or twice per month; if I was lucky, I would get one or two. My federal parole officer would give me permission to travel across the state line as long as I was traveling for legitimate business reasons.

Cowboy eventually plead guilty to some of the charges in his case—the federal prosecutors dropped the continuing criminal enterprise charge in return, resulting in a total sentence of only eleven years. If he behaved himself, my brother would be eligible for parole in 1989. As far as I was concerned it was a miracle, in lieu of the amount of time he could have received.

Most of the other Arkansas members had plead to charges that resulted in sentences which would allow them to return home in just a few years, but one received a twenty-year sentence. All in all, the prosecution of the Bandidos in Arkansas was a lot less fruitful than the federal authorities had hoped for and predicted.

In February I got permission from my parole officer to go to Mardi Gras for a much needed, long overdue vacation. I drove to Longview, Texas, and hooked up with a Bandido who lived there that I had originally met in Little Rock. Frances "Lenny" Bonner was a wild man, always on the edge, who lived in the fast lane. We traveled together by car to Galveston Island—our mission was to meet with Bandido El Presidente Ronald "Ronnie" Hodge so I could possibly get permission to start a new chapter in Tulsa. It was Mardi Gras time on the island, as it was everywhere along the gulf coast. Every house we went to, we were one step behind Ronnie.

At one of the houses I ran into a young Bandido, John "Big John" Lammons, who I had first met in Muskogee, Oklahoma, in 1980 when I was a Rogue. John was a hangaround then for a local motorcycle club called the Drifters. They wanted to be assimilated, and I was one of the Rogues that had been sent to Muskogee to check them out. At the time I thought John was the best of the bunch, better than all the Drifters put together, but he was too young—only sixteen-years old—to be a patch holder. Running into him was a fluke, and turned out to be one of the highlights of my trip.

While we tried to catch up with Ronnie, Lenny and I wasted some time watching the Mardi Gras festivities. When Lenny had to leave for a little while, he dumped me in a van with a few Bandidos and asked them to watch me. It was the first time I met Bandido Trash, and within a few minutes he was all over me, asking me obnoxious questions. At one point I thought I was going to have to fight my way out of there when he accused me of being a cop, but then learned he was only kidding to check my reaction.

Lenny and I finally caught up with the El Presidente a few days later at Trash's house on the north side of Houston. Ronnie and I sat in the living room by ourselves, while Sargento-de-Armas Dave from South Dakota watched us from the other side of the room.

It was actually the first time Ronnie and I had ever met in person, but we had talked on the phone many times through the years. Since all of the Oklahoma Outlaws were in prison then, I thought it would work to my benefit, but in the end it worked against me. Ronnie decided that a new chapter in Oklahoma would have to wait until one of the Outlaws got out of prison. His decision was based on the respect he had for the organization, but more specifically the respect he had for Little Wolf, who was still the president of the chapter even though he was incarcerated.

I learned that his relationship with Little Wolf went back many years, and Ronnie didn't want to sacrifice it by starting a chapter behind his back. At the time I was surprised, but that turned out to be very typical of Ronnie, as I would learn in later years. The El Presidente suggested that I move somewhere in the Bandido Nation to become a member, but I told him I wanted to stay in Oklahoma and would wait for permission to start a chapter there, no matter how long it took.

We agreed that Oklahoma would be an ideal place for Bandidos coming home from prison to reside while they were on parole, for I could get them a place to live and a legal job. I would also do some legal investigation work for the national chapter, and in return would be welcome anywhere the Bandidos were, almost as if I were a Bandido. Although things didn't work out as I had hoped, I knew someday I'd get the green light to start the new chapter.

In April former Rogues Tulsa president Marvin Brix died unexpectedly in the middle of the night from a brain hemorrhage. I was shattered, for Marvin was one of my closest friends and confidants, and was going to become a Bandido whenever I got permission to start the new chapter. On Wednesday April 23rd we buried my brother under a tree in a cemetery in south Tulsa. Tattoo Tommy, who had taught Marvin the art of tattooing, came over from Memphis to bid him farewell, and five of the six pallbearers were former Rogues.

Searching For My Identity: The Chronological Evolution
Of A Troubled Adolescent To Outlaw Biker

By the summer of 1986 I had temporarily put the idea of starting a new chapter behind me, and focused all of my energy on making a legal living by buying, fixing and selling rebuilders. I traveled back and forth to Little Rock on a regular basis, and developed a small business capable of paying the bills that was considered visual means of support in the eyes of my parole officer.

Lee's house burned down one night that summer while he was out of town. It wasn't a big surprise to anyone, for it was old. The place was insured, so it presented an opportunity for us to reconstruct it the way Lee envisioned it to be. He spent the summer building the new house, and I got my feet wet in the construction business helping him whenever I could—it set the stage for bigger and better things to come.

In the fall I had the good fortune of running into Howard Camron at the salvage car auction. He was a small guy with a dynamic personality who owned an auto salvage and rebuilder business in northeast Oklahoma called Oak Hill Auto Salvage. We hit it off immediately, and I soon started working for him on a regular basis, traveling back and forth from Glenpool to Jay. I would work twelve to sixteen-hour days for Howard, a few days a week, to supplement my income. Oak Hill was an amazing place out in the middle of nowhere. We would take a brand-new Lincoln Towncar that had been badly wrecked, completely disassemble it, cut the car in half through the windshield posts, replace the frame, weld on a new rear clip, and repaint the car. From the time it arrived at the shop, to the time that the vehicle was ready for sale, usually took no more than ten days.

In January of 1987 I had a brand new 1987 Chrysler Fifth Avenue in my inventory that was ready to sell. A business associate at the downtown Ford dealer was interested, so I went there to sell it. The buyer called the auto theft unit at the Tulsa Police Department, and asked them to check if the car was stolen. As soon as the auto theft detective heard my name, he dispatched two rookie detectives from the squad to investigate. The rookies promptly decided the car was stolen, which was funny, because it wasn't.

I was adamant that the vehicle was legal, so they allowed me to call their supervisor, Dewayne Smith, who was the same detective who had arrested me as I walked out of federal court in January of 1983. I told him the history of the car, explained that it wasn't stolen, and told him I had a receipt for all of the parts I had bought from a local salvage yard. He asked me to go get the receipts and meet him at the auto theft impound lot with the car, as soon as I could. I told him I would be there in an hour.

When I arrived at the impound yard it didn't take long to figure out what had happened; one of the parts I bought had a serial number on it. The car it had come from had been stolen, recovered, and sold to the local salvage yard before I purchased the part. The only problem was that no one had ever removed the parts car from the stolen vehicle list, so it appeared as though I had changed the serial number on the car.

The supervisor then informed the two rookies that I was one of the best auto thieves he had ever encountered, and that I was an expert at changing serial numbers. Detective Smith asked me if I would show the two new detectives where all the hidden serial numbers were on the car, so I did. Doing so made the two look like idiots, and I got a small amount of satisfaction in return.

By May I had outgrown the small shop at the Glenpool house. Teresa and I moved back to the north side of Tulsa, into a house I lived in for a few months back in 1981. I had bought the house about six months before I went to prison, but during the last six years had rented it out to pay the mortgage. Now that the renters were moving out, it presented a perfect opportunity for us to move in. The home was located in a little town called Turley just north of the Tulsa city limits, sat on almost an acre, and was only a few blocks from Lee. The home had three bedrooms and a garage that was twice the size of the one I had been working out of. I had come full circle, and it felt good to finally be back home.

The summer started off with a bang. Howard Camron got into an altercation with his wife, Karen, in the middle of the night inside their home at Oak Hill Auto Salvage. Karen and Howard were separated, and Karen had already moved most of her belongings out of the house. While Howard was in bed sleeping with his new girlfriend Faye, Karen snuck up to the house and fired a shotgun through the wall of the bedroom, narrowly missing them both. When Karen entered the bedroom and attempted to shoot them again, Howard took the shotgun from her and hit her in the head with it. Although Karen left the property a little beat up, she walked to a friend's car parked one-hundred yards away under her own power. A few days later Karen died from the injuries she sustained in the fight at Howard's house.

The police immediately charged Howard with manslaughter, but weren't fortunate enough to find him at home when they arrived with the arrest warrant. I started moving some of his cars off the property to get them ready to sell, to prevent the police from seizing the vehicles. There was a little-known Oklahoma law in existence that enabled law enforcement authorities to seize anything that could possibly be sold to facilitate a getaway—in this case it was Howard's entire auto salvage. I wanted to get enough cars off the property to fund his bond and pay for an attorney.

On the second day I was stopped by the police on my way to Tulsa three miles east of Jay on Highway 20 while driving one of Howard's car haulers loaded with cars. A friend of mine who had volunteered to help load and unload that day was sitting in the passenger seat, so we both got out to see what was going on. Surrounded by law enforcement authorities with a half-dozen guns pointed at us, we rapidly deduced that they thought I was Howard. I laughed at the cops and asked them what they thought they were doing, but the police weren't in a joking mood, and both of us were immediately handcuffed and thrown in the dirt. They soon realized that I wasn't Howard and released us, but impound the car hauler and cars on it. I asked the officer in charge how we were supposed to get back to Tulsa, and he told us to walk—we were left on the side of the road to fend for ourselves.

A few days later Howard turned himself in and spent a few days in jail before I was able to get my Tulsa bondsman to make the fifty-thousand dollar bond. We hired a prominent Tulsa attorney to represent my friend, and life slowly returned to normal at Oak Hill Auto Salvage.

For the rest of the year I continued working full-time as a mechanic at Oak Hill Auto Salvage and my shop in Turley. I specialized in full-size Ford pickups, Lincoln Towncars, and of course, Harley-Davidson motorcycles. I didn't get rich, but I was living comfortably. I traveled whenever I could, and tried to visit the Little Rock Bandidos who had been released from prison as much as I dared while on federal parole.

Quite often I let my adopted dad drive some of the cars for a while after I fixed them. While I was incarcerated, Warren and Dolly had sold their home in Connecticut and moved to Tahlequah, Oklahoma. Warren was my version of quality control—while he did the job for free, it enabled him to drive a new car for nothing.

I supplemented the income from my auto and motorcycle rebuilding business by doing paralegal work for some of the attorneys I knew in Tulsa. I would do research in the evenings for complicated post-conviction appeal briefs, sometimes even ghost write the entire brief myself. When I was finished, the attorney would just sign his name on the document and submit it to the appeals court in Oklahoma City as if he had done it himself. I was also making money doing legal people searches using an information service company in Nashville, then selling the information I received.

In late summer I traveled to Connecticut to record my third vinyl LP record *Crossbar Hotel* with my friends Kurt Newman and Mario Figueroa. Kurt, Mario, Andrew "Andy" Rutman, Lou Sabetta and I recorded the entire album at Grace Recording Studios in Hamden. We completed the recording process in one long weekend, but this time the sound we captured was professional and I was extremely proud of the results.

While I was in Connecticut Pete Hansen and I thought up an excellent birthday gift for his older brother Skip on his thirty-eighth birthday. We both wanted to do something really special, something that he would never forget. When we stopped by Skip's house and asked to borrow his extension ladder, Pete and I were pleased that it never crossed his mind to ask us what we needed it for.

We took the ladder to Skip's stained-glass business, which was up on the second floor in a commercial building located on a main street going through town. We made up a banner that said

Celebrate Skip's 38th Birthday - Free Food and Beer on the 2nd Floor, and then used Skip's ladder to climb up to the outside of the second-floor window, where we securely fastened the banner. The next day must have been great, because the window overlooked a major intersection with a traffic light. All day long people stopped in to wish Skip a happy birthday, asking for free food and beer in the process. The beauty of the gift was that there was no way that Skip could remove the advertisement, because he was unable to leave work to retrieve the ladder!

On the way back from Connecticut I stopped in Dayton to visit Hambone at the clubhouse for two days. I hadn't seen the Outlaws chapter president since the early eighties when I was a Rogue, and it turned out to be the last time I ever saw him.

Chapter 11

Waiting On The Bandidos

January 1988 To December 1989

I started off 1988 by celebrating at a New Year's Eve party hosted by a former Rogue in Tulsa. It was a good party, and I thought at the time that the new year looked promising. Most of the Little Rock Bandidos were home from prison, but Cowboy wasn't scheduled to go to a halfway house for another year. I was thinking about marrying my girlfriend Teresa and settling down. We had gotten used to living in Turley, and my various businesses were producing more than enough income to sustain our frugal lifestyle.

I was still working at Oak Hill Auto Salvage with Howard, rebuilding cars and motorcycles at my shop, researching and writing legal briefs, and locating people; I named the three businesses Header, Connecticut Bike Specialties and Paralegal Services. I made the decision to become totally legitimate, and started filing income tax returns for my business like every other normal American.

My parole officer was generally staying off of my back, and allowing me to travel for almost any occasion, as long as I linked the travel to some aspect of my business. I used some of the extra money to start remodeling the house, poured additional concrete outside the shop to use as work space, and installed a hot tub inside the den. Before long I had an excellent place to work, as well as a nice place to live and relax.

Cowboy's girlfriend Sissy said goodbye in early spring, and to assist him in facilitating the breakup, I advanced her some money to move back to Texas. Sissy had promised to pay back the money when her income tax refund arrived, so when she called to say she had the money, I figured I'd better get it as soon as possible. I flew to Dallas on a Southwest Airlines flight and met her at the airport, spent about an hour there, and flew right back to Tulsa. All I took with me was my briefcase, where I placed the check that Sissy gave me for the money she owed. I even got advance permission from my federal parole officer to travel to Dallas and back.

When I landed at the Tulsa airport I got a big surprise. As soon as I got off the plane, two undercover police officers confronted me. They told me that they had received a tip that I was carrying drugs or drug money in my briefcase. I asked them if they had a search warrant, and they told me that they could easily get one. Being a guy with lots of legal experience, and considering the fact that I was working for a half-dozen prominent criminal defense attorneys, I told them to get a warrant. I figured that I would sit there for an hour, and they would give up and let me go.

Although I had no drugs or drug money and was totally legit, I was still quite recalcitrant. The two police officers had rapidly turned into almost a dozen, all undercover. They had been stationed all over the airport waiting for me to arrive. I thought that they must have been expecting a huge drug bust, and I wondered who had given them so much erroneous information.

It was like I was in the middle of a cheap movie, surrounded by police in the airport. It turned out they wanted to take me downtown for questioning, and to see if they could get a warrant to look inside my briefcase. I'm sure you can imagine the entire pack escorting me through a busy airport—what a circus show! When we finally got outside the terminal, I decided it would be easier to just let them look in the briefcase, than wait for them to get a warrant. I also thought it would be fun to see the look on their faces when they found the cashier's check.

I told the officer in charge that I had changed my mind, and that I didn't have the time to waste hanging out with them. I let them look inside the briefcase, where all they found was the check. They asked to search me, and I let them. Of course they found nothing at all and were obliged to let me go. It ended up being a colossal waste of time, but at least I felt vindicated when I saw how disappointed they were.

In April Howard Camron fired his Tulsa attorneys and hired an eighty-two year old attorney from Jay to represent him at his upcoming manslaughter trial. Howard had become addicted to methamphetamine, and was convinced that the justice system in Delaware County was controlled by the Masons. He told me that since the judge and the prosecuting attorney were Masons, he hired a Mason to represent him. What a mistake that turned out to be.

When it came time for trial Howard was so whacked out on meth that he ended up stealing the firearm that was the state's star piece of evidence during a noon recess. It only took thirty minutes for him to get caught and admit what he had done. Howard's elderly attorney told the jury what had happened to cover his ass and avoid implications of impropriety. After Howard's attorney spent most of the remaining trial sleeping, Howard was convicted and the jury recommended a prison sentence of thirty years.

With a few of Howard's friends and a few of mine, we liquidated his business. We sold everything we could, then had an auction at the end to sell what was left. We sold the house, all of the salvage cars, the property, some of his tools, and paid off everything he owed. We were able to keep his prized 1964 Chevelle SS and all of his basic mechanic tools, and when we were done, Howard had about thirty-thousand dollars left. We packed all of his tools and personal belongings into an old school bus, then drove it to Missouri where we left the bus, Chevelle, and money in the care of his brother Dwight.

Later that summer I met a twenty-five year old biker from Germany. Dieter Tenter was an intelligent entrepreneur who was in the United States to buy a load of used Harley-Davidson motorcycles. He had done some business with a friend of mine in

Kansas, who brought him to Tulsa to meet me. I let Dieter and his German friend stay with me for a few days, and treated them as though they were family, just like I did with all bikers in my world. I made sure that no one took advantage of him, and helped him to buy two Harleys.

By now the Bandidos were stopping by to see me on a regular basis. I would usually see a bunch of them before Sturgis in August, or just afterwards. If any of the Arkansas, Mississippi, Alabama or Louisiana Bandidos were traveling through Oklahoma, it was a sure bet they would be stopping by for a meal and a place to rest.

I decided to marry Teresa on the 8th of August in 1988. I wanted to get married on a day that I could easily remember, so I picked 8-8-88. We had a conventional biker wedding in the backyard, and invited seventy-five close friends and family to witness the ceremony. The motorcycles were lined up in two rows, and we used the bikes as an aisle to walk down. We had the reception afterwards in the house and yard, and Teresa and I ended up eating some LSD to cap off the night before we opened the wedding gifts. By the time we woke up the next day we had no idea who gave us what present because of the acid!

By the time Christmas rolled around I was getting antsy. Cowboy was getting ready to be released from prison and transfer to the halfway house in Little Rock. I had also accepted a contract to establish a state-of-the-art collision center, which would be

Tulsa's first one-stop shop for wrecked cars. Up until that time if your vehicle was wrecked and you wanted it fixed, your auto would have to go to more than one shop depending on exactly what repairs were needed. For example, it might have to go to a frame shop, a body shop, an upholstery shop, and a mechanic's shop— with our new business model every aspect of the repairs was located under one roof. My title was general manager, and I was in charge of setting up the business and running it day to day. The name of the shop was One Stop Collision Center, and we planned to open it in January.

The new year started out great when Cowboy got transferred to the halfway house in Little Rock despite the worst ice storm to hit there in ages, and I opened the new body shop on time and within budget. On January 20th of 1989 members of a rival motorcycle club assassinated my good friend Hambone, who was the national vice-president of the Outlaws. I didn't hear about his death until three weeks after the murder, so I was unable to attend the funeral.

In mid-February I woke up one morning with a sore neck, and as the month progressed it got worse and worse. In early March the pain was unbearable, and I finally broke down and went to see a doctor. It turned out that my body hadn't been getting enough calcium, and as a result, three vertebrae had started to break apart. In essence I had a broken neck, and had been walking around with it for almost a month. I was extremely lucky that I hadn't been paralyzed in the process.

During the emergency neck surgery, the doctor took some bone from my hip and fused the three vertebrae together. I then had to wear a wonderful neck collar for three antagonizing months. It was a job just to bend over and write a check, much less anything else. To do so I had to stand up and bend over to see what I was writing. I was thankful that my job was 90% decision making and only 10% check writing.

In June Cowboy was released from the halfway house he had been confined to for the previous four months. I went to Little Rock to see him but had to be driven there in a car, for I was still in the neck brace. During the visit we went to a kick ass rock n' roll concert by the river. Jim "Jim Dandy" Mangrum, the lead singer of Black Oak Arkansas, was a friend of ours, so it turned out to be a great place for a reunion after more than four years apart.

By the end of the year Cowboy was getting used to his freedom and was actually doing well. He had moved in with a female friend of mine who was an editor and roving reporter for Supercycle magazine—her name was Marla Garber, and she rode her Harley more than most men I knew. Supercycle was, at that time, the chief competitor to Easyrider magazine. Marla rode her motorcycle all over the country, typically putting more than fifty-thousand miles on the odometer each year, and she had a dog named Scooter that rode on the motorcycle everywhere she went.

I got Cowboy involved with my wrecked car rebuilding business again, but this time we did it legally. Both of us even got our respective federal parole officers to grant permission for us to see each other for business purposes. Although we could only associate for business and not socially, the arrangement gave us plenty of time to hang out, and in no way hindered our social interaction. After a few months we convinced both parole officers that it was okay for me to visit Marla, as long as Cowboy went to his bedroom and I stayed in the living room. Too funny I have to admit. We were both on top of the world at the end of 1989, but there still wasn't a chapter in Oklahoma. After more than eight years, I was still trying.

Chapter 12

Waiting On The Bandidos

January 1990 To December 1991

After the holidays I bought a female Akita puppy and named the dog Kat—everybody laughed when we hollered for Kat and a dog came running. My one-year contract at One Stop Collision Center was over, and since I was now in the rebuilder business again I built a new car hauler from of a wrecked 1988 Ford one-ton cab and chassis which was capable of hauling two cars.

By this time the Little Rock Bandidos were all back on the streets except one, Michael "Abe" Jones, who was still in federal prison as a result of the indictment in 1985. Abe still had lots of time left to do, but everyone expected he would be home by the end of the decade. On January 27th Abe beat the feds by dying of natural causes, but we were consoled by the fact that he had gotten the last laugh.

The club buried Abe the first week of February on a blustery, cold day just outside of Little Rock. It was a traditional Bandido funeral, and he was buried close to another Little Rock Bandido so they would be able to keep each other company for eternity. It was the first actual Bandido funeral I had ever attended, and there were a lot of Bandidos there from all over the country. After the funeral there was a big party, but Cowboy and I had to leave early because of our federal parole status. Notwithstanding, some of the Bandidos followed us back to Cowboy's house to socialize.

One of the brothers who joined us there was a snake expert from Texas. Cowboy wanted Robert "Snakeman" Humphries to show him how to handle his new rattlesnake. When Snakeman dropped the rattlesnake on the floor in front of us, I almost had a heart attack. There were about a half-dozen of us in the room, and everyone except Snakeman and Cowboy held their breath during the show. After a ten-minute basic course in snake handling, which to me looked more like snake flipping, the show was over. The pissed-off rattlesnake went back in its cage where it belonged, and we all went back to breathing.

On February 10th Lee got a job as a salesman at a Ford dealer in Tulsa, which was ironic because he had served a federal prison sentence for auto theft and was a convicted felon. Since he had been released from the halfway house in early 1986, Lee had been heavily involved with the purchase and sale of rebuilders. The only difference was that he did it legally this time.

As winter turned into spring I finally got enough money saved to build a new shop in the back yard. It was one-thousand square feet, and was divided into two sections. The front section was for working on cars, trucks and bikes. The remainder was storage area with multiple racks and bins to store parts for cars, trucks and motorcycles. By mid-April it was completed, and making money became a whole lot easier with larger work space and the new car hauler.

Early one afternoon my attorney called and wanted to know if he could come by and sleep for a while. Apparently William "Bill" Patterson had too much to drink over the lunch hour, and needed a quiet place to sleep it off, a place where no one would ever know or tell. Being the good friend I was, I waited for Bill to go to sleep then patiently painted his fingernails bright pink. While the attorney slept, I took some 35mm photos of him that clearly showed his pink fingernails.

A few hours later Bill woke up and we had a good laugh, but I failed to mention the fact that I had taken the photos. I waited a few months until it was his birthday, had the best photo blown up into a giant poster, and had the poster framed. I invited Bill to a birthday lunch at a friend's popular downtown restaurant, which was a convenient and frequent lunch spot for an assortment of legal professionals. I had previously made arrangements with the owner, Buzz Dalesandro, to replace one of his wall decorations with the framed poster of Bill.

When Bill and I arrived for lunch, Buzz directed us to sit at a table in front of the poster, and Bill was positioned in a seat which looked directly at the giant-sized photo. We then ordered lunch while I waited for Bill to notice the practical joke on the wall. It only took a few minutes before Bill knew he'd been okey-doked. It was a fantastic birthday present, definitely one that he would never forget. Years later I heard that his young son found the poster hidden away in a closet at Bill's home, and Bill had to explain to him why his daddy was wearing pink fingernail polish. I wish I could have been there to see that!

I drove up to Kansas City in March and bought my first new bike, which had never been wrecked and was literally brand-new. The guy who owned it was in trouble and needed money, and I wanted a new Harley Softail. The bike was blue and silver, and I loved the color scheme.

In late April I packed up my guitar and drove to a bar in south side Tulsa one night to play guitar live for the last time in my life. Some friends of mine were in a rock n' roll band, and the lead guitar player convinced me to join them onstage in front of an audience. I wasn't ever much into playing live, but this time I let my inhibitions down and had a blast. We played a few popular cover songs and a few tunes from the *Crossbar Hotel* record, and I ended up playing with the band for almost an hour.

The 1st of May was Lee's birthday, and this year I had a really good idea to okey-doke him. I hired a stripper to show up at the Ford dealer where he worked and ask him to show her some cars. The dancer brought a small music box which she stashed in her belongings. I had one of the salesmen let the other salesmen know about the joke, and gave him a camera to take some photos.

When the girl picked out the car she wanted, unsuspecting Lee took her back to his cubicle to sign the papers. When she wanted to give him a blow job in return for the down payment money, I was told he looked befuddled. Before he figured it out she turned on the music and started dancing. The prank was so successful I decided to make it an annual ritual.

I packed my bags in June for a long overdue motorcycle trip. I had a friend in Florida who wanted to move back to Tulsa, so I volunteered to bring down one of the trucks I had in inventory at the time which had a twelve-foot flatbed. Because the trip was for business, my parole officer gave me permission to go. I loaded my new Harley on the truck and took off for Florida.

After I unloaded the bike and dropped off the truck with my friend in Tampa I rode south to Highway 41, which was known as 'alligator alley', but by the time I headed east on the narrow two-lane road it was dark. Before long I saw a giant hump in front of me which I initially thought was a speed bump. When I got closer I realized it was a giant alligator enjoying the heat from the asphalt. The tail of the beast was hanging off the road, so there was no way to get by on that side. There was just enough room for me to ride past the business end, so I put my left leg up next to the gas tank and rolled the throttle. The Harley God must have been with me that night because the gator never moved—I figured it wasn't the reptile's first encounter with a motor vehicle.

After spending two nights with an old girlfriend in the Florida keys, I rode north up the east coast to Daytona to visit an old female friend and her husband. She worked as a dancer at the

Shark Lounge in the heart of Daytona, and I had a lot of fun hanging out at the Shark for free while I was in town. It was like old times again, except that I had a little more than a year left to go before I would be free. I had already been on federal parole for more than four years, and was amazed I had made it this far without going back to prison.

From Daytona I headed west to Mobile on I-10 and stopped in to see the Bandidos. Even though I had spent most of the time with Buddy when I had stayed there in 1979 and 1980, there were other Bandidos I had met and knew well enough to call on for a meal and place to lie down. I had also been recently introduced to a Bandido from Louisiana I wanted to visit—his name was Doyle Reaux and he lived in Lafayette.

After Mobile I stayed with Doyle and his family for a few days, and enjoyed the Cajun food his wife cooked while I was there. From Lafayette I rode north to Shreveport where I stopped in for a few hours to visit Bandido Ed "Eatin Ed" Younkers. From northern Louisiana it was a beautiful six-hour ride through the mountains of southeast Oklahoma back home to Tulsa.

Over the years I had repeatedly tried in vain to get permission to go to Sturgis for Bike Week, but my federal parole officer would never let me go. In July of 1990 I tried to outsmart him, and instead asked for permission to visit Yellowstone National Park in Wyoming. By then he knew me too well, and although he granted me permission to travel, he made sure to tell me in writing that I couldn't go to Sturgis to see the Bandidos.

Instead of going to Yellowstone, I went west to Amarillo to see a Bandido who had recently been let out of prison. I had been introduced to James "Tucker" Atkins in 1983 but didn't ever get to meet him. At the time a stripper from Connecticut wanted to visit me in Oklahoma, but didn't have the funds to travel conventionally. Along with one of her girlfriends, she intended to hitchhike all the way to Tulsa, but instead fell asleep inside a truck and wound up in Houston.

The dancers called me from south Texas wondering what they were going to do. I called Cowboy, and he called Bandido King Crab in Houston. Thirty minutes later the girls were in safe hands with a Bandido named Woody. Cowboy had no idea who he was, which was strange, but the strippers called the next day to ask if it was okay for them to stay in Houston with Woody. I really didn't need any more strippers working for me then, so I told Woody he could keep the girls as long as he took good care of them.

A few years later while Cowboy was locked up in federal prison he told me he had finally met Woody. Tucker had been eluding the authorities when I gave the two girls to him, and at the time was using the name Woody to confuse law enforcement authorities. We agreed that as soon as he got out of prison, either he would come see me or I would go see him. Since Tucker was

139

now out of prison and his parole officer wouldn't let him travel, I found the opportunity to be a good time for us to meet. We got to spend a few days together, and it turned out to be a much better trip than going to Sturgis.

After returning from Amarillo, my wife talked me into getting a companion for Kat. We traveled to the woods of eastern Oklahoma in August, and bought a male Akita with large paws who was the last puppy left from his litter. We named him Axle, after Axl Rose from the rock band Guns n' Roses.

Later that month Kurt Newman came to Tulsa to visit me for a few days. Kurt had recently relocated from Connecticut to southwest Missouri, and was now the proud father of a new baby girl. I let Kurt borrow my new Harley Softail for the weekend, which turned out to be a mistake, for he had too much to drink on his first night out with the crew. While riding home from a party we had attended, Kurt miscalculated an exit ramp off the highway and hit the raised median that separated the exit from the highway.

The median acted as a ramp, and Kurt and my bike flew through the air for a few seconds before they crashed to the ground, ultimately causing my friend's ankle to fracture. The motorcycle skidded on its side down the exit ramp for two-hundred feet, finally coming to rest in the middle of the road. I learned of the incident when a stranger called to let me know that Kurt was in the hospital, and my Harley was lying in the middle of an exit ramp in downtown Tulsa.

I picked up two biker friends that lived nearby, and we drove to the accident site where the police allowed us to load the totaled bike into the truck. We then followed the Oklahoma Highway Patrol officer to the hospital, where I talked the trooper out of charging Kurt with drunk driving—I successfully convinced him that Kurt had enough problems already, since he totaled my bike.

In late December, just in time for New Year's Eve, Dieter Tenter from Germany arrived for another visit and to buy more Harleys. To celebrate the holiday we drove to Fort Smith to see a rock band called Judge Parker. Two brothers, Larry and Arthur Pearson, had started the band in 1988. Larry was the lead singer, and Arthur was the best lead guitar player I had ever known.

When I had first met them, they were playing with Jim Dandy and Black Oak Arkansas. When Jim and Black Oak played in Oklahoma, Jim always called me or came by to say hello if he had the time. The brothers had somehow wound up in jail in Wagoner, and Jim had called on me to get them bailed out in time for the show. As promised, I got the rock duo bailed out and delivered to the show in the nick of time, and since then, we had become good friends.

In the first week of February I awoke to my dogs barking loudly. Both Akitas were in the back yard, one at one side of the house and the other at the opposite side. The rear fence actually wrapped around to the front edge of the house, so both dogs had

141

overlapping views of the front yard. I looked out through the window and all I saw was law enforcement officers and police cars. I figured I was going back to prison for a bullshit parole violation, since I only had a few more months to go before my parole term was over.

When I opened the front door the first thing the officer in charge wanted to know was the whereabouts of Howard Camron. I told him that Howard was incarcerated at Conners Correctional Center in Hominy, Oklahoma, and suggested he go there to see him. As I started to shut the door, the cop informed me that Howard had escaped from prison the day before, and they thought he was hiding in my house. The officers standing on my front porch step wanted to search the house and property, so I asked them if they had a search warrant. They didn't have a warrant, but assured me they could get one—I doubted that they could, told them to get a warrant and slammed the door. They never got a warrant, but even if they had, they wouldn't have found Howard hiding in my house.

At the time my former employer was across town hiding in a friend's attic, but I didn't hear about that until a few days later. Howard had boldly walked out of the prison with all of the visitors at the end of visiting time, as if he was a visitor. From the prison parking lot he had caught a ride back to Tulsa with some people he knew, and then hidden at their house for a few days until the publicity died down.

Searching For My Identity: The Chronological Evolution
Of A Troubled Adolescent To Outlaw Biker

Although Howard kept a low profile in Tulsa for a while, he had a strong desire to go back to his hometown in northeastern Oklahoma. We kept him in the Tulsa area for as long as we could, but in late April he finally went back to Jay to visit friends and relatives. It wasn't long before Howard decided it would be a great idea to throw a welcome home party at a friend's house in Jay— the same town where he had operated Oak Hill Auto Salvage and killed his wife in self-defense.

When the sun came up the house was surrounded by law enforcement officers. The police had heard about the party, and arrested Howard for escaping from prison. He eventually plead guilty to escape charges and got two more years added on to his original sentence. Howard was then transferred to the maximum-security prison in McAlester to finish serving his thirty-two year sentence. He was finally released in 2005 after serving more than seventeen years in prison.

In February of 1991 I convinced a business associate to form a partnership with me to build Tulsa's first gentlemen's club, which was a high-class night club and restaurant that had strippers for entertainment. When I first pitched the concept to Mike Emerson he said, *"What? People pay to watch girls dance and remove their clothes? Who would do that?"* I had located an old restaurant in the heart of Tulsa at 3902 South Sheridan Road which was a perfect location. The place was for sale, and appeared to be properly zoned for a sexually-orientated business.

Searching For My Identity: The Chronological Evolution
Of A Troubled Adolescent To Outlaw Biker

A bank in western Oklahoma had owned the property for quite some time. The building had been abandoned for years, and was completely vandalized. I got a friend at the City of Tulsa to write a letter saying that the building couldn't ever be rebuilt, and then Mike and I bought the dirt it sat on for a song and a dance. We then set out to repair the building by bringing it up to code, and got permission from the City of Tulsa to allow us to do so. Mike provided the financing and encouragement, and I took care of all of the construction, zoning issues, and inspections.

Since Mike was in the insurance salvage business, we utilized his vast resources to supply materials whenever we could. We used a load of damaged automotive exhaust pipe to build all of the interior railings, and carpeted the entire facility with rolls of carpet that were missing a large swath of thread about a quarter-inch wide—we figured that in the dark no one would ever notice the missing thread. Everything went as planned until we encountered an interesting zoning issue we had never foreseen. There was a zoning law we were aware of that required our sexually-orientated business to be more than three-hundred feet from a residentially zoned piece of property, but who would ever have thought I-44, the interstate highway adjoining the property, was sitting on residential property? Notwithstanding we eventually got the zoning application approved, and finished the construction. *Scarlett's* opened at the end of the summer after we had spent almost a million dollars. The nightclub was seven-thousand square feet of sheer elegance, and we were extremely satisfied to have successfully raised the bar for all strip joints in the Tulsa area.

At the time we were building the club, another section of the new zoning law was forcing an older strip joint across town to close their doors after more than twenty-five years in business. I knew the manager there, as well as most of the dancers who worked for him, and got them all to come to work at *Scarlett's* when we opened. Mike and I even timed the opening of our place to coincide with the last day of the bar that was closing, so the employees wouldn't miss any work.

My adopted dad finally died from his battle with leukemia on April 30th of 1991. Warren had been sick for the last year, but had gotten worse the first week of April. Throughout his entire life he had been a huge New York Giants football fan, so in mid-April I contacted the Giants' corporate office in New York and explained the situation. I asked them if it would be possible for them to do something special for Warren, and they told me that they would try. I gave them my contact information, and a week later I received a letter from the Giants head coach, Bill Parcells. It was addressed to my dad, so I took the letter with me to the hospital where I read it to Warren.

Halfway through the letter he started crying—when I had finished, Warren told me that it was the best thing that had ever happened to him in his life. I hoped the happiness I brought him that day helped a little to offset the bad things I had done to him when I was young, but in reality I'm sure it was too little, too late. Shortly thereafter I brought him home from the hospital to stay with me, and he died a few days later with my mom at his side while I held him in my arms. A week later the newspaper where my dad worked published an article about Warren and the letter he received from New York Giants head coach Bill Parcells.

On the 1st of May it was once again Lee's birthday, and he was still working at the Ford dealer. This year I splurged and sent two dancers to strip and help him celebrate. No tricks this time, just two knockouts for him to reflect upon for a few minutes. In mid-May the June issue of Supercycle Magazine hit the newsstands with a story about my music. Cowboy's girlfriend Marla, using the pseudonym Kat in honor of my Akita, had authored a two-page article about the Warren Winters Band and the *Crossbar Hotel* record album.

I finally completed my federal parole term on June 15th of 1991. After being either in jail, on bond, and on parole for more than twelve years I was finally a free man. I felt like I had a brand-new lease on life, and could now go anywhere I wanted without asking permission from my federal parole officer. I couldn't believe that I had stayed out of trouble for so long.

Back in Little Rock Cowboy was very much back in the swing of things, too much so I was starting to think. He and Marla had parted ways, and he was now hooked up with a girl named Cheryl. She was from the streets, and it didn't take long for my

146

brother to go back to his old ways. I was positive that Cheryl was dragging him backwards, but couldn't convince my brother it was so. Cowboy was happy, so what the hell—I closed my eyes and hoped for the best.

Now that I was free of federal supervision I decided that it was time for another vacation, but this time it was a quick one. I packed up the Harley and rode to Arkansas to attend the Labor Day Rally at Lake Leatherwood in Eureka Springs. There I met up with all of the Arkansas Bandidos, and we had a blast for a few days in the sunshine and warm weather. One night Cowboy and I ingested some LSD, and ran around all night laughing and howling at the moon.

In November I got into a big fight with Axle which caused me to get almost one-hundred stitches in my upper arms. By now he weighed more than one-hundred twenty-five pounds, was extremely territorial, thought he owned everything including the house and yard, and wasn't scared to prove it. The Akita had bitten me between the shoulders and the elbows, and tore nasty gashes in the outside and underside of both arms. When the doctor finished stitching me up, I couldn't use either of my arms; I couldn't even wipe my ass. In honor of the fight one of my friends made a t-shirt for me that said *DOG TRAINER* on the back in big letters, and *Axle's Little Eddie* on the front. It seemed as though everyone thought it was funny except me.

Searching For My Identity: The Chronological Evolution
Of A Troubled Adolescent To Outlaw Biker

In December of 1991 I asked Edd Lackey, who was a Jacksonville Outlaw serving time in federal prison, to make five leather plaques as Christmas gifts for Cowboy, Jack-E, Trash, Tucker and Big John. The plaques were engraved with the Fat Mexican logo and had the respective bottom rockers for Arkansas, Louisiana, Texas, Texas, and Texas. I also took the liberty of having one more plaque made with an Oklahoma bottom rocker, which Cowboy said he would keep for me until the chapter became a reality. Cowboy's plaque had a little extra—it said *Charter Member Eleven Years*—which was a testament to the time he had been in the club.

Bandido Trash in Houston received an additional gift from me—a female puppy from Axle and Kat which he ended up calling Honey Dog. The Akita, who was a few months old, actually rode to Houston in a BMW car that belonged to David "Rooster" LeJeune, who was a Louisiana Bandido. On the way to Houston Rooster stopped to spend a few hours visiting some Bandidos in Longview, Texas, and forgot to let the dog out of the car while he was there. Honey Dog thanked him by tearing up the interior of the expensive car, and destroying the armrests on the door panels. Rooster wasn't very happy about it, but couldn't do anything to Honey Dog because he was afraid of making Trash mad. Honey Dog made it to Houston okay, and brought Trash many years of happiness.

Chapter 13

Waiting On The Bandidos

February 1992 To January 1994

I started out the new year by heading south in mid-February to deliver the plaques to Jack-E in Baton Rouge, Big John in Galveston, and Trash in Houston. This time my wife came along, which was extremely unusual. Teresa always said she wanted to go with me on my excursions, but when it came time to go she always came up with an excuse to stay at home in Tulsa.

While visiting the Bandidos in Baton Rouge I made a life changing decision to no longer ingest methamphetamine. Although I'd never been a meth addict, I had used the drug occasionally to keep me awake and alert when traveling for a few days.

When we got home from Texas my wife returned to her job as a bartender at *Scarlett's*, and I went back to working my ass off. I was now the booking agent and manager for the Judge Parker Band, as well as running Paralegal Services, Connecticut Bike Specialties, and Header. I had my hands full, and every phone call required me to change my hat—one minute I was talking about Harleys, the next legal work, and a few minutes later I'd be booking the band; it was exciting, and there was never a dull moment.

Searching For My Identity: The Chronological Evolution
Of A Troubled Adolescent To Outlaw Biker

In March the Bandidos sent a Vice-Presidente to Tulsa for a few days. Lawrence "Larry" Borrego was a member of the nomads in addition to his duties as a national officer. We spent a few days together, and a few nights at *Scarlett's* watching the strippers. I was hoping that his presence would signify the club was ready to do something in Tulsa, but my hopes were premature. I heard years later that Larry had reported back to the Bandidos that there was nothing in Oklahoma worth having.

Later that month I let Axle inside the house while my wife was at work. I had gotten over my injuries from last fall, but had developed a healthy respect for the Akita since the fight. He had developed an arrogant attitude since the incident, and when I urinated in the backyard, he would immediately piss over my urine. I should have known that we couldn't live on the same property together for long.

Just before bedtime I told Axle to go outside, but instead of being obedient, he raised the middle finger of his paw to let me he owned the house and the yard. I walked across the room to grab him by the collar and the fight was on. It didn't take long to figure out I was in deep shit, especially after I tried to stick my hand in his mouth to break his jaw.

Whoever had told me the story was full of shit, or forgot to mention how to get your hand past all those teeth. I grabbed the stun gun off the table and tried to shock him, but that was a mistake I won't forget. Up until that point Axle wasn't too angry, but when

I nailed him with the stun gun he kicked it into overdrive. I vividly recalled the previous ass-kicking and rapidly deduced that if I didn't do something different, I'd soon be headed back to the doctor's office for stitches again. I grabbed my wife's gun from the bedroom, but missed the Akita on the first shot and blew a hole in my living room wall. The next two shots put an end to Axle's life, but he got the last laugh, for he shit, pissed, and bled all over my living room carpet.

Cowboy married his girlfriend Cheryl in April. My wife was the maid of honor and Wiggs the best man. The marriage was a major political event in the biker world, and attracted motorcycle club members and independent bikers from all over Arkansas and a small group of Mongols from Tulsa.

When I got back from Little Rock I replaced Axle with another male Akita puppy. Thunder had a much better disposition than Axle, and I planned to learn from past mistakes and raise him a little different than Axle. He grew up to be a dynamite dog with a great personality, and was completely snow white with the exception of the black around his eyes and muzzle.

To celebrate the Memorial Day weekend I rode south to Mississippi for the annual Gulfport Blowout. There was always a large contingent of Bandidos there, as well as one of the best Harley drag races in the country. A few members of the club participated in the drag races, and by sheer coincidence I got a chance to see the Judge Parker Band play at the Crazy Horse Saloon in Biloxi.

In June of 1992 my Little Rock brother fell in love with Suzanne, who was a stripper at *Scarlett's* in Tulsa, and not long after Cowboy and Cheryl got divorced. He moved into a little one-bedroom house with Suzanne not far from where I lived, and started the laborious process of convincing his Arkansas federal parole officer that he should be allowed to transfer jurisdictions.

Shortly thereafter another Bandido from Louisiana moved to Tulsa. Joseph "Joe-E" George had been convicted in Louisiana of an auto theft charge, and as a condition of his probation he was told to move out of Louisiana. Cowboy eventually convinced his parole officer to let him transfer to Tulsa, and Joe-E and Cowboy both secured legal employment. Tulsa was rapidly becoming a great place for Bandidos to serve out their parole or probation, and once again I was starting to think that a Bandidos chapter in Oklahoma was within reach.

In August some of the Louisiana Bandidos stopped in Tulsa on their way to Sturgis for a night of rest. Joe-E, Cowboy, and I were happy to see Bandidos Dane, Osco, Billy and Dave from the Baton Rouge chapter. Two weeks later Bandido Rooster stopped in to visit for a few days. He was broke from the trip to Sturgis so I got him a temporary job on a construction crew as a laborer.

Searching For My Identity: The Chronological Evolution Of A Troubled Adolescent To Outlaw Biker

Before noon the foreman called to tell me that the Louisiana Bandido was asleep in a closet inside the building they were working on. Rooster had locked the closet door figuring that no one would miss him or be able to find him. The foreman fired him on the spot, but agreed to let him continue sleeping. When the construction crew left to go home that night Rooster was still asleep in the closet. In the middle of the night he woke up and came back to my house, and started complaining that the construction crew had left him there. He seemed surprised to find out that he had been fired before noon for sleeping on the job.

In September I made a deal with Bruce "Fuzz" Terreson, who owned a Harley dealership in Pennsylvania, to purchase a leftover brand-new 1992 FXR convertible. The blue bike had a set of detachable saddlebags, as well as a detachable windshield. After picking up the Harley I cruised down I-81 to eastern Tennessee, then headed west on I-40 to the mountains of Arkansas where I met Teresa and some of the Tulsa crew near Eureka Springs. In early December Teresa announced she was pregnant, and that our child would be born in late July or early August of 1993.

Once again I welcomed in the new year with the Judge Parker Band in Fort Smith. Larry and Arthur Pearson put on another dazzling show, and I let my guard down and got on stage with them to sing harmony on a Judge Parker favorite called *My Missouri*.

Less than forty-five days later during a blinding snow thunderstorm, a bolt of lightning hit the house while Teresa, Thunder, Kat and I were in the shop working. The lightning strike caused a power surge in the electrical wiring and started a fire in the den. We had no idea that the house was burning, and by the time we figured it out, the fire had been burning for ten or fifteen minutes. The first sign something was wrong was when we heard glass break and the dogs started barking.

I initially thought somebody was breaking into the house, and that the burglar had broken the back-sliding glass door to gain entry. When I came flying out of the garage it was difficult to see because of the smoke, but I could see flames coming out of where the sliding glass door had been an hour earlier. The hot tub was even on fire! I got the garden hose out, hooked it up, and desperately tried to put out the fire, but it was way more than I could handle. A few minutes later the fire trucks showed up, and not long after the fire was out.

The den, kitchen and rear of the two-car garage was a total loss, and the fire had burned a hole through the roof. The rest of the house sustained severe smoke and water damage, and it took the insurance adjuster two days to go through everything that had been damaged. The few things we saved were sent to a special facility where the smoke smell was removed from each item.

The insurance adjuster told me that it would take a construction crew more than a month to get started repairing the damage, but I knew some of my friends, business associates, and I could fix it faster. The adjuster allowed me to rebuild the house myself, and within ten days of the fire we had cut the house in half, bulldozed the north side into a pile of debris, and removed the roof from the south side because of the smoke damage. In early March we poured a new concrete slab for the bulldozed end of the house, and by the end of the month we had it all closed in from the weather. By the middle of May the outside was painted, the interior of the house was finished, and we were able to move back in. All we lacked were finishing touches to the exterior landscaping.

The whole time we were working on the house Teresa and I lived in the back shop, where I had converted the work area into a bedroom and office. The shop had heat, but no running water. My adopted mom was living across the street, so we used Dolly's house to eat and shower. To complicate our situation we had to keep the dogs in the shop with us, and Kat chose that time to have another litter of puppies. Between Teresa being pregnant, all of the construction work going on, and the whining of the new puppies, it was a wonder I got any sleep at all.

I finished the house project just in time to take a motorcycle trip to Mississippi. It was Memorial Day weekend again, and time for the Gulfport Blowout. This time I planned to meet Tattoo Tommy from Memphis there. We hadn't seen each other since Marvin's funeral, and I eagerly anticipated the visit. Tommy and I had spent a lot of time together when I was visiting Arab in 1983 and 1984, and we had originally met when I was traveling between Florida and Oklahoma in 1979. The Gulfport Blowout was a blast, and as always the Bandidos had a camp there and their racing team participated in the drag races.

In early July I started a construction project for one of my neighbors. He had watched me rebuild my home, and decided he wanted me to build his new house. I told him I could build it in about thirty days, but it would be about forty days before he could actually move in. We started the house on July 6th and he moved in during the second week of August. I was actually getting the drywall ready for paint when my daughter was born at the end of the month.

At the same time I was finishing up the house project and trying to get used to having a baby in the house, some of the Louisiana, Arkansas, Alabama, Mississippi and eastern Texas Bandidos converged on my house while on their way to Sturgis. It was the first week of August, and it just happened to be raining. So instead of getting a break between the small packs as I usually did, a bunch of Bandidos wound up staying at the house while waiting out the thunderstorms.

Cowboy, Joe-E, and I took care of forty Bandido, while my wife stayed in the bedroom nursing Taylor. When the pack finally pulled out early one evening two days later, we breathed a sigh of relief. It had been no easy task to build my neighbor's house, work on a wrecked truck I was rebuilding, and take care of my wife, new-born daughter, and the brothers at the same time.

Three days after the pack left I took off for Sturgis like a bat out of hell. I left on my fifth wedding anniversary, but since Teresa had her hands full taking care of Taylor, she didn't seem to care. I had been able to reserve a cheap room in an old motel in downtown Rapid City close to the Bandidos clubhouse, so I spent a few days there hanging out with the brothers and the Bandidos racing team at the drag strip.

At the drag races I ran into an old friend of mine from Florida. Beau was a retired Outlaw from Joliet, Illinois, and we had known each other since 1980 when I was a Rogue and he had stayed with me in Tulsa. At the time the Outlaw had gifted me a beautiful hand-carved club made from cedar. Although it was really a walking stick, I kept it strapped to the handlebars of my bike for many years to use as a weapon when the opportunity presented itself. It was the last time I ever saw Beau, for he was killed by a drunk driver while riding his Harley a few months later.

I came up with a great idea to start manufacturing rolling chassis kits in the fall of 1993. By then it was getting difficult to sell rebuilders, and I was beginning to think that the industry was dying. I convinced an Ohio motorcycle frame manufacturer to provide me with Harley frames that included a seventeen-digit serial number almost identical to the 1HD1 serial number used by Harley-Davidson. In the United States the first four digits of a serial number always designate the manufacturer of the vehicle, and my frames had a 1SD1 serial number.

I took the paperwork provided by the frame manufacturer to the tag agency—the motor vehicle department in Oklahoma—where I was able to get titles that said Harley-Davidson was the manufacturer. On the title where you would normally see the model, it said Fatboy, Heritage or Superglide instead of Dyna or Softail. If you didn't note the minor difference in the beginning of the serial number and the model names, you would think you were looking at a real Harley title.

I was ecstatic for I had found a legal pot of gold and it didn't take long to capitalize on it. With the exception of the frame and engine cases, I used original Harley parts and even provided the buyer with a factory Harley transmission case. I sold almost one-hundred of the chassis kits before the party was over. Harley eventually notified the state that Oklahoma couldn't issue a title that designated Harley-Davidson as the manufacturer unless the serial number started with 1HD1.

I took off after the holidays to deliver some of the frame kits I'd sold to Michigan and New England, but couldn't have picked a worse time to travel. It had been an unusual snowy winter, and Michigan had gotten its share of the white stuff by the time I arrived. From Michigan I thought I'd be smart and cut across Canada to save some time—what a mistake that was! When I crossed the border, custom agents searched the car and found a rolling chassis kit in the trunk. The authorities made me declare it, and I had to post a bond to prevent me from selling anything while I was in Canada. The bond cost a little more than one-hundred dollars and severely cut into the financial resources I had budgeted for the trip. I definitely saved time crossing Canada, but it cost me to do it. I should have stayed in the United States and taken the long way around the lake.

In Buffalo the weather was worse than Michigan, and the snow piles were the largest I had ever seen. I couldn't figure out why anyone would want to live there. I spent two days visiting the local Outlaws chapter, showing the president how to research courthouse records. From there I traveled to Boston on the last weekend in January to attend a motorcycle parts swap meet where I had planned to meet a retired Outlaw from Florida. I met two outlaw bikers at the swap meet who were getting ready to launch a new chapter of the Outlaws in Boston—it would be their first chapter in New England and a point of major contention with the Hells Angels who had dominated the area for decades.

From Boston I drove north to New Hampshire to hang out with Chris Westerman at his new home in the woods just outside of Laconia. I had originally met him at Grace Recording Studio in Connecticut when I was recording *Crossbar Hotel* in 1988. Chris had a new wife and had built a fantastic recording studio in his home. The home was a spiritual place that sat on top of a snow-covered hillside—it was peaceful there and I didn't want to leave.

Searching For My Identity: The Chronological Evolution
Of A Troubled Adolescent To Outlaw Biker

Before heading to Connecticut, I traveled west to Vermont and stopped in for a day to visit another old friend of mine and his family. Richie Doolittle had originally introduced me to Stanley Lynde in 1974, around the same time I bought my first Harley. Stanley owned a motorcycle shop in Brattleboro, and over the last nineteen years we had bought and sold a lot of Harley parts from each other, and spent a lot of time together. New England in the winter was fun to visit, but by now I was missing sunny, warm Oklahoma, so I headed south on I-91 to New Haven.

I spent a few days in Connecticut visiting Harry "Skip" Hansen, who I had known since I was eleven—he had been riding motorcycles for decades and was a member of the Vietnam Vets motorcycle club. For years I had been trying to convince him to move to Oklahoma, but this time my timing was perfect, for Skip finally broke with tradition and promised me he would relocate.

From there it was south through New York City to visit Frankie "Harmless" Pattica in New Jersey. Although Harmless had been an Outlaw in Jacksonville, he had been extremely fortunate, for he wasn't one of the many Outlaws in Florida that were arrested by federal authorities in 1981. After the bust Harmless had retired and headed back to where he had grown up. Before he became an Outlaw he had been a member of the Breed motorcycle club, and now he was a member again. I spent a few days there catching up on old times and meeting his Breed brothers.

Searching For My Identity: The Chronological Evolution
Of A Troubled Adolescent To Outlaw Biker

The next stop was Mario Figueroa in New Jersey, who had
been a roommate of mine in Oklahoma in 1984 and played bass on
Crossbar Hotel. From Mario's house I traveled west to visit Fuzz
and his crew at Terreson's Harley-Davidson in Shillington,
Pennsylvania. I had originally met Fuzz in the late seventies, and
he had sold me the blue 92 FXR.

It was one hell of a trip and I had a blast seeing my old
friends, but by now I couldn't wait to get back to warmer
temperatures. I arrived home just in time for the worst snowstorm
Oklahoma had seen in fifty years—eleven inches of snow in one
day. The city was completely snowed in, paralyzed for days until
the snow melted. It didn't matter to me, for it was good to be back
home.

Chapter 14

Waiting On The Bandidos

March 1994 To December 1994

By early spring my daughter Taylor was eight months old, and being a dad for the first time was starting to sink in. One day while I was filling in some genealogy papers I started wondering if I needed to state her lineage as biological or adopted for my side of the family. The obvious decision was biological, but to do that I would have to ascertain the identity of my real parents.

I had already started thinking about locating my biological parents and started working on the process. While on my recent trip to New England while I was passing through Hartford, I stopped and did some research at the local library and court records office. As a result I discovered that there were two different types of birth certificates in Connecticut—a short one and a long one— on the long form is the name of the doctor that certified the birth.

While the authorities always change information when a person is adopted, they typically don't change the time and date when you're born or the name of the doctor that delivered you. A few weeks after I got back to Tulsa my long form birth certificate, which I had ordered at the vital records office in Hartford, arrived in the mail. I had never seen it before, and to my pleasant surprise at the bottom of the certificate was the name of the doctor. I was extremely fortunate for his name was unusual.

Searching For My Identity: The Chronological Evolution
Of A Troubled Adolescent To Outlaw Biker

I ran the name through the resources I had for locating people and came up with a few possibilities. Within an hour I located the doctor and was surprised that he was still alive. He told me all of the birth logs were stored in the attic of his house, and he thought he could locate my birth record in few days. Two days later he called to inform me that my mother's name was Jackie.

Since my parents had divorced shortly after I was born, I knew my mother had filed for divorce before then. Cross-referencing dates in Hartford at the records office, I had recorded the names of parties involved in two-dozen divorce files that could possibly be my parents. Searching the list of names I soon found a female named Jackie who had divorced a guy named Forrest, and the names of both my maternal grandparents.

Since it was likely they were my biological parents, I utilized my people locating resources again and quickly found my grandmother in Massachusetts. The next day I contacted a friend's daughter who worked at the phone company in New England, and she checked my grandmother's phone records. The majority of the long-distance phone calls listed on the statement were to a number in Austin, Texas. Thinking that the Austin phone number was likely to be my biological mother, I made the call. My real mother was shocked to hear from me, and told me I had three half-sisters in Texas and a half-brother in Boston, Massachusetts.

My biological father was much harder to find. In spite of the fact that he also had an unusual name, he moved a lot. When I finally managed to catch up to him in California, he was extremely happy I had found him and told me I had a half-sister in Michigan. When I learned he had been a musician and was in the construction business, I was shocked. As a result of locating my biological family, I spent the spring and early part of the summer getting acquainted with my five siblings.

By now both my automotive rebuilder and people locating businesses were running out of gas, but Connecticut Bike Specialties was booming due to the sale of the rolling chassis kits. I was producing them ten at a time, which was a full-time job in itself, but at least I was home to watch Taylor, who sometimes hung out with me in the shop while I was working.

My wife and I drove to Austin to meet my biological mother, brother, and sisters over Memorial Day weekend. It was an interesting holiday celebration for us, since it was the first time we were all together in one place. Jackie was an antique book dealer, two of my sisters were homemakers, one sister was a production assistant in the movie industry, and my brother was a manager at a research laboratory. The entire weekend Teresa was freaked out about traveling for the first time without Taylor—I should have paid more attention for it was a sign of things to come.

Bandido Jack "Jack-E" Tate moved to Tulsa in June—he was functioning under an assumed name and traveling with his girlfriend. Jack-E was on the run from the feds for a minor parole violation, but wanted to make absolutely sure that it was only a

Searching For My Identity: The Chronological Evolution
Of A Troubled Adolescent To Outlaw Biker

Panhead Chopper 1975

Prospect Patch 1976

Hulbert July 4th 1976

Searching For My Identity: The Chronological Evolution
Of A Troubled Adolescent To Outlaw Biker

Dolly 1977

Dave Gruber 1979

Rogues Patch 1979

Florida 1979

Searching For My Identity: The Chronological Evolution
Of A Troubled Adolescent To Outlaw Biker

Rocky 1980

Enid 1980

Harley Gas Tank 1980

Warren & Dolly 1982

Searching For My Identity: The Chronological Evolution Of A Troubled Adolescent To Outlaw Biker

Leavenworth FPC 1982

Marvin 1982

Arab Memphis FCI 1983

Warren Winters 1983

Searching For My Identity: The Chronological Evolution Of A Troubled Adolescent To Outlaw Biker

Glenpool 1986

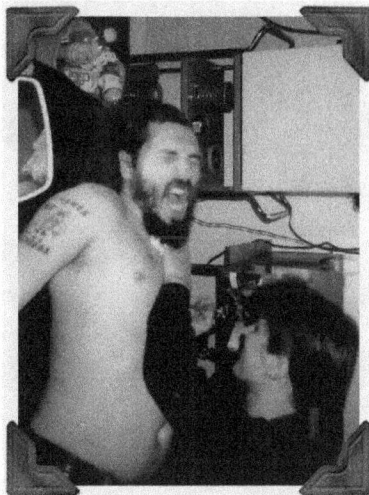

Memphis 1986

Warren Winters 1987

Searching For My Identity: The Chronological Evolution Of A Troubled Adolescent To Outlaw Biker

Warren 1988

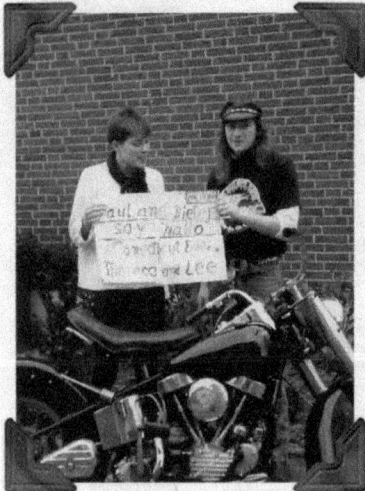

Dieter Tenter & Wife 1989

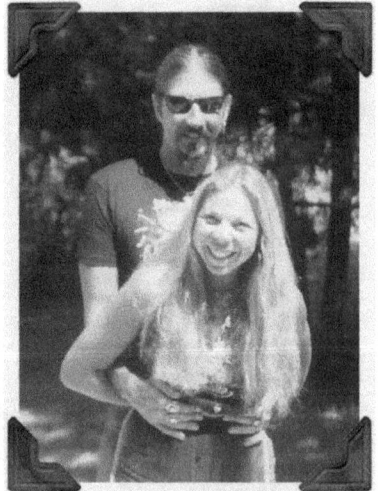

Cowboy & Marla 1989

Searching For My Identity: The Chronological Evolution Of A Troubled Adolescent To Outlaw Biker

Warren Winters 1990

Lee & Stripper 1990

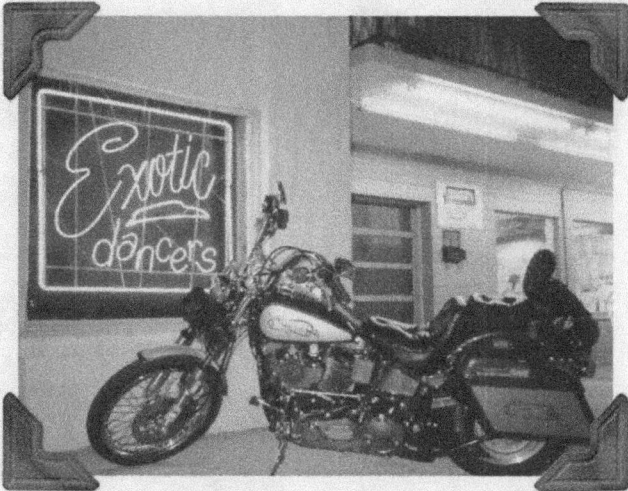

1989 Softail Shark Lounge Florida 1990

Searching For My Identity: The Chronological Evolution Of A Troubled Adolescent To Outlaw Biker

Tucker Amarillo 1990

New York Giants 1991

Arkansas Plaque 1991

Searching For My Identity: The Chronological Evolution
Of A Troubled Adolescent To Outlaw Biker

Axle 1991

Bandidos Sturgis Ride Tulsa 1993

Searching For My Identity: The Chronological Evolution
Of A Troubled Adolescent To Outlaw Biker

Dolly & Taylor Christmas 1993

Lee 1994

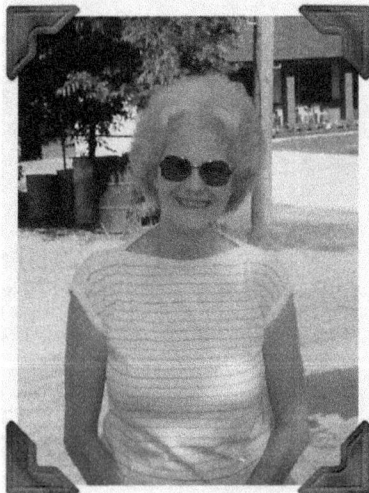

Dolly 1994

Searching For My Identity: The Chronological Evolution Of A Troubled Adolescent To Outlaw Biker

Forrest 1994

Pete 1994

Skip 1994

Searching For My Identity: The Chronological Evolution Of A Troubled Adolescent To Outlaw Biker

Taylor & Rolling Chassis Kits 1994

Fuzz 1994

Searching For My Identity: The Chronological Evolution
Of A Troubled Adolescent To Outlaw Biker

Forrest 1995

Shirt 1996

Wizard's Custom Harley 1996

Searching For My Identity: The Chronological Evolution Of A Troubled Adolescent To Outlaw Biker

Big John 1996

Jack-E & Lee 1996

Lee 1997

El Presidente Craig 1997

Searching For My Identity: The Chronological Evolution
Of A Troubled Adolescent To Outlaw Biker

Malisa 1998

Les 1998

Oklahoma Chapter 1999

Searching For My Identity: The Chronological Evolution Of A Troubled Adolescent To Outlaw Biker

Muskogee Medical Center Daycare 1999

OK Riders 1999

German Stripper 1999

Searching For My Identity: The Chronological Evolution Of A Troubled Adolescent To Outlaw Biker

Four Corners 2000

Europe Presidente Jim & Sargento-de-Armas Diesel 2000

Searching For My Identity: The Chronological Evolution Of A Troubled Adolescent To Outlaw Biker

Europe Vice-Presidente Kok

El Presidente George 2000

parole violation. He planned on laying low for five years to let the statute of limitations expire on any other charges the feds might be considering, then turn himself in for the parole violation. The Louisiana Bandido had a large RV trailer that he pulled behind his truck, and was able to travel, to a degree, when and where he wanted. For about eighteen months while he was on the run he called Tulsa home.

I had met Jack-E years before in Pascagoula, Mississippi. A mutual friend had introduced us on one of my many trips to the Gulf coast. Bandido James "Goldie" Cutrer had called me one day and asked me to stop in for a visit as soon as I could arrange it. He told me he had a brother in trouble that needed my assistance. The brother turned out to be Jack-E, and he wanted to pick my brain about his legal options. Jack-E and I spent a few days together, and from that day on we deliberately sought each other out whenever the opportunity presented itself.

In the summer of 1994 I started thinking again that maybe the time had come to get the Oklahoma chapter kicked off, if I could just get permission from the national chapter. Even though Cowboy and Joe-E were on parole, and Jack-E was on the run, they were all living close to me, and were available and willing to supervise. Lee had told me that he was interested, and so was a friend of mine from Michigan, John Fisher. All I really needed was to get Skip to move to Tulsa and I would have my dream team ready to go.

Searching For My Identity: The Chronological Evolution
Of A Troubled Adolescent To Outlaw Biker

Since I had first asked El Presidente Ronnie for permission to start a chapter in 1986, I had asked him about it a few more times. I was persistent, knowing it was my destiny to become an Oklahoma Bandido. Every time I inquired about starting a new chapter I was given the same answer—we'll talk about it when the Oklahoma Outlaws get out of prison. At the time Ronnie was incarcerated in federal prison for participating in a murder conspiracy and El Vice-Presidente James "Sprocket" Lang had taken his place. The new Bandidos boss also declined the opportunity to start a new chapter, but I wasn't surprised, for I didn't know him well. Now Ronnie was out of prison and poised to take over the club again, or so I hoped. I thought that if he was El Presidente again, my chances would be much better.

Cowboy had broken up with his girlfriend Suzanne and was in love again, this time with a stripper named Shawnda. In July they got married at a ranch just outside of Tulsa. The ranch was actually the home of Suzanne's parents, for Shawnda just happened to be a good friend of Suzanne's. Once again I didn't think the marriage would last long. I was also getting concerned, for Cowboy was using meth again. I wondered how long it was going to be before he got busted, and how much time he would get in prison when he got caught.

In early September my biological father packed up everything he owned and moved from California to Tulsa in a spur of the moment decision prompted by a divorce. I was glad to see him relocate because I wanted to get to know him, but it sure was strange having my real father near me after so many years of not knowing him. Later that month a Bandido from Lubbock stopped by for a few days to visit. I had recently helped Scott "Hollywood" Crawford get off federal paper, and he wanted to say thanks in person.

Around that time Skip finally decided to move from Connecticut to Oklahoma. He packed everything he owned into a U-Haul trailer, and a friend of ours helped him get to Tulsa. As soon as he arrived he moved in with us for a few months, but soon found himself a young girlfriend and a house in Tulsa. At the time I was convinced that the move saved his life, and still believe that today. Skip had been in a big rut living in Connecticut, but being in Oklahoma gave him a new lease on life.

In late October Skip and I traveled to Eureka Springs to attend the wedding of our childhood friend Kurt Newman, who had played drums on all three of my record albums. If you have never been there, Eureka Springs is a beautiful place, an old hippy commune surrounded by forests, located in the Ozark Mountains of northwestern Arkansas. The actual wedding was held in an old hotel on top of a hill. Surrounded by a bunch of small artistic shops, the setting was ideal.

The following month we decided to sell Skip's old FXR, so we went to Dallas to participate in a huge motorcycle auction. It was held every year at the Parker Ranch in Plano, just north of

167

Dallas. The Parker Ranch is where the TV show *Dallas* was filmed, so it was kind of strange being there to auction off the bike. In spite of the fact that it needed work, the Harley still looked good with its tiger-striped red and black paint job, which were the colors of the Vietnam Vets motorcycle club. Now that he was living in warmer territory and planned on riding more, Skip was going to need a more reliable motorcycle that wouldn't break down. We sold the FXR for a fair price, then bought a brand new 1995 Harley FLHT Standard from a Tulsa dealer. The money that he received for the FXR almost paid for the new bike, and my brother was thrilled.

The year ended with a visit from Bandido Dane and his girlfriend Missy. Dane was a young Bandido from New Orleans that I was fond of. He was on his way home from California, and stopped in to visit for a few days. He had already taken care of me on a couple of my trips down south, and it felt good to be able to return the favor. Seeing Dane reminded me of one night a year ago when I was visiting him in the French Quarter, where he worked at a jewelry store and lived. We all went out to eat that night—the restaurant he chose was famous for its menu so there was a long line out the door down the sidewalk. I told him I was hungry and didn't want to wait, but Dane just laughed as we passed everybody in line to get to an employee he knew at the door.

After greeting Dane the employee went inside and approached the party he had just seated. The doorman told them that there had been a huge mistake, and that they would have to go back to the front of the line. Our party was then led to the table the employee had just vacated for Dane. When I looked at the menu prices I had a major case of sticker shock, but he patiently explained there were two sets of prices in the French Quarter—one price for tourists and another for residents. Dane told me not to worry and to order anything I wanted, which I did. The food that night was fantastic, and now I finally had the chance to return the hospitality.

It was an unusual Christmas that year. I had my biological father Forrest, Skip, my adopted mom Dolly, Teresa, and Taylor with me for the holidays. It had been decades since I had so much family to share the holidays with.

Chapter 15

Waiting On The Bandidos

January 1995 To August 1995

I started out 1995 by taking a trip to Germany to visit my friend Dieter. He had been to the United States a half of dozen times, and stayed with me for a day or two every time. One time he even brought his wife Christiane and young daughter Malisa with him. For years he had invited me to come visit, so when I finally found some cheap plane tickets I jumped at the opportunity.

I hadn't been to Germany since I had been in the Army in 1973, but still remembered bits and pieces of the language. After arriving in Frankfurt, Dieter first took me to Kirch-Gons where I had been stationed in the Army. Ayers Kaserne, also known as 'The Rock' was still basically the same, but I was quite surprised to find that the base was now open to the public—anyone could go on or off the base at any time without being stopped by a soldier. When I was there, there had been a front gate staffed by military police, and the only way in was by proving that you belonged there. The highlight of the trip was seeing where and how Dieter and his family lived, but meeting his German friends and going to the biggest swap meet I had ever seen in my life was memorable.

Dieter and some of his brothers had rented a booth at the swap meet where they were selling their used Harley parts. At first I wondered why the spectator aisles were one way only, but in a few hours I learned why. There were more people there than I could have ever imagined, and by the early afternoon I was shocked to see total gridlock in the aisles. There were so many people in the building that no one could move, and the only way in was when someone actually left. There was not one inch of empty space in the aisles.

While at the swap meet I learned how to say *"Do you speak German?"* and *"I don't speak German because I'm a stupid American"* in German. Someone would ask me a question about a Harley part that was for sale, assuming I was from Germany. I would answer by asking if they knew how to speak German, in the German language. The customer would always look surprised and answer *"Yes, I do."* I would then tell them in fluent German, *"I don't speak German because I'm a stupid American"*. The reactions on their faces provided us with a constant source for entertainment all weekend long.

From Germany Dieter and I traveled by train to see a business associate in Vienna that had come to Oklahoma and bought some Harleys from me. Hans had never met Dieter, and Dieter and I had never been to Vienna. The Austrian gave us a grand tour of Vienna for a day—we saw old churches and buildings in the downtown area. We were both amazed at the beauty of the city, and the fact that a few five-hundred year old buildings were still standing. Although the bombing during World

War II had reduced the city to rubble, most of the buildings had been restored to what they looked like before the war.

I hated leaving Germany, but needed to get back home where I had a mountain of problems waiting. My marriage was in tatters, and Teresa had moved out of the house to her sister's place for a few months last year. She and I were now back together but things weren't the same. My wife was doing a lot of strange things with Taylor, not willing to work, and running in circles all the time—there were days when I thought she was insane—I would be reading the newspaper, and she would confront me in the living room and accuse me of talking bad about her on the phone, but I wasn't on the phone, I was sitting there reading the newspaper. I couldn't figure out what was wrong at the time in spite of all the warning signs that were flashing in neon around me.

When I got back to Tulsa, Forrest had bought a dilapidated house a few blocks from me and was in the process of rebuilding it. He was extremely talented and capable of accomplishing most aspects of the remodel—wooden stud framing, electric wiring, plumbing, drywall, paint, and roofing were elementary tasks to my father, who was in his early sixties. It took him a while, and sometimes he forgot where he was at during the construction process, but eventually he completely rebuilt the residence by himself. Forrest seemed to enjoy living in Tulsa, and didn't seem to miss California. He had played drums for years in New York and California, and was now playing with a small band at a Tulsa nightclub. I got to see him quite often, and it was a good feeling to get acquainted and learn where I came from. I was amazed at how much we were alike, and soon figured out that half of me was learned behavior and the other half was hereditary.

In April I rode south to Hallsville for the annual Harley drag races to get together with the Bandidos, and spend some time with the new El Presidente. Since Ronald "Ronnie" Hodge had recently died unexpectedly from a massive heart attack and El Presidente James "Sprocket" Lang had been indicted by the feds and was headed to prison, Craig Johnston from Longview, Texas, was running the club.

When I finally got a chance to talk to him, my hopes for a new chapter were dashed again. By now almost everyone in the Bandidos nation knew I wanted to get an Oklahoma chapter going, but they also knew that Ronnie wanted to wait until an Outlaw from Oklahoma City got out of prison. Craig, like Ronnie, had no desire to do this behind their back, but did agree to reconsider the chapter if and when Little Wolf got out of prison. Since I expected the Oklahoma City Outlaw to be back on the streets in two more years, we agreed I would talk to him then.

I took off just after noon to ride home from Hallsville, figuring that I would make the five-hour ride and be home for dinner. I had ridden my 1992 FXR all over the country, and never once did I have any mechanical problems. But sooner or later everyone breaks down somewhere, and this day happened to be my day. As I was enjoying the ride on a desolate stretch of highway thirty miles south of Henryetta, Oklahoma, my battery decided to give up the ghost. I coasted to the side of the road in the middle of nowhere.

I was fortunate to see a house in the distance that I was able to walk to in ten minutes, and even more fortunate when I found someone there willing to let me use the phone. I was able to call a friend in the rebuilder business who had a car hauler. By 6PM the Harley was loaded up and I was on my way to Okmulgee to meet my wife who had driven down from Tulsa in our truck. We rolled the bike off the back of the car hauler into the bed of the pickup, and by 9PM the bike and I were back in Tulsa safe and sound.

Later that month my sister Kitty from Flint, Michigan, came to Tulsa with two of her girlfriends to meet me for the first time. Kitty was Forrest's daughter but had a different mother, so she was technically my half-sister. I was sitting in my living room with Kitty and her friends socializing on April 19th of 1995 when a news flash appeared on the television news—the Alfred P. Murrah federal building in Oklahoma City had been blown up. We spent the entire day watching the events unfold, and were fascinated when we heard there was a Michigan connection, which later proved to be false.

A friend of mine at the Harley dealer called me in May to tell me that a local recording studio was looking for a couple of Harleys to record that day. The studio was Long Branch Studios, and it just happened to be where part of my second album *As I Was* had been recorded in 1984. Because it was raining hard that day, the motorcycle riders the recording studio had hired to record chickened out and didn't show up. The Harley shop called knowing that I could find someone, and since it was about music I volunteered. I talked Skip into going, and we both got there within two hours. We rode our bikes right into the studio, and the actual recording of the bikes went off without a hitch—it was the ride home that got us into trouble.

I took a short cut because it was raining and we were cold. Being wet is one thing, but being wet and cold is another. The only problem was that we couldn't see very well because it was raining so hard. Skip was unfamiliar with the route, and there was a stop sign located at an unusual intersection. When I began to stop for the stop sign Skip never stopped, and plowed right into the back of me. Fortunately his front tire lined up perfectly with my rear tire, and what happened next must have been comical to anyone that had been watching.

The impact pushed the bike out from under me, and when my hand could no longer reach the clutch the bike went back in gear. Simultaneously my right hand rolled the throttle, and as I came off the back, the bike did a wheelie through the intersection without me on it. I landed on my feet, but the Harley went off the road into the soft mud of a drainage ditch. Skip never went down, although I believe that it must have taken everything he had to keep from doing so.

After making sure we were both okay, Skip and I dragged the motorcycle out of the ditch. The accident and the recovery were over in less than two minutes, but our next thought was to get the hell out of there before someone recognized us—we were both extremely embarrassed. As soon as we got home and got the bikes into the garage the phone started ringing. Sure enough one of the local neighbors had seen the whole thing and recognized us, and now the cat was out of the bag. Before long everyone was calling, laughing about our misfortune. One good thing came out of the incident—I got a new custom paint job courtesy of Skip's insurance company!

In June I traveled to Austin to attend my sister April's wedding and celebrate my birthday. On the eve of the wedding my future brother-in-law convinced me to let him take a ride on my recently repaired Harley. I warned Steven about the power the bike had, but he was adamant that the horsepower wouldn't be an issue. I felt that it would be a great wedding present letting him ride the bike, so against my better judgment I handed him the keys. Off he went down the road while I waited at the house with his father standing next to me. Just after I heard him shift into second gear, there was silence. Steven had miscalculated a serious bend in the road, missed the curve and crashed. His father and I jumped into a truck and drove as fast as we could to the curve, where we found my brother-in-law about ten feet off the road in the woods.

My future brother-in-law was visibly shaken and extremely embarrassed. He had multiple abrasions and an injured arm, but fortunately no broken bones. The bike was surprisingly not damaged too bad—Steven's pride was hurt more than the bike. It took an hour but I was able to make a few minor repairs that enabled me to ride it back to Tulsa. When I got home a few days later, a custom painter I knew was able to touch up the paint job without too much trouble.

Steven had no choice but to go through with the wedding, and it looked like he had been beat up by a professional boxer. His arm was in a sling and his head covered in road rash. All of the wedding photos clearly showed his injuries, and in some you could see Steven wincing in pain. Their honeymoon was in Hawaii, and the salt water caused my new brother-in-law massive pain, so he was forced to watch his new bride go swimming every day without him. It was certainly a wedding present they'd never forget!

On June 30th of 1995 Cowboy's former girlfriend and roving editor for Supercycle magazine, Marla Garber, was killed instantly while riding her motorcycle in, of all places, Connecticut. The crash occurred along a gradual curve on Route 6 in Andover when Marla crossed the centerline and hit a tractor-trailer head on. I was saddened to hear of her death for she had been a good friend, a frequent visitor to my home, and had written articles about my music for Easyrider and Supercycle magazines.

I packed the bike into the truck and hit the road in late July, and headed southeast. I needed some breathing room because my wife was driving me nuts. I still hadn't figured out that she was addicted to meth, so her behavior from my perspective bordered on the insane. We planned for her to join me somewhere on the road before I got to New England. My first stop was Dalton, Georgia, and the West Yellow Knife Trading Post, which handled insurance loss liquidations.

There was a music equipment loss that had just arrived, and I had been given an opportunity to buy whatever I wanted before anyone else. I picked up Larry and Arthur Pearson from the Judge Parker Band on my way through Fort Smith, and the three of us went guitar and amplifier shopping in a ten-acre warehouse for the better part of a day. From Dalton we drove back to Nashville, where I got to see the brothers perform a live show.

After parting with Larry and Arthur I drove east through Tennessee, and then north through Virginia into Pennsylvania, where I stopped to see Fuzz at the Harley dealership and John "Sam" Cirulli in Shillington. From there I stopped in New Jersey to see Tommy "Rookie" Sands from the Breed motorcycle club and Mario Figueroa, my former roommate who had also played bass on the *Crossbar Hotel* album. When I left Mario's house I went straight up the coast all the way to Maine, where I spent a few days with Randall "Stash" Perkins and his family. Stash was a retired Outlaw from Jacksonville, who I hadn't seen since my trip to Buffalo and Boston a few years before.

From Maine I drove to New Hampshire where I spent a few days with Chris Westerman at his house in the mountains. I always loved his home and the tranquility the surroundings instilled, and the recording studio in the basement was a bonus. While I was there I tried unsuccessfully to get Teresa on a plane again to join me. Every time we had made a reservation she missed the flight, and my wife used every excuse imaginable to explain why she couldn't get to the airport on time. One time she told me that the driveway had to be washed before she left, and the cleaning operation had caused her to miss the flight. I should have heard the methamphetamine talking, but I didn't. I finally got tired of hearing her excuses and headed west to Michigan.

In Michigan I got to meet Kitty's family for the first time, and to see how and where they lived. My sister and her husband had three kids, and I enjoyed the visit in Flint tremendously. While I was there I tried again to get my wife to fly to Michigan, but again I was stonewalled with incomprehensible excuses. I was amazed at her persistence in not getting to the airport on time, in spite of the fact that she repeatedly claimed she wanted to. By now she and I had made almost a dozen plane reservations and she had missed every flight.

Searching For My Identity: The Chronological Evolution
Of A Troubled Adolescent To Outlaw Biker

From Kitty's I traveled west one-hundred fifty miles to Saugatuck to see another friend. John Fisher was a talented master carpenter who had been introduced to me by Cowboy when they both were in federal prison together. John was getting tired of the cold Michigan weather and was thinking seriously about moving to Oklahoma. I wanted another chance to see him in person, to convince him to move and become a Bandido in the new chapter I hoped to get permission for in the near future.

While at John's I totally gave up on my wife ever getting to the airport, but to prove the brilliance of meth-based decision making Teresa went to the airport at the last minute and flew to Detroit without telling me in advance. After all the failed plans we had made since I left Tulsa, it turned out that she wanted to be with me for our seventh wedding anniversary.

The only problem was that the trip to the Detroit airport was three hours from Saugatuck each way. When Teresa called me at 11PM with the surprising news that she was now in Michigan, I was worn smooth out and tired of her shit. I asked her to get a hotel room, and told her we would either pick her up in Detroit or get her to Saugatuck in the morning.

The next day she boarded a bus headed west to Kalamazoo, and John and I rode our bikes from Saugatuck to meet her at the bus station. Although I was happy to see her, it didn't take long for my happiness to wane—before long the insanity that hovered around her like a dark cloud was back with a vengeance. If only I had known at the time that she was addicted to meth I probably would have handled the situation differently.

By the time we got back to Tulsa a few days later I knew that I had reached the end of my rope. I instructed my attorney to proceed with the divorce I had been pondering for many months, and on August 25th of 1995 I officially filed the paperwork. It was a sad day for me, for I was in love with my wife but still had no idea what had gone wrong. The only thing I knew for sure was that I was no longer willing to put up with the insanity that had become an everyday adventure. I had hoped that filing for divorce might be the catalyst that would propel her to get some help, but to get help you have to first realize you need help, and Teresa had no idea that she needed help.

The next night Lee took me out on the town to talk and see what he could do to help. Somehow I convinced him that I had everything under control, and we got back on our bikes. We left the club side by side, and as we got out on the main road we both took off like rockets—our version of a drag race. Although both Harleys were quick I was hoping that mine was faster. In just a few seconds Lee was nowhere to be seen. I pulled over as soon as I could, and looked back to see him coasting down the street. It took him a minute to catch up and explain that he had broken a rear drive belt just as he hit second gear. It provided me with a little dose of laughter after such a crappy day.

Chapter 16

Waiting On The Bandidos

August 1995 To May 1997

In the summer of 1995 Dolly and I decided to go into the construction management business together—Blockhead City Construction Company. In August our new company landed a contract to install the masonry work at a new Office Max in Joplin, Missouri, and by September 1ˢᵗ the project was off and running. I traveled back and forth to Joplin from Tulsa for a little more than a month to manage the installation of the concrete block walls for the new store.

Although I had to provide and pay for the materials, the Tulsa masonry crew agreed to be paid two dollars for each and every block installed. I then made an agreement with the general contractor to pay me four dollars for each and every block installed, insuring a profit. The only catch was that in commercial construction it normally takes ninety days to get paid, so I borrowed everything I could from every source I had to get the job finished on time, and to pay the labor crew and material supplier in full. Then I sat back and starved for ninety days until my seventy-five thousand dollar check arrived just before Christmas.

Filing the divorce paperwork drove my wife and I further apart, and by mid-September Teresa and my daughter had moved back in with her sister Vicki on the south side of Tulsa. Things had gotten worse between us, and there was nothing I could do to alleviate the cloud of craziness that surrounded her. It wasn't long before I discovered that Teresa owed more than fifty-five thousand dollars on her numerous credit cards, and that the majority of the debt had been spent on cash advances used to purchase meth. I was shocked beyond belief, and could have kicked myself in the ass for not having realized the cause of her insanity.

I did everything I could to make sure that Taylor was okay, and tried as best I could to get Teresa some help while attempting to restore our relationship. I was a firm believer that I had married her for better or worse, and just because I had discovered the worse it was no time to run. At least now I knew that she wasn't insane, and that the meth had contributed significantly to the craziness. I contacted the drug dealer that had sold my wife the majority of the methamphetamine, and instructed him to never sell her any type of drug again. I had known Steve McBride since I had arrived in Tulsa in 1975, and he had been there when I got arrested leaving Arby's on my Harley chopper. I couldn't believe it when he informed me that Teresa had spent more than thirty-thousand dollars purchasing methamphetamine from him in the last year.

In October Forrest convinced Teresa to move into his house, where there were two extra bedrooms—one for her and a separate bedroom for my daughter. Throughout most of the week he was away on business, and Forrest was generally home every other weekend. Since his house was a few blocks from mine it was easy for me to see Taylor. Their living arrangement also provided me the opportunity to frequently attempt to convince my wife that our relationship could survive, but she soon turned to alcohol for comfort rather than get help for her substance abuse issue. As she sunk farther into her world of drug and alcohol abuse, our marriage continued to deteriorate.

Christmas was uneventful. Although I did get to see Teresa and Taylor the usual holiday spirit just wasn't there. I wished for a Christmas like I had known in years past, but recognized it for what it was—for the kids. I put all my heart and soul into making sure that Taylor enjoyed the day in spite of what her parents were going through.

In February of 1996 a custom bike painter I knew well called me up and requested my immediate assistance regarding a situation with a bike he was building. Terry "Wizard" McConnell had hired a motorcycle shop across town to assemble the bike for him, and the facility had not performed their obligations in a timely fashion. The shop was giving him the cold shoulder, and was now ignoring all of his phone calls. Every time he had confronted them about the bike building schedule, they gave him excuse after excuse for not getting it done. By the time he called me, Wizard was ready to strangle the shop owner.

The custom Harley was going to be one of the most expensive bikes that had ever been built in Tulsa, and would be worth twenty-five thousand dollars when it was completed.

Wizard wanted his bike done in time to display it at Daytona Bike Week in Florida, but there were only a few weeks left before the event, and it had dawned on him that there was no way the shop would complete the assembly in time for the show. It was time for a miracle and Wizard knew that I could pull a rabbit out of a hat.

I took a wrecking crew, a truck, and a trailer, and drove across town to the shop that was building his bike and walked uninvited into the shop area. Without asking for permission, we immediately started loading the parts to Wizard's bike into the truck and on the trailer. Although we were prepared for a worst-case scenario the shop owner decided the best thing to do was sit back and watch, and fifteen minutes later we were headed across town to my shop. We didn't waste any time, and immediately set to work on the assembly of the bike. Wizard sent over one of his hotshot apprentices, Ian Wilhelm, who helped me a lot with the assembly and running errands over the next two weeks.

I was extremely fortunate that another old friend, Mason Morton, was building the engine. If Wizard had contracted that same shop to build the engine, the custom Harley would never have been completed on time. The premier engine builder was a lot like me and didn't screw around, and about the time I got as far as I could with the assembly Mason delivered the engine. From then on it was a walk in the park, and in a week the bike was complete and running except for the gas tank, which Wizard was putting the finishing touches on. I actually delivered the bike to him the day before he had originally scheduled the bike to be shipped to Daytona, and within a few hours the gas tank was installed and the bike was ready for its journey.

In mid-March, as a result of the contacts I made while working on the Office Max project in Joplin, I landed a new contract for the demolition of a Dillon's grocery store in Wichita, Kansas. We only had four weeks to remove everything in the building, leaving the roof and walls intact. It was right up my alley, and I took a skeleton crew from Tulsa to supervise the local temporary labor force I hired to complete the job. One of the supervisors was Skip, who was now living with his new girlfriend in a house he bought just south of Muskogee, Oklahoma.

I divided the temporary laborers into four manageable teams, then punched a hole in the front of the building for all of the large debris containers. For about three weeks we destroyed everything in the building, saving all of the copper electrical wiring and water pipes, as well as anything else of possible value for future resale. At one point Skip was operating a bobcat loader pushing around the debris dumpsters when the whole back of the bobcat caught fire. I thought for a minute that he was going to get burned alive, but he escaped with no injury and we were able to put the fire out without calling the fire department.

While I was working in Wichita Teresa wasn't employed, but had Taylor in daycare every day so she could party. All of that came to an end on March 22nd when my wife showed up drunk at

4PM to pick Taylor up. The manager wisely refused to allow her to take custody and instead called the police. My wife was lucky, for the police didn't see her driving so they couldn't arrest her for DUI. Fortunately for Taylor the officers made Teresa call someone to get her, before they let her take my daughter home.

The next day my divorce attorney, Jonathan Sutton, went to court and got a temporary order for me to take immediate custody of Taylor. Until Teresa stopped getting high there was no way I was going to let Taylor be near her. I had no choice but to bring Taylor to Wichita, and to simultaneously take care of her while I managed the demolition of the grocery store. Between all of us, especially her Uncle Skip and grandfather Forrest, we handled the situation well. It was the first time I had ever had the responsibility of taking care of a child long-term by myself. Although I had frequently taken care of Taylor when she visited, I had never experienced anything like this.

The guys on the jobsite helped a lot, and we worked together to keep Taylor occupied, happy, and in a normal routine for a child her age. Taylor loved being there and had lots of fun. She played in my jobsite office while I answered the phone and did paperwork. Forrest snuck out occasionally during the day and brought her to the playground at the local park. If I had to change a diaper or put Taylor down for a nap, everyone turned a blind eye to the single father with custody.

Searching For My Identity: The Chronological Evolution
Of A Troubled Adolescent To Outlaw Biker

Teresa was willing to do anything to get her daughter back when she decided to get help for her substance abuse addiction in the first week of April. She also signed the divorce decree, which now included an additional paragraph that precluded her from ingesting drugs or alcohol while Taylor was in her care and custody. As part of the divorce decree I did what I thought was right for my daughter and agreed to let my former wife have custody as long as she didn't get high, provided Taylor with a suitable living environment, and kept my daughter in a daily routine that was suitable for a child her age. Teresa rented an apartment on the south side of Tulsa and the three of us settled into divorced life.

As soon as I finished up the demolition job and returned to Tulsa I purchased an old abandoned house across the street from Forrest's house on North Victor. Since my house had been sold and the closing date was scheduled in sixty days, it was time to find a new home and for me to make some money, so between April and June I totally remodeled the old house. Forrest had also sold his house, but he was going to be out of town on a construction site for six months. Our plans were to temporarily move his belongings into two rooms at the new place across the street, and we would live there together until he found another place to live.

In May I took a break and headed off to Fort Smith to relax with Larry and Arthur again, and to see the Oak Ridge Boys live in concert. They were playing at a new place in Fort Smith called

the Red Roper, which was the largest nightclub I had ever seen—
the owners had spent a million dollars building the facility. The
three of us hung out with William Lee Golden all night and had a
blast. It was good to get out of town and get away from work for a
few days.

In late June I moved out of the house on North Madison in
Turley, which I had owned since 1981. I felt just a tinge of sadness
as I packed up the last load and moved to the house I had
remodeled across the street from Forrest. A few days later I moved
all of my father's belongings into mine, since he had been
conveniently absent when moving time came. By July 1st
everything I owned, as well as everything Forrest owned, was in
the newly remodeled home on North Victor. Although I was ready
to start my life anew I really didn't have any idea how to go about
it.

The first week of August was extremely interesting. Larry
called and asked me if I would be willing to produce a music video
for the Judge Parker Band at the last minute. Once again I had been
asked to pull a rabbit out of a hat, and again I stepped up to the
plate to answer the call. The video shoot was scheduled in less than
a week, but I had absolutely no experience in producing a music
video. I knew the project would be a challenge, but took the job
even though it didn't pay a dime. I'd been thinking about taking a
vacation to southern Louisiana anyway, so I figured since Fort
Smith was right on the way, now would be a great time to go.

The filming took place at the Red Roper nightclub where we saw the Oak Ridge Boys just a few months before. The name of the song was *Guitars and Girls*, so I suggested Larry round up as many girls and guitars that he could, and we would just roll the dice. I came up with different ideas to film all night long—some of them worked and some didn't. In the end some of my ideas made the final cut, but the rest wound up on the editing room floor.

At one point I caught an unauthorized guy filming the proceedings with a handheld video camera. It turned out that he was a tourist from Germany who was visiting the area and had heard about the video shoot on the local radio station. Not knowing any better he wandered in and just started recording without asking. So I made a deal with him—he could continue filming as long as he was willing to do something for me—send a copy of the video to Dieter in Germany.

Dieter had been to quite a few Judge Parker concerts while visiting the United States, and was a huge fan. I never expected the German tourist to go through with his part of the bargain, but a few months later Dieter called me ranting and raving about this wonderful videotape he had received in the mail. I hadn't told him about the German tourist, never expecting the tourist to send Dieter the tape. After I explained the whole story, he was very appreciative of what had transpired and we had a good laugh.

From Fort Smith I headed south to Louisiana to see the Bandidos in Baton Rouge and Lafayette, and then headed west to

190

Beaumont, Texas, to visit my sister Deedee and her husband Rick.
I then stopped in Galveston to see John "Big John" Lammons, and
talk to him again about starting a chapter in Oklahoma. It had now
been sixteen years since I had first discussed the concept with
Bandido Buddy in 1980. Big John suggested that it would be a
good time to bring the subject up at the drag races in Ennis, Texas,
which were scheduled for the first week of October. The Galveston
Bandido agreed to talk to the national chapter, and since Jack-E
from Louisiana was going to do the same I thought I might have a
chance.

While I was in Fort Smith and touring the Gulf coast, Lee
was on his way to Sturgis with another friend of ours—Bill Beaty
had married the widow of former Rogue Marvin Brix in May of
1987. On the way home from Sturgis Lee got a flat tire coming
across Kansas in the heat of the day. They decided to raise the bike
up using the kickstand as a fulcrum, but the kickstand broke off
and Lee was trapped under the weight of the motorcycle. It must
have been quite the sight to see for all of the passing cars on I-70
that day, and I sure wish I could've been there.

Being the nice guy he was and thinking of me, Bill first ran
to his bike to retrieve his camera. Lee was screamin at Bill,
pleading for him to help remove the motorcycle. But Bill did the
most sensible thing he could considering the circumstances—he
first took some photos—then helped get the motorcycle off of Lee.
In his haste to take the photos Bill forgot to remove the lens cover,

191

so the wonderful images never got developed. I was deeply saddened at Bill's thoughtless action and scolded him for leaving the lens cover on. What I could have done with those images...

I set off for Austin in early October to visit both of my sisters there, and on the way home attended the drag races at Ennis. I spoke to El Presidente Craig about getting permission to start the chapter, and got invited to present the concept to a large contingent of national officers in a press box above the racetrack. There were Bandidos present from all over the world who asked me all sorts of questions. I rode out of there that evening on top of the world, because I had finally been granted permission to officially start talking to people, to find out exactly who was seriously interested in becoming a member of the new chapter.

November was a great month—I was well on track to putting together a crew that would become the first chapter of Bandidos in Oklahoma. I had convinced John Fisher to relocate from Michigan, and he had rented a house not far from me. I had sold the house on North Victor I was living in, and had bought a wreck of a house about ten miles east in a little town called Owasso. It was a booming town with one of the best school districts in Oklahoma. The house sat on more than three acres and had a good-sized shop to work out of, but was infested with wild cats, fiddleback spiders, and thousands of wasp nests. In addition to the massive amount of construction work that was needed, there was also more than three-hundred thousand dollars in federal tax liens attached to the property.

On December 1st my biological father and I moved into the abandoned Owasso house and started to remodel it. I had taken possession of the property through a federal tax deed, and it superseded all of the liens except the first mortgage. I purchased the first mortgage from the bank for thirty-thousand dollars and then got my real estate attorney to do a quiet title action which terminated all of the liens and cleared the title. By Christmas Forrest was sleeping in the living room and I was residing in one of the bedrooms, and we had one bathroom working and the laundry functioning, but the rest of the house was a construction zone. There were huge holes in the roof all over the house, and we had garbage pails set under them to catch all of the water when it rained. Teresa and I were starting to see each other again, and Taylor was adapting well.

By February of 1997 I had accumulated quite an impressive roster of potential members for the new chapter which would be based out of Tulsa, but unfortunately Robert "Cowboy" Crain and Joseph "Joe-E" George were not among them. Cowboy had gotten so whacked out on meth he had been arrested again. He was destined to do another stretch in prison, but this time courtesy of the state of Oklahoma. After he was finished with the state prison sentence, he then had to go finish the time that remained on his federal prison sentence. Joe-E had also gotten whacked out on

193

meth, been thrown out of the Bandidos, and was destined to be arrested on federal drug charges in the near future. The potential members of the new chapter were:

Edward "CT Ed" Winterhalder	Owasso
Lee "Lee" McArdle	Tulsa
Harry "Skip" Hansen	Muskogee
Louis "Bill Wolf" Rackley	Broken Arrow
Earl "Buddy" Kirkwood	Sapulpa
Joseph "Little Joe" Kincaid	Muskogee
Mark "Bones " Hathaway	Sapulpa
John "Turtle" Fisher	Tulsa
Joseph "Popeye" Hannah	Muskogee
Keith "Keith" Vandervoort	Tulsa

At the end of February Turtle and I took off for Florida and Daytona Bike Week for the last time as independent bikers. We spent a day together in Daytona, and then went to Orlando where David "Dave" Gruber worked at Disney World. Dave had been a member of the Rogues with me in Tulsa, and we had known each other since the late seventies. He got us into Disney World for free through the employee gate, and then into the Indiana Jones show where Dave worked. My old friend had previously arranged for me to get picked out of the audience to participate in the show, but I wasn't aware of the fact. I had to do a bunch of crazy stuff to entertain the crowd on stage, while Dave and John laughed their asses off. Since Turtle wanted to visit some of his personal friends in Jacksonville, we split up for the rest of the trip. I headed west on I-10 to Baton Rouge, where I talked to Jack-E about getting the Oklahoma chapter off the ground.

In April the Bandidos sent Vice-Presidente Larry to visit Tulsa again. Big John came up from Galveston, and most of the potential new chapter members sat down with the two Bandidos to answer questions the guys had about the club. Larry informed us that it would be a long time before we would become Bandidos, but in the meantime he would see what he could do about getting permission for us to wear support shirts—in his opinion that was all we were worth.

A week later Craig assigned Vice-Presidente George Wegers from Washington state to oversee the new chapter, effectively saving us from the axe of Vice-Presidente Larry. I had met George a few months earlier when he had come to town with California AIM attorney Richard Lester for an Oklahoma Confederation of Clubs (COC) meeting. Richard and George had stayed at my house, and we had gone to the meeting together, in spite of the fact that I wasn't a Bandido.

At the confederation meeting George had got into a shoving match with Roger Wiley, who was a member of the Rogues in Tulsa. I guess Roger didn't realize who George was or didn't notice the expensive gold Bandidos necklace he was wearing. After the Vice-Presidente was introduced at the meeting and gave a little talk about clubs getting along, a humble Roger ate a large helping of crow pie during a walk with George as he begged for forgiveness.

George's attitude was a whole lot different than Larry's, and it was his intention to get the chapter started. By now John "Little Wolf" Killip from Oklahoma City was out of prison and had given me his consent, so in April everyone rode to Hallsville, Texas, to attend the annual drag races as a chapter for the first time. For the occasion we all wore ball caps we had made that said *Sooner or Later—Oklahoma,* and the Oklahoma part of the ball cap mimicked the shape of a bottom rocker.

While we were at the racetrack the Bandidos national chapter was in Longview meeting with the Outlaws national chapter. During that meeting the Outlaws officially gave their blessing for us to start the new chapter. We later heard that some of the Oklahoma Outlaws were totally against it, but their national president, Harry "Taco" Bowman, told the Bandidos they could have the new chapter and he could care less about Oklahoma.

The stage was now set for what was yet to come, but we still had no idea when we would actually become Bandidos. In early May Vice-Presidente George notified us that we all needed to attend the Gulfport Blowout in Biloxi, Mississippi, for the upcoming Memorial Day weekend. George told us that he would drive to Tulsa from Washington state, and then personally make the ride down to Biloxi with us. Everyone wondered if our chapter would be chartered while we were at Gulfport, but for me it was hard to believe that my dream was about to come true almost eighteen years after I met my first Bandido in Mobile.

We were all brimming with excitement when we left for Gulfport on Thursday evening. We rode over to Little Rock and spent the night at Bandido Leo "Murray" Murray's house. Six of the potential new Oklahoma members made the ride down to Biloxi with George and two other Washington state Bandidos, Hoot and Thumper, but four of the guys from Oklahoma didn't make it. The next day we rode from Little Rock to the gulf coast getting into Biloxi early Friday evening. We hadn't planned on going there so no one had thought about getting motel rooms in advance. By the time we rolled into town the only rooms we could find were more than one-hundred fifty dollars per night. So we got two rooms, packed three of us into each, and split the cost between us.

To our surprise everyone at Gulfport was told there was going to be a new probationary chapter in Oklahoma, but none of us received our patches. We met plenty of Bandidos who were excited about the new chapter, but we also met a bunch of Bandidos that weren't. The ride back to Tulsa was a long one because we all had expected to get patched. To complicate the ride home Turtle's bike broke down in southern Arkansas. He had forgotten to check his battery water and it had boiled dry. We were dead in the water, and Little Rock was our only option for rescue.

Searching For My Identity: The Chronological Evolution
Of A Troubled Adolescent To Outlaw Biker

It didn't take long before George and I got in an argument. I was used to traveling this stretch of road and knew the only thing to do was to call Little Rock, but George insisted that we figure out some other way to rectify the situation. We tried everything we could, but it was Memorial Day and there was no help available or any stores open in this rural area. I eventually called Murray for help in spite of the fact that George had specifically told me not to.

I knew that if I didn't call Little Rock we would be there for the next few days trying to fix something that couldn't be fixed. George was livid, but soon resigned himself to the fact that help was on the way. We loaded the broken Harley into the back of Murray's Ford Ranchero and finally got into Little Rock just before 10PM. Once again we spent the night at Murray's, got John a new battery in the morning, and rode home to Tulsa the next day. When we arrived in Tulsa the Vice-Presidente summoned all of us to a meeting at my house the following night. George told us that it was important and everyone had to be there.

Chapter 17

Bandidos Motorcycle Club Oklahoma

May 1997 To March 1998

On Wednesday morning May 27th a FedEx package arrived from Texas addressed to the Vice-Presidente. By the shape, size and feel of the box, I thought the day I'd been waiting for so long had finally come. Rumors were flying and the anticipation was like a cloud surrounding us when everyone gathered at my house that evening for our first weekly meeting. George had told us that we had to act like a chapter even though we weren't Bandidos yet, and part of this mandate meant that we would have weekly meetings that were referred to as church or card games.

After George called the meeting to order he told everyone that the patches had arrived and the first order of business was to choose our chapter officers. After everyone voted I was selected to be president, Buddy the vice-president, and Skip the sergeant-at-arms. Lee volunteered to be the secretary, and the Vice-Presidente appointed Turtle as road captain.

Because I was president and had been around the organization for a long time I was given an Oklahoma bottom rocker in spite of the fact that I was a probationary member—everyone else received probationary bottom rockers. The next day everyone had the patches sewed on to their vests, and we were on top of the world.

Searching For My Identity: The Chronological Evolution
Of A Troubled Adolescent To Outlaw Biker

Our first trip together as the official Oklahoma chapter was to Baton Rouge, Louisiana, for the all Harley motorcycle drag races in the middle of June. George flew back to Tulsa—he had left his Harley at my house to fly back home to Bellingham for three weeks—and joined us for the ride to Baton Rouge from Oklahoma. It was exhilarating to finally be a Bandido after almost eighteen years, and I savored the ride and the time I spent at the event. Probationary Bandido Bones entered his bike in the drag races, but was eliminated in the second round.

Later that month at our initial Oklahoma public appearance we set up a booth at the first annual BACA (Bikers Against Child Abuse) fundraiser where we sold t-shirts and ball caps emblazoned with the words *Support Your Local Bandidos*. We had two banners made for the event that read *Bandidos MC Oklahoma*, which we hung on the fence on either side of the booth.

Our intent from the beginning was to provide the public with a positive perception of the club. Some of us, who had previously been members of other motorcycle clubs, wanted to make sure we didn't repeat the mistakes that had been made in the past. For example, we had no intention of beating people up for no reason at all. On the contrary, we agreed to do everything we could to avoid a fight—we were adamant that we didn't want to alienate the public. Our presence at the BACA party that Sunday afternoon met accolades of approval from everyone except the Rogues. Some of them set up chairs directly across from us, and then proceeded to take photos all afternoon. One of them got stupid drunk and made a complete idiot of himself.

Jerry Nelson kept approaching the new brothers and making threats about what was going to happen now that the Bandidos had a chapter in Oklahoma. We later learned that they were upset because we had moved into their territory without first getting their permission, but the Bandidos didn't need their consent because the club wasn't a 1%er organization—even if they had been, the Rogues didn't have enough horsepower to tell us no.

Almost all of the Bandidos present at the BACA fundraiser wanted to give Jerry a serious attitude adjustment. Keith had to battle to keep his temper in check, for he knew Jerry well from when they were Rogues together—we ultimately had to physically restrain Keith from kicking the shit out of him in front of everyone. The only thing that saved Jerry that day was the fact that we were in the middle of a BACA fundraiser at which we were supposed to be helping abused kids.

In late July of 1997 the new Oklahoma chapter hosted a get together at my house in Owasso for a bunch of Bandidos from all over the United States. It had been a last-minute decision by the national chapter to come to Tulsa and support us at the Bikers Against Diabetes (BAD) rally which was being held that weekend at Mohawk Park. El Presidente Craig, Sargento-de-Armas Terry "Scrufty" Larque, and Galveston president Big John were a few of the almost sixty Bandidos who made the journey to Tulsa.

201

Searching For My Identity: The Chronological Evolution
Of A Troubled Adolescent To Outlaw Biker

We had planned to show up at the BAD event in mass, to make sure everyone and every motorcycle club in Oklahoma knew about the chapter and to make a statement. But the BAD Rally was a huge flop and only three-hundred spectators showed up. Our scouts reported back to us that there were almost as many members of law enforcement present as there were spectators. So instead of going to the rally, we opted to take a leisurely motorcycle ride from Owasso to a yuppie biker bar and restaurant at 34th Street and Peoria Avenue in an area of town known as Brookside.

At 6PM we fired up the Harleys and headed out from my house. The pack of more than seventy-five bikes traveled west through Owasso up into the hills of north Tulsa, before navigating the streets of downtown Tulsa and heading south on Peoria Avenue to the nightclub parking lot. The rumbling of the bikes sounded like thunder and shook the buildings in the downtown area as if there had been an earthquake.

Our entrance into the bar was electric as we occupied every empty chair in the place. The few chairs that had been occupied by customers soon became vacant, and we filled those as well. The Bandidos completely dominated the popular biker hangout, and everyone spent a quiet evening there drinking, eating, and relaxing. Pleasantly surprised by the unusual absence of police resources in Brookside, we later found out the cause of our peaceful adventure—a massive contingent of law enforcement officers had gathered at Mohawk Park to greet us when we rode into the event, and hadn't been allowed to leave all evening anticipating our arrival.

After getting tired of being seen and hanging around on Brookside, we started to disperse around midnight. Some of the brothers went to their motel rooms, some hit the road to get an early start back home, and the last group planned to go back to my house for the night. Just as we were walking out to our bikes to leave the Tulsa Police Department gang squad arrived. They had waited for us all day and night at Mohawk Park, and finally heard that we were at the bar on Brookside. By the time they raced across town to catch a glimpse of us we were leaving, and they only got a few photos of the new Bandidos Oklahoma chapter.

I spent the spring and summer of 1997 remodeling the Owasso ranchette, and between the two of us a lot of the major problems were resolved. My biological father and I also added a new addition to the house, consisting of a fourth bedroom, a third bathroom, and some additional eating space in the kitchen.

I took a job late that summer with a local property company to remodel nineteen residential properties simultaneously. The contract kept me busy big time, but also provided me with the necessary legal funds to pursue my life as a Bandido. While I was working my ass off fixing the nineteen properties, I was also working on the house.

At the end of the summer the national chapter decided that the Oklahoma chapter would benefit from the presence of a

Bandido from the nomad chapter. Their intention in sending us the nomad was to make sure we understood the Bandido way, but in the end the decision caused us much grief and discontent. In spite of the fact the supervising Bandidos were friends of mine, they had no authority to tell me what to do, but thought they did. It came to a head within a few weeks when Bandido Earthquake and I got in a hell of an argument. To solve the dilemma El Presidente Craig told Earthquake that he was there as an advisor and couldn't tell me what to do.

In October of 1997 my former wife once again dove off into the world of alcohol and meth. As a direct result I petitioned the court and got full custody of my daughter. This time I knew it wouldn't be temporary and that I had arrived at a major crossroads in my life. I had to figure out if Taylor was more important than being a Bandido, and I needed to make the decision fast.

I was already doubting my leadership abilities as a chapter president, and knew that Lee wasn't the best choice for secretary. After explaining the situation during a phone call with the Vice-Presidente, I resigned my chapter presidency and attempted to quit the club. George refused to let me leave, and appointed Lee to run the chapter for a few weeks until George was able to come to Tulsa.

When the Vice-Presidente arrived he diplomatically helped set the stage for a better-organized chapter, which simultaneously allowed me get a handle on my life. As a chapter we hammered out our differences—Lee was voted in as president and I became the secretary, which allowed me to spend less time on the road as a Bandido. Every member of the chapter agreed to do what they could, to give me more time at home to take care of my daughter who was four years old. I was impressed with the way that George handled the issue, and proud of the fact that everyone thought enough of me to support this unconventional solution to my unusual situation.

November 1997 was a month of major highs and lows. As I settled into being a single dad with custody and my major child-rearing responsibilities, I started going to the Parent Child Center for much needed guidance in how to be a parent. I also put the finishing touches on a new music CD which I titled *The Best Of Warren Winters – Forever & Always*. Forever & Always reflected what I said to my daughter Taylor each night as I tucked her into bed—*I love you Taylor, forever and always, until the end of time.*

The music CD was a compilation of the best songs from all three of my record albums, as well as a few studio tracks that had never been published. The songs covered a time span of almost twenty years from 1979 to 1997, as well as a broad range of musical styles. For the cover I took photos of Taylor and me walking down the street in front of my home while I carried my guitar. I used the club colors, which were referred to as red and gold, for accent colors in the title block. The finished product marked the closing of an era, for I no longer possessed the desire to continue being a musician.

Searching For My Identity: The Chronological Evolution
Of A Troubled Adolescent To Outlaw Biker

On November 27th my heart broke when my adopted mom Dolly died peacefully in her sleep—there was no hint of impending doom in the last weeks of her life. I spent my last moments with her just before I left for a trip to Texas with Taylor. I asked Dolly if she wanted to join us, and she told me that she was looking forward to spending the holiday with her friends at church, and she wanted to stay in Tulsa. When Dolly wouldn't answer the door on Thanksgiving Day, her friends from church gained entry to the house where they found her lying serenely in bed. It appeared that my mom had gotten into bed and just stopped breathing. The way she died was a fitting end for a wonderful woman who had spent her entire life in the devotion of others.

I learned of Dolly's passing while I was visiting my sisters in Austin, late in the afternoon on Thanksgiving Day. Ironically my biological father was the one who actually broke the news to me. I had a hard time maintaining my composure that evening and was quite surprised at Taylor's grasp of the situation. Even at the tender age of four Taylor did all she could to comfort me on the long ride back to Tulsa. When I wrote her obituary with a heavy heart the following day I said, *"Dolly was a generous, kind, and loving parent, full of life, laughter and courage."* Although she had spent her entire life battling diabetes and the last ten years of her life blind, never once did she complain.

Christmas was a somber event, and the only reason I got through it emotionally was Taylor. For me it was my first

206

Christmas without Dolly—she had always been either with me or just a phone call away. This Christmas though, there was no calling her, and I found that I really missed her. Taylor came through again and consoled me every time my emotions got the best of me.

By March of 1998 I desperately needed a vacation and decided to visit Dieter—being a Bandido and a single parent over the winter had literally kicked my ass, and I was wore out. I made reservations to fly from Dallas to Frankfurt, Germany, and two close friends of mine in Dallas, Greg and Bridgett Johns, volunteered to take care of Taylor for the week I would be gone. They had known my daughter since she was born, and had two daughters her age that Taylor could play with while I was away. Taylor and I drove down to Dallas, and before I knew what hit me I was landing in Frankfurt.

Chapter 18

Bandidos Motorcycle Club Oklahoma

March 1998 To November 1998

Getting off the plane after a ten-hour plane flight from Texas I had to force myself to stay awake and find my land legs again. I was thankful to find my German brother waiting for me after I cleared customs. As tired as I was, I was able to stay awake and enjoy the four-hour car ride from Frankfurt to Lengerich—it was exciting to be back in Germany again, and good to be away from the pressure and stress of daily life at home.

I spent a few days hanging out with Dieter and his family, and went to school with his daughter Malisa who was in the fourth grade. Malisa had told the kids in school that her Uncle Ed was visiting from America—some of them refused to believe it and called her a liar. When I volunteered to accompany her to school to prove that she was telling the truth, my niece was elated. The next morning when two long-haired bikers walked into the school by her side, each holding one of her hands, the fourth-grader was beaming.

After Malisa's schoolteacher and Dieter volunteered to translate, all the kids in her class gathered in a circle to ask me questions about the United States. I was surprised at the warm welcome I received and the interest the children had. Before we left Dieter took a great photo of me with Malisa, her entire class, and Malisa's teacher.

The next day we traveled by train from Lengerich to Copenhagen, Denmark. Since July of 1995 when Sweden president Mikael "Joe" Ljunggren had been shot and killed, the Bandidos in Scandinavia—Denmark, Norway, Finland and Sweden—had been embroiled in a violent war with the Hells Angels. There had been many casualties on both sides from homemade bombs, hand grenades, anti-tank rockets, knives and gunfire. Dozens of members from the two organizations were either in prison or on the run for participating in the carnage.

The Bandidos has suffered terribly, for in addition to Joe, four other members had been murdered during the biker war. Finland vice-president Jarkko Kokko had been shot and killed in January of 1996 at the Bandidos clubhouse in Helsinki. Bandido Uffe Larsen had been shot and killed at the Kastrup Airport in Denmark—Bandido Lars Harnes, the president of Norway, was shot in the chest at the Fornebu Airport in Norway an hour later but survived the attack—on March 10th of 1996. Prospect Jan "Face" Krogh Jensen was shot and killed in Drammen, Norway, on July 15th of 1996, and Bandido Bjorn Gudmandsen was shot and killed in Liseleje, Denmark, on June 7th of 1997.

In the fall of 1997 after months of negotiations the Bandidos and Hells Angels had wisely agreed to a truce, and Bandidos European Presidente Jim Tinndahn and Danish Hells

Searching For My Identity: The Chronological Evolution
Of A Troubled Adolescent To Outlaw Biker

Angel Bent "Blondie" Nielsen shook hands during a live television press conference to cement the deal. As part of the agreement the Hells Angels and Bandidos in Copenhagen set up a joint clubhouse for a year, as additional proof to the world that both sides were serious about keeping the peace. Since I was going to be the first American Bandido to visit Denmark since the war ended, we wondered what kind of reception we were going to get.

I wasn't sure how we would be received by Danish immigration and customs agents at the border, so we planned to enter the country disguised as tourists. To facilitate the plan I made sure all of my Bandido shirts and jewelry were well-hidden in my luggage, and didn't contact anyone from the organization until after we arrived. I also wasn't sure how the Hells Angels would react to my presence, since most Bandidos in Denmark were still quite apprehensive about the truce and were operating under the premise that violence between the two clubs was still likely to occur.

To cross the border it was necessary to get on a massive ferry since there's nothing but water between Denmark and Germany. Imagine my surprise when the train stopped and we were told to get off, and I found myself inside the bottom of the ferry. The ferry was so big it carried the entire train, in addition to another level completely full of cars, trucks and motorcycles!

After a short thirty-minute ferry ride and another two-hour journey on the train, Dieter and I were greeted at Central Station in Copenhagen by a contingent of Bandidos who were surprised to see an American Bandido in Denmark. The Danish brothers were quite concerned with my safety and surrounded us with guards the entire time we were there. In a small café near the train station I met Swedish Bandido Jan "Clark" Jenson from the Helsingborg chapter for the first time. Clark was a former Hells Angel who had found the Bandidos to be more suited to his way of life, and we got along great. After a short meeting and cup of much needed coffee, we agreed to get together again as soon as possible.

The first night we were in Copenhagen Dieter and I attended a reception for a Danish Bandido who had gotten married earlier in the day. I was surprised at how well most of them spoke English, and how easy it was to communicate compared to what I had experienced in Germany. I was also surprised at how young most of the Danish brothers were—the majority of them were in their twenties and thirties.

During the party I met so many Danish Bandidos I couldn't remember most of their names, but I did retain one of them. Jacob "Big Jacob" Anderson was a new member on furlough from prison who went out of his way to make sure I felt at home. He was incarcerated for attempting to blow up the Hells Angels clubhouse in Titangade with a thirteen-pound radio-controlled bomb in July of 1996, and we agreed to write each other while he finished his prison sentence. Although I held up my end of the bargain, Big

Jacob never wrote me back and I was able to harass him about it for years to come.

After only a few hours at the wedding reception Dieter and I were prematurely rushed out the back door when local police raided the party. After spending the night in Copenhagen, we got a tour of the famous Christiana section of Copenhagen with a Bandido as our guide. While in Christiana Dieter and I were able to temporarily play the part of hashish dealers for an impromptu photo session at one of the many legal open-air drug kiosks.

One of the brothers appointed to keep us safe went out of his way to show the two of us all over Denmark. With Jan "Buller" Sorensen as our guide, we experienced Danish life and food as though we lived there, and were able to cross over into Sweden to visit Clark at the Helsingborg clubhouse. Buller made his living buying and selling Harley-Davidson motorcycles, so we talked a lot about motorcycles and agreed to explore the prospect of wholesaling Harleys from country to country.

Buller offered to drive the two of us back to Germany, and after enduring the day-long train ride from Lengerich to Copenhagen we jumped at the chance to relax in a car for the ride back to Germany. Dieter and Buller planned to check out motorcycles in Germany while we were there, and further explore the possibility of starting a legal motorcycle business with each other.

Searching For My Identity: The Chronological Evolution
Of A Troubled Adolescent To Outlaw Biker

During my visit to Denmark I had spent some time with the national president for the Bandidos in Europe. When I had told the Presidente I would be returning to Germany for a few days before I flew back to America, Jim asked me to contact a motorcycle club there called the Ghostriders. The Bandidos were very friendly with the Ghostriders, and Jim thought that a visit from an American Bandido would promote the friendship. After a short two-day visit I went back to Germany to visit the Ghostriders.

I initially made contact with Armin "Armin" Geffert, who had a good grasp of the English language. With Dieter as my guide we drove from Lengerich to Dortmund, which was located in the Ruhrpott area of central Germany. There we met up with Armin, Diesel and Leslav "Les" Hause, all full patch members of the Ghostriders. At the time they were the second largest motorcycle club in Germany—only the Bones motorcycle club exceeded them in size and strength. Les was the national president, Diesel was national sergeant-at-arms, and Armin was national secretary.

Diesel owned a tattoo shop in the heart of Dortmund, so we met in a small café nearby. After getting to know each other, Les offered to let me his Harley. Although I was freezing, the German bikers were oblivious to the weather conditions, and informed me that it was a nice day for a ride. I graciously accepted the use of the motorcycle and rode side by side next to a Ghostrider for a few miles across town. At the time I was unaware that Les was taking photos as he followed us in a car. The images would eventually become famous, for they were the only photos ever taken of an American Bandido riding with a Ghostrider.

Les ended our afternoon outing by inviting me to a party that was going to be held a few days later by a new prospect chapter in Kassel. I promised that I would show up, but first I needed to travel to Luxembourg to visit a brand-new chapter there—a long-time Luxembourg motorcycle club called Les Copains had recently patched over to Bandidos.

The next morning I set out for Luxembourg by myself via train and arrived there early that evening. It didn't take long to locate a member of the local chapter, for this time I had called ahead to warn them of my arrival. When we got to the clubhouse I was quite surprised to find myself in front of a multi-storied building in a nice area of Esch Alzette. The first floor was a bar that was open to the public—the entire second floor was their clubhouse, and the third and fourth floors housed an apartment for Angus, the chapter president.

I spent a total of two days with the brothers in Luxembourg, and although there was a distinct language barrier, with the help of Bandidos Pirate and Mario who could both speak a little English, everyone got along fine. I visited the local Harley dealer, got introduced to techno pop—a type of music heard throughout Europe, but not popular in the United States—ate some unusual home cooked food, and visited a Luxembourg doctor who helped me sort out a minor health issue.

Searching For My Identity: The Chronological Evolution
Of A Troubled Adolescent To Outlaw Biker

Early Saturday afternoon Pirate and I drove to Germany where we planned to rendezvous with Les, Armin and Diesel in Kassel. Late that evening we arrived at the Kassel clubhouse, where I found the language barrier to be intense. Although Pirate was fluent in German, English and French, we both had a lot of trouble keeping up with the conversation. The Kassel guys were all prospects, and weren't quite sure what to make of their two Bandido visitors. The highlight of the evening for me was watching an obnoxious guest get thrown out of the party.

The next day the Luxembourg Bandido dropped me off at the Frankfurt airport before heading back to Esch Alzette. It had been a great trip, but I was eager to get back to Texas and Taylor. Although I had talked to my daughter nearly every day while I was in Europe, I was missing her a lot and knew she needed to see me. I fell asleep on the plane, and before I knew it we were landing in Dallas. It was about 3PM by the time I cleared customs, and again I had a bad case of jetlag. After picking Taylor up in Carrollton, I somehow drove the two-hundred fifty miles back to Owasso before I collapsed from exhaustion.

I didn't spend much time at home before I headed to Hallsville, Texas, for the drag races in early April. While the troops partied at Hallsville, all of the Bandido presidents gathered at a house in Longview for a mandatory meeting, where they decided that Vice-Presidente George would be the new El Presidente after Craig reported to federal prison to begin serving his ten-year sentence. It would be a major turning point for the Bandidos motorcycle club in the United States, and a dynamic shift in club policy would soon follow, for George's philosophy was quite different than his predecessors.

The new El Presidente believed that change was a good thing for the club, and that all motorcycle clubs needed to get along. He was an active participant in the national Confederation of Clubs, which was a new organization that was attempting to convince all motorcycle clubs to peacefully coexist. George also adamantly believed that to be a successful Bandido, a member had to maintain a critical balance between the club, employment and family, or being a Bandido long-term wouldn't work. George was involved with a Harley dealership in Bellingham, Washington, so he knew first-hand how important it was to balance the club and employment.

This reasoning was sound, for if a member lost his family he would carry that burden with him, and it would likely be an expensive load to bear. If a member lost his job, then he would be a Bandido without money. A member without employment would soon turn to illegal enterprises, and before long that member would more than likely be arrested and sent off to prison. The new El Presidente wanted to break the cycle, and was willing to guide the club through the internal turmoil that was sure to follow when changes are made.

George also wanted the club to grow, but to facilitate this vision the organization had to change in a big way. In order for new members to have the desire to join, older members had to open up and accept them. There also had to be some type of attraction, and policy change was going to be the only way to assure potential members that the club was worth joining. At the time there were less than one-hundred fifty Bandidos in the United States—only a third of them thought like George, another third were dinosaurs that thought the Bandido ways of the sixties should continue forever, and the last third were generally stuck somewhere in the middle. The new El Presidente also realized that to effect major change there had to be minor changes to club policy made every day.

The decades-old traditions of pissing all over a new member and his club colors when he received his full patch, beating up prospects and hangarounds, and intimidation and extortion of prospects, hangarounds and independent bikers was strictly forbidden. He also understood that the club needed new members who were men of respect, and not pieces of shit. To facilitate this rationale potential members had to be treated better, for in the outlaw biker world, to get respect you had to first give respect.

Last of all but not least, the new El Presidente was not a fan of methamphetamine. He believed, as I did, that meth was the most dangerous enemy the club had ever encountered and it had the potential to cause the total destruction of the club unless something was done to prevent its use. At a minimum I secretly hoped the sale and distribution would soon be a patch pulling offense, but knew that was something the club would likely never mandate.

I was elated when I heard that George was going to be the next El Presidente, and decided to do whatever I could legally to assist him in getting the job done. I knew that he was going to be a good leader as long as he kept focused on his plan to change the club—and the older members that hated him didn't kill him. At the same time I was worried that he too would eventually be corrupted by the absolute power he possessed, like so many that came before him.

In late April I was in the right place at the right time when I bought a two story, twenty-six hundred square foot house on five acres of land in Sperry, a small suburb about ten miles northwest of Tulsa. The house had been heavily damaged in a fire, but most of the damage was confined to the second floor. I got Skip to help me, and together we rebuilt the entire house. A week after it was completed I sold the house to a young couple who had bad credit, by carrying the mortgage myself. To do this legally, I utilized a provision of Oklahoma real estate law commonly referred to as a contract-for-deed.

May was a blur between working on the Sperry house and the Owasso house where I was living, and the trips I took as a

Bandido. The Oklahoma chapter attended the Pawhuska Mayfit and the Red River Run in Red River, New Mexico, on back to back weekends. Close to the end of the club's general meeting assembly at Red River that Sunday around 3PM, we celebrated big-time when we were handed our Oklahoma bottom rockers and 1%er diamonds. It had been a year since we had started the chapter in Tulsa, and now there were only six of us left—Lee, Bill Wolf, Turtle, Buddy, Joe and I had survived. Popeye, Keith, Skip, and Bones had left the club in good standings, going their separate ways for various reasons.

At the end of a hectic summer I traveled by car to Texas for a myriad of reasons. First and foremost it was going to be my daughter's fifth birthday, and I planned to take her to Sea World for a birthday present. I also needed to see my sister Julie who was dying from a rare form of lung cancer called mesothelioma. A Bandido I knew well was also heading to prison for many years, and I wanted to see him before he went.

I was quite fortunate when Bandido Bones, who had an annual family pass to Sea World, decided to accompany us there and act as our guide. Taylor got to see the dolphins, and was able to feed one by hand for a few precious minutes while I watched. That night Bandido Ramon and his girlfriend threw Taylor an impromptu birthday party, going way beyond the call of duty when they provided her with a birthday cake and a few presents.

On the way back to Tulsa we spent two days visiting Julie—it would be the last time I would see my sister alive. In spite of the horrible disease which had ravaged her body, she was alert and coherent for most of the time we were there. I was thankful for the short time we knew each other, but sad that I hadn't known her longer. Shortly after I left Austin in early August she passed away, leaving this world for a much better place. I knew in my heart that Julie would now be one of my guiding angels, watching over me for the rest of my days on earth.

In October I landed a job for a Dallas based construction company, building a new child care facility for the Muskogee Regional Medical Center in Muskogee, Oklahoma, which would be my first cradle to grave construction project. I felt challenged by the fact that I had been brought in at the last minute, and that I was a single dad with custody of a five-year old daughter. I soon got into a routine dropping Taylor off at a Koala daycare near my house at 6:30AM, then driving the fifty-five miles to the jobsite in Muskogee typically arriving an hour later. I would leave every day at 4:30PM, pick Taylor up before 6PM, then head to the house and make dinner for the two of us. It was a hectic pace to say the least, but I persevered.

I went to the Bandidos Thanksgiving party which was held in Austin for a change. During the event it was decided that I would be put in charge of publishing a new monthly newsletter for the organization. The newsletter had been originated ten years prior by a Bandido named Rawhide, but never amounted to much more than a page or two of news. Bandido Super Dave from Baton Rouge had recently attempted to rejuvenate the concept, but hadn't achieved much success due to the fact that his computer equipment was antiquated and his knowledge insufficient.

I was to have total control over the content and authority to get the entire Bandido world coordinated, but had no authority to make the USA chapters submit monthly news. Over the next few months I got most of the Australia, Europe and USA chapters to agree to publish a monthly newsletter, and was able to coordinate the publishing date for each region to coincide with each other. It was a monumental task to accomplish, as most of the older USA Bandido members thought the newsletter was a total breach of internal security—they were worried about what would happen if law enforcement or our enemies got hold of it. We placated those angry brothers by reassuring them that the published news would never contain any information that would benefit the police or our adversaries. An example of what could be published was general news like *Baytown Bob broke his leg last Friday and is now at home in Corpus resting.*

Chapter 19

Bandidos Motorcycle Club Oklahoma

December 1998 To July 1999

I had high hopes for Christmas in 1998 with the arrival of Kitty, her husband Michael, my nieces Amanda and Kaitlyn, and my nephew Robert, who had traveled from Michigan to Tulsa by plane to spend the holiday with us. My biological father ruined it as soon as they arrived in a horrific display of anger vented towards Kitty, Michael and me, in the kitchen of the home I shared with Forrest and his new Romanian wife. In front of everyone, Forrest screamed, shouted and swore like a deranged, demented man, smashing a bookshelf and all that it contained in the process.

Everyone retreated to my bedroom where the adults tried to calm the children, who were obviously scared to death. After sorting through our options we made the decision to vacate the premises, and retreat to the peace and tranquility of my construction site in Muskogee, where I proudly showed off the child care facility I was building. We decided to eat Christmas dinner in the dining area at the Muskogee Regional Medical Center—at less than three dollars per person the meal was the least expensive Christmas meal I had ever purchased, and also one of the best. We were all surprised at how good the food was, and thankful Forrest was nowhere to be seen.

When we returned to the house Forrest seemed to be a changed man, and was acting like nothing had ever happened in spite of the damaged bookcase that had been reinstalled on the wall. In the spirit of the holiday season, notwithstanding his actions earlier that day, everyone gathered around the fireplace in the living room to open the Christmas gifts as a family. Although we acted like it was a joyous occasion, in reality we were wondering how soon Hyde would turn back into Jekyll. Thankfully all went well for the rest of the night, albeit surreal, and the next day I took Kitty and her family to the airport for their return flight home.

For them the horrible trip wasn't over. By the time they got to St. Louis, where they were scheduled to change planes, an unexpected winter blizzard had arrived. The snow caused the entire airport to shut down, and Kitty's family ended up spending two days and nights in a pricey hotel where their only option for food was extremely expensive room service. Eventually the storm let up and the planes resumed flying, but by then there were thousands of other pissed off passengers wanting to get to their original destinations as fast as they could. After waiting many more hours, my sister and her family finally got back home to Flint where they relished the memory of the worst Christmas vacation they could have ever imagined.

I spent the first three months of 1999 supervising the construction of the child care facility, attending all required Bandido functions, and trying as hard as I could to be the best dad for my daughter who was now five-years old. In addition to all the daily demands ongoing in my life I enrolled Taylor in counseling at the Parent Child Center to help her cope with the absence of her mother. I had always been upset that Taylor didn't come with an owner's manual, so while Taylor was in her weekly sessions with the therapist, I spent a quiet hour in the library reading books and learning everything I could about raising a child to improve my parenting skills. Years later I would look back at this decision as one of the most important things I ever did for my daughter and myself.

The entire chapter had more than enough of Turtle by the time March rolled around. He had become addicted to meth and was so far out there no one could talk to him. I remember the chapter discussing Turtle's mental condition due to his constant ingestion of meth. We would joke that Turtle wasn't out in left field, he was beyond the bleachers and the parking lot. After giving him a last chance for the tenth time, Lee finally kicked him out of the club and pulled his patch.

But sadly we were dealing with the meth head, and not the man—Turtle decided that he didn't want to leave the chapter quietly. His expulsion turned into a fiasco, and instead of paying the chapter the small amount of money he owed, the former Bandido told us all to get screwed. That incensed Bandido Joe, our sergeant-at-arms, who decided the chapter would seize his bike to even the score and settle the debt. The only problem was that Turtle was nowhere to be found, and when he did turn up he was so whacked out on meth he was unpredictable and extremely volatile. Joe didn't want to die for something as trivial as a small debt, but on the other hand it was a matter of respect.

El Presidente George solved the problem by instructing Lee to repossess Turtle's Harley by filing a civil replevin action at the Tulsa County Courthouse. A replevin lawsuit is how every car, truck and motorcycle dealer handles a repossession when the vehicle can't be located. Although the attorney successfully prosecuted the replevin action and the Court ordered the return of the motorcycle, the former Bandido dismantled the bike and sold all the parts for more meth. The chapter never did collect the money that Turtle owed, or locate what was left of his motorcycle. His methamphetamine addiction finally got the best of him less than a year later when he was indicted by the feds for drug trafficking and firearms possession offenses.

By April I had pushed myself as far as I could, so when a Bandido Mississippi Charlie died in Washington State, I jumped at the opportunity to travel there for his funeral. On April 23rd Taylor experienced her first plane ride, and the two of us arrived in Seattle after a short layover in Salt Lake City. While we were there Taylor and I stayed with Bandido TJ, his wife Cheryl, and her two daughters—one of the girls looked so much like Taylor they could have been twins. I attended the funeral and after-party for Charlie, and spent a little time hanging out and relaxing with TJ while the girls kept Taylor occupied.

As soon as I returned to Oklahoma it was back to the grind and my daily routine. I could see light at the end of the proverbial tunnel though, because now the construction of the child care facility was in its final stages. I was determined to see it completed and open on schedule no later than July 1st. For once in my life I was happily employed, and had become friends with two of my employers, Mike Crowe and Mike Lewis. Both Mikes were decent down to earth regular guys that were easy to relate to and great to work with. Later that summer I was able to get both of them a fantastic deal on brand-new Harley Softails without having to endure the mandatory six-month waiting period that was common at that time in Texas.

In spite of the fact that the Oklahoma chapter wasn't gaining any new members, over the winter of 1998 and spring of 1999 we established two chapters of a new motorcycle club in Oklahoma that we proudly called the OK Riders. Their presence initially helped us look like we were larger than we were, and eventually turned into a training program for future Bandidos, like a minor league baseball team is to a major league team. Most citizens weren't able to distinguish the two clubs—to them the patches were all the same because both had red and gold colors—and to our surprise a lot of law enforcement officers also thought the same.

Searching For My Identity: The Chronological Evolution
Of A Troubled Adolescent To Outlaw Biker

In reality the OK Riders patch had the opposite colors as the Bandidos. The club colors were red on gold, and the OK Riders colors were gold on red. In addition the Bandidos center patch was a Fat Mexican, and the OK Rider center patch was a cow skull with snakes set inside of a diamond.

We intended from the outset to make this club a support club for the Bandidos, yet different from all the rest of the red and gold support clubs across the United States, for we guaranteed that its members would not be treated like shit. For years the Bandidos had used support clubs to do all of their dirty work and had treated support club members as their personal slaves. Our innovative approach to the treatment of support club members sent shock waves throughout the Bandidos nation, and eventually changed the way most support club members were treated.

Even though we were a national 1%er motorcycle club and didn't need their permission, we did the right thing and approached the three major Oklahoma outlaw motorcycle clubs to ask for their blessing. We were surprised at the initial opposition we received, but with persistence and perseverance we eventually got the Rogues, Outlaws and Mongols to accept the concept.

The first OK Rider chapter was based in a tiny Oklahoma City suburb called Jones, but the bottom rocker said Chandler because the chapter's president lived there. Another chapter followed shortly thereafter just outside Tulsa in the town of

227

Claremore, which had been the home of famous humorist Will Rogers.

Both OK Rider chapters grew like weeds—this was because their members were not being treated like shit and the chapters were led by seasoned motorcycle club veterans Charles "Snake" Rush and Raymond "Ray" Huffman. OK Rider Snake had been a member of the Rogues back in the seventies, when Bill Wolf and I were Rogues, and OK Rider Ray had once been a member of the local Mongols chapter in the early nineties.

Lee and I wanted the OK Riders to have a different focus— in essence an extension of what we preached all the time, so the OK Rider bylaws dictated that:

1. No methamphetamine addicts are allowed to be a member of the club; and

2. To be a member you must have visible means of support, meaning you either have a job, a pension or your wife/girlfriend needs to be employed in a capacity that provides sufficient income to support your lifestyle; and

3. Your family and employment come first; and

4. You would not be treated like a slave by a Bandido.

At the time Lee and I were convinced that the procedures and requirements to be a member of the Bandidos and the OK Riders would prevent the typical drug dealer and law enforcement problems that all of the other outlaw clubs experienced on a regular basis, but in hindsight our perception was a giant miscalculation.

Searching For My Identity: The Chronological Evolution
Of A Troubled Adolescent To Outlaw Biker

At the end of April I had so much on my plate I was in a constant state of exhaustion. In addition to the construction of the child care facility, being a single dad with custody, and a Bandido, I had also been instructed by El Presidente George to increase my involvement with the Oklahoma Confederation of Clubs (COC).

George wanted me to get the COC in Oklahoma rolling, but this was no small task. In Oklahoma, as in the rest of the country, most 1%er outlaw motorcycle clubs could barely tolerate each other. Most of them hated the others' guts, and some clubs were in a state of war killing each other's members on a regular basis. Getting methamphetamine fueled bikers to sit down in one room and talk about life was a monumental concept, but if anyone could get it done it was going to be me and the Bandidos.

In May of 1998 I attended the annual meeting of the National Coalition of Motorcyclists (NCOM) in Texas at which there was a meeting scheduled for the Confederation of Clubs. In advance El Presidente George had asked members of the Pagans, Outlaws, Hells Angels, and Sons of Silence to attend the COC meeting and not start fighting with each other while they were there. All of the major 1%er organizations sent representatives to the Dallas convention, which was held in a large nine-story hotel near the Dallas-Ft. Worth airport. Bandido George guaranteed the safety of each major club member personally, and to make sure nothing happened the Bandidos were in charge of security for the duration of the event.

Searching For My Identity: The Chronological Evolution
Of A Troubled Adolescent To Outlaw Biker

On the first day of the gathering I personally attended individual meetings between George and the other clubs. First George and I met with representatives from the Hells Angels, then the Pagans, then the Sons of Silence, and finally the Outlaws who arrived with a large contingent of members expecting trouble. The El Presidente and I convinced each club to send two members of their respective organizations to a meeting that was going to be held in a Bandidos suite.

The next day, for the first time in history, representatives from the five major 1%er outlaw motorcycle clubs in the United States were present in one room at the same time. At the time I was a new Bandido and wasn't allowed to attend the actual meeting, but I learned a lot from the experience. I was told afterwards that not much was discussed, but all five clubs did agree to stop fighting each other and to open lines of communication, which everyone hoped would prevent future conflicts from getting blown out of proportion.

After the meeting was held there seemed to be tranquility amongst the major clubs, which passed on by example to the smaller organizations, so by the spring of 1999 there was some limited participation in the Oklahoma Confederation of Clubs by the Outlaws, Rogues, and Mongols, and a lot of participation by the Bandidos and OK Riders. At the beginning of the year I had been voted in as the legal liaison for the Oklahoma COC—part of my duties were getting all the Oklahoma motorcycle clubs involved with the COC, and trying to keep the ones that were involved from having arguments that would lead to violent altercations.

For years the Sons of Silence had been locked in a mortal battle with the Outlaws, but over time I had cultivated friendships in both organizations. In early May I personally invited members from both organizations to be our guests at the annual Pawhuska Rally which was going to be held in the middle of the month. It took a lot to get them to agree to show up, but eventually we got it done. A contingent of Outlaws arrived from Indiana and Ohio to join their Oklahoma chapter, and a larger group of Sons of Silence members arrived from Kansas and Colorado. I put the Outlaws next to our camp on the hill, and the Sons of Silence in front of us. We later learned that two full patch members of the Sons were undercover ATF agents that had infiltrated the organization.

To get the Outlaws and Sons used to being in the presence of each other, I made sure that there was an Outlaw, a Bandido, and a Son together for each guard duty shift at the main entrance to the Bandidos camp. It wasn't long before the talk between the three outlaw bikers turned to pretty women, the weather or motorcycles, and friendships were born. By the end of the weekend it wasn't unusual to see an Outlaw hanging out with Son or vice versa. The entire 1%er outlaw motorcycle club world in the United States was rocked by what we accomplished that weekend, and how well everything turned out. I had taken a huge chance coordinating this, but in the end it was a major turning point in the history of 1%er clubs in the United States.

At the end of June I completed the child care construction project in Muskogee. I was very proud of it, primarily because I had done something for children that would last a lifetime. It felt good to have given something back to the world after taking so much from it for so many years. I took a week off, but soon was assigned new construction projects, both of which I could manage from the office in my home. This was a blessing because it allowed me more time to take care of Taylor, and gave me the income I desperately needed at the time to keep up the Bandidos lifestyle I was living.

The first construction project involved the replacement of an existing fire alarm system in the hospital at Fort Huachuca in Sierra Vista, Arizona. The second project was the new installation of a fire sprinkler system for another Army hospital at Fort Leonard Wood near Rolla, Missouri. I was going to be the project manager for both projects simultaneously, which required a ton of paperwork since both were federal government construction projects.

As I dived headfirst into both assignments my biological father and his Romanian wife decided to move out in early July and get a place of their own. Forrest and I had been sharing the Owasso ranchette while we rebuilt it, but the remodeling process was long over and now it was time to part ways. I was ecstatic because a serious bump in the road had disappeared overnight. For quite a while I had wanted to find a new female partner—by now I had totally given up on reestablishing a relationship with my former wife—and this allowed me to start the search.

I had been unable to do this previously because of the impression my father's Romanian wife would likely make on any female that entered my life. She deliberately contributed absolutely nothing to the household, and because she was in her mid-twenties and Forrest was in his mid-sixties, she had him waiting on her like she was some type of royalty. There was no way I could tolerate a female that didn't contribute to the household financially, emotionally and physically—and no female in my life would be willing to contribute while Forrest's wife lived there and did absolutely nothing.

Chapter 20

Bandidos Motorcycle Club Oklahoma

July 1999 To November 1999

In the middle of July I cashed in some of my Southwest Airlines rapid reward miles, and flew with Taylor to Michigan for a few days of relaxation. While I was there El Presidente George called and told me that he had to fire me from the national chapter. I had been appointed an El Secretario at the Red River Rally in New Mexico over the Memorial Day weekend, but hadn't sewed the new El Secretario bottom rocker on to my vest.

The decision didn't matter to me for I never had the need to show everyone I was a national officer. On the contrary I actually dreaded the attention the rocker would bring, both from regular members of the club as well as law enforcement. On the other hand it was nice to see that I was being recognized for everything I was doing. I had been executing secretarial duties for the national chapter off and on for the last year and the bottom rocker didn't change my job assignments.

George still wanted me to continue working for the national chapter—he just wanted me to do it while I wasn't in it. He told me that Big John from Galveston had cried the blues about me being a part of the national chapter, and to pacify him I had to transfer back to the Oklahoma chapter. Years later I learned George lied to me about what the Sargento-de-Armas said, and that

Big John hadn't said anything. At the time I was just another former national officer in a long list of former national officers, except my tenure had probably been the shortest.

I flew back to Tulsa and left my daughter under the care and supervision of my sister Kitty in Michigan. Although it felt good to temporarily not have the responsibility, on the negative side I missed her a lot. With some extra time on my hands I turned my attention to finding female companionship. Although I was surrounded by strippers and women with no self-esteem, and had numerous offers from club ol' ladies that wanted to set me up with their girlfriends, there wasn't a large selection pool of suitable candidates to consider. First and foremost I needed a positive role model for Taylor, but I was also determined to find an intelligent younger female that didn't have a history of substance abuse or mental health issues. I had heard of computer dating, which was a relatively new concept at the time, and decided to give it a try. I quickly located a dating website devoted to the biker lifestyle where I tested the waters over the next few months.

At the end of July I drove up to St. Louis, stopping on the way to check on my jobsite at Fort Leonard Wood. I caught a Southwest Airlines flight to Detroit, picked Taylor up at my sister's home, and then we flew back to St. Louis. It was Taylor's sixth birthday, and you can imagine her surprise when the stewardesses on the plane sang *Happy Birthday* to her over the intercom system, with most of the passengers joining in. After arriving in St Louis we drove to Branson, Missouri, where she and I planned to spend a few days celebrating her birthday. We both had a blast at Silver Dollar City, but the highlight of the trip was the outdoor slide and pool at the hotel we stayed in.

Two weeks after we got home Taylor got on the school bus for the first time and headed off to the first grade, and I was thinking about how fast time was flying. It was now much easier to take care of her and there were no more daycare expenses to sustain. I got lucky when I found a woman I liked on the dating website who was interested in me. Caroline Haynor was twenty-one years old, intelligent, good-looking, independent, and fresh out of United States Army after a three-year enlistment. She lived near Savannah, Georgia, where she was going to college and working at a car dealership—my only problem was the distance between us and the fact that she loved horses more than Harleys.

I invited Caroline to Oklahoma for the Pawhuska Rally in September, and then utilized one of my Southwest Airlines rapid reward tickets to get her plane fare for free. On the day she was supposed to fly out of Jacksonville, Florida, there was a hurricane. Trusting in decisions I made from a thousand miles away, Caroline raced southwards on I-95 while thousands of cars headed the opposite way to escape the dangerous storm. Everyone going north that day must have thought that she was crazy. Arriving at the Jacksonville airport with only minutes to spare, she caught the very last plane out before the airport was completely closed down. She had dodged a bullet, and we both took it as a sign from the Harley God that this was meant to be. After a slight error on her plane ticket was resolved in Baltimore she landed on time, the day before Pawhuska started.

We awoke at 5AM in the morning to the startling sound of Bandido JW Rock—who was shot to death by a Houston Bandido while he was sleeping in 2003—scratching on our window screen, hollering for me to get up and let him in. Caroline just about had a heart attack but soon calmed down when she found out who he was. After I opened the door for the Bandido from Austin and got him settled, I tried to explain to Caroline what it was like being a Bandido, but that's hard to understand when you've never lived this kind of life before. Over the next few days I knew that she was in for a crash course on being the girlfriend of a 1%er—in the club girlfriends and wives were referred to as a PBOL, which is an acronym for Proud Bandido Ol' Lady. I wasn't sure how she would react but knew one thing for sure—it was going to be interesting to see how she would when faced with the stark reality of outlaw motorcycle club life.

Pawhuska went well for us, as well as everyone else. For once the other Bandidos in the chapter and some OK Riders pitched in to supervise the operation of our magnificent camp on the hill that overlooked the main party site. The only snafu in the operation was when I went there to check on things Thursday afternoon, and found that Buddy hadn't arrived to secure the campsite as he had been ordered to. We should have seen it coming, for by now Buddy was immersed in the world of methamphetamine, and doing anything on time wasn't his way. I was extremely pissed off, but made some on the spot decisions and held down the fort until reinforcements arrived. I was looking forward to enjoying myself for the first time, because at every Pawhuska Rally I had attended since I'd become a Bandido I'd been in charge of the entire camp—food, security, drinks and all the other responsibilities that come with a campsite for one-hundred members of a major 1%er outlaw motorcycle club.

Upon my return from Pawhuska I was quite dismayed because I couldn't locate my daughter, who was on a court-ordered, unsupervised visit with my former wife. When I finally made contact with Teresa, I found out that Taylor was in the hospital because of her asthma, undergoing periodic breathing treatments. After my initial tendency to blame my former wife for Taylor's predicament subsided, I learned the situation likely wasn't something my former wife could have prevented, and realized that in the future I needed to be alert for anything that could cause an asthma attack. Visiting my daughter in the hospital that Sunday night I realized how much she meant to me, and I was thankful that Taylor had survived and was going to be okay.

A few days later she was released from the hospital and all was well again until a woman from the Oklahoma Department of Human Services (DHS) showed up at my door. Apparently DHS had received a complaint concerning my refusal to buy a one-thousand dollar breathing machine that an administrator at the hospital thought we needed, but there was absolutely no need for the apparatus and I refused to buy it. While Taylor was in the hospital I had done a lot of research on the situation and talked to Bandido Doc, who was a licensed pediatrician in Laredo, Texas. He told me that because she was only slightly asthmatic the breathing attack had more than likely been a fluke. My Bandido brother sent me a carton of inhalers which were worth their weight in gold, and promised to be there whenever I needed advice regarding my daughter's health.

After letting the DHS representative look all around the house and explaining my situation in detail, including the fact that we were both attending the Parent Child Center on a regular basis, she rightfully concluded that everything was in order. Thankfully the complaint was dismissed, for in Oklahoma DHS has the power to immediately remove a child from the home and place the child into foster care for an indefinite period of time.

Caroline had already returned to Georgia before I met the incident with DHS, and her trip home was uneventful. The hurricane hadn't done much damage along the I-95 corridor, and everything at her home was just like she left it. We remained in close contact throughout the rest of September and early October, talking on the phone frequently and exchanging emails daily. I liked her a lot, and was hoping that she felt the same and that things would work out between us.

On October 1st all members of the Bandidos and OK Riders met at OK Rider Cub's home just outside of Jones for a mandatory meeting, where we voted in the first new members in the history of our chapter. Former OK Rider Hank "CC" Leasure, David "Doc" Mullikin, and Robert "Ree" Thomas were now probationary members of the Bandidos Oklahoma chapter. We also took photos for our annual Christmas card which came out great. It was a time of joy for all of us, but if we had opened our eyes we would have seen the writing on the wall.

In the middle of October I convinced Caroline to leave Georgia and move in with me. The week before Halloween she made the long drive to Oklahoma by herself to bring her old beat-up Ford pickup truck, the horse trailer, and her horse to Owasso. She stayed in town for a day, then got in my new pickup and pulled an enclosed cargo trailer all the way back to Georgia—my Harley was strapped down inside and we had plans to ride it.

In addition to her intelligence and independence, I admired her tenacity, fortitude, moral compass and character, and thought the relationship was bound to work if this was any sign of how it would be in the future. Caroline had also never smoked a joint, experimented with drugs, or drank a drop of alcohol—she was definitely going to be a positive role model for Taylor.

Searching For My Identity: The Chronological Evolution
Of A Troubled Adolescent To Outlaw Biker

A day after she arrived back in Georgia I flew to Jacksonville, Florida, and met her at the airport. We drove north to Savannah, packed up all of her furniture, clothes and Harley Sportster, and took off fully-loaded southbound for Daytona, Florida. We wanted to spend a few days there in the sun and warm weather experiencing the annual Biketoberfest during Halloween before we returned to Oklahoma for our first winter together.

While in Daytona we hooked up with Lee, who had flown from Tulsa to Orlando, and then paid a visit to the local Outlaws clubhouse. We spent the afternoon there with Smitty and Fuzzy, both longtime members who I had known for twenty years. By the time two Bandidos from Alabama stopped by to have a few beers and relax a few hours later, the music was blasting and the clubhouse rockin'. The next morning we met up with another old friend who used to be a Rogue back in the late seventies, Dave Gruber, who I hadn't seen since he okey-doked me at Disney World. Our stay in Daytona was way too short, and by the end of the day we were already on the road making the long, slow drive back to Oklahoma.

As soon as we returned to Owasso and got Caroline settled, I took off for a week in late November and went to Europe again where I attended the patch over ceremony for the Ghostriders in Germany, who had now decided to become Bandidos. Because I had been sent by the European national president to visit the Ghostriders in 1998 I had a personal interest in this important event

241

in German biker history. The patch party was held in Dinslaken at the clubhouse, which had been a Ghostriders clubhouse the day before. The atmosphere was electric, and Bandidos from all over the world were there. I was shocked to see Big John had made there from Galveston, Texas, along with Bandido Knucklehead Dave.

The Sargento-de-Armas had me laughing my ass off when he told me about the gift he had brought for the new German Bandidos. As always, Big John was running late when it came time to take off for the airport in Houston, so at the last minute he grabbed a Bandidos plaque off the wall and threw it in his bag. By the time he got to Germany he realized that the plaque had been a Christmas gift from me, and to compound the mistake he realized I was going to be at the party.

The easiest thing for him to do was tell me the story and hope that it was going to be okay. It was so typical of Big John to do something like this, and what was I going to say anyway, that it wasn't okay? After all he wasn't known as Big John for nothing— as far as I was concerned he could have done whatever he wanted to, but I appreciated the respect he showed, and without hesitating I told him not to worry about it. From that day on it was an inside joke between the two of us.

When it came time for the actual ceremony, during which each chapter was handed an official plaque to mark the occasion, we all went into a huge room at the clubhouse. We were packed in like sardines—there were more than two-hundred Bandidos there.

Searching For My Identity: The Chronological Evolution
Of A Troubled Adolescent To Outlaw Biker

European Presidente Jim gave each chapter a plaque and a big welcome to the Bandido nation. I was proud to be there, and prouder of the fact that I had helped the Ghostriders become Bandidos. After the ceremony it was time to bring out the dancing girls, and some of my German brothers had reserved a seat for me right up front. At the time I thought the courtesy was an outstanding gesture on their behalf, but I should have known I was the object of a global practical joke conspiracy.

No sooner had the first beautiful stripper got on the stage and started to dance, she came directly to me and led me back up on the stage to a chair that she had strategically positioned to entertain my brothers. As you can imagine I was like a lamb being led to slaughter, and happier than a pig in shit in spite of the fact the joke was on me. With everyone cheering her on and hundreds of cameras taking extortion-quality pictures, the stripper performed an exquisite show using me as the center piece.

Months later I was informed that the celebration had been featured in a German magazine called *Biker News*, and in the article there was a photo of me. Like an idiot I asked El Secretario Armin to mail a copy the magazine to me, and he did. He must have laughed his ass off all the way to the post office, because the photo of me in the article was with the stripper. Armin also added an assortment of compromising photos of me and the stripper to the page where my photo was.

Searching For My Identity: The Chronological Evolution
Of A Troubled Adolescent To Outlaw Biker

Ordinarily this wouldn't have been an issue at all, but it just so happened that when the magazine arrived I was out of town for work, so Caroline asked me over the phone if she could open the package and look at the magazine. I had previously told her it was coming, never figuring that there was a photo in the magazine of the stripper and me, much less the additional photos that had been added. You can imagine the horror on my girlfriend's face when she opened the magazine and found all the pictures—life at home was a little uncomfortable for the next few days, but thankfully it didn't take her long to realize the practical joke was just Bandido entertainment.

I did get to spend a night and day at Armin's home while I was in the area, and then spent my last twenty-four hours in Germany with Dieter in Lengerich. It was good to see my brother and his family again, and get some much-needed rest before I took the long flight home. After Dieter dropped me off at the airport, twelve hours later I was back in the United States looking forward to going back to work and being with my family.

Chapter 21

The Beginning Of Bandidos Canada

April 1999 To January 2001

It was springtime in Washington State—I thought that it always rained there, but this was one of those rare and beautiful days of unexpected sunshine. It was April of 1999 and the day I first met my brother from Quebec. We were both in the Seattle area to attend the funeral for a Bandido who had died while having sex with his girlfriend, Mississippi Charlie.

The Canadian biker could have been anyone in the red and gold world, but the first thing I noticed was that his patch had red stitching around the edges. The center patch on his vest was an eagle, and the top rocker, bottom rocker, and center patch were silver on black. When I maneuvered closer to introduce myself I realized that I was looking at a full patch member of the Rock Machine motorcycle club—the first one I'd ever seen. The outlaw biker introduced himself in a heavy French accent and told me his name was Alain, but I later learned his full name was Alain Brunette.

We talked for a little while and then parted ways. I tried unsuccessfully to find him again after the burial—I wanted to spend more time with the biker from Canada but had no idea why I found myself intrigued. There was no way I could have known at that time what an important part of my life he would become.

The next Rock Machine member I ran into was in New Mexico during the Red River Rally in late May of 1999, and I was surprised to see that the colors of their patches had now changed—they were red and gold, no longer silver and black. I had recently heard a rumor that the Bandidos in Europe had designated them a hangaround club, and the Rock Machine had changed their patch colors to red and gold.

A hangaround club is an existing club that wants to join a larger motorcycle club. Being accepted as a hangaround club puts everyone in the biker world on notice—in motorcycle clubs as well as the rest of the biker world—the smaller club wants to be affiliated with or assimilated by the larger club. After a minimum of a year the Bandidos vote to ascertain whether all members of the smaller club are worthy to wear the patch. If the vote is affirmative then the bikers in the smaller club become probationary members in the Bandidos.

In mid-November 2000 I traveled to Europe for two reasons. First, to attend a world meeting that was going to be held in Denmark, and second, to attend the one-year anniversary party for the German Bandido chapters who were going to receive their Germany bottom rockers after being probationary members for a year.

Whenever I traveled to Denmark I typically flew into Frankfurt, Germany. The German customs and immigration authorities paid much less attention to motorcycle club members

246

than the officials at the Copenhagen airport. Dieter picked me up at the airport and I spent a night with him and his family before I met up with some German and United States Bandidos. To make the drive from Germany to Denmark we traveled by minivan.

Before we got out of Germany a car pulled alongside—the passenger started making all sorts of hand signals—then the vehicle pulled in front of us. An illuminated screen popped up at the bottom of the rear window which told us to follow them to the next exit. At the time I was informed it was an unmarked police car and that we were being pulled over, but no one had any idea why—we just assumed it was because we were Bandidos. Surprisingly the police interaction was only because the driver had been speeding through a construction zone on the autobahn interstate highway. Our driver got rewarded with a speeding ticket which included a hefty fine.

We eventually arrived at our destination in rural Denmark around 7PM, shortly after dark. Although I was still suffering from jet lag and didn't feel well, I was glad to see Bandidos there from all over the world—many had become good friends of mine. Sargento-de-Armas Helge, Sargento-de-Armas Johnny, and Clark were from Sweden. Presidente Jim, Vice-Presidente Michael "Mike" Rosenvold, El Secretario Gessner, and El Secretario Munk were from Denmark. Vice-Presidente Les and Sargento-de-Armas Diesel were from Germany. Presidente Jason Addison and El Secretario Larry were from Australia. El Presidente George, El

Searching For My Identity: The Chronological Evolution
Of A Troubled Adolescent To Outlaw Biker

Vice-Presidente Jeffrey "Jeff" Pike and me were from the United States. Because this was a world meeting that only national officers could attend I had been temporarily appointed El Secretario.

The gathering was held in the middle of nowhere inside a house that was surrounded by trees and armed Bandidos. Once we arrived we weren't allowed to leave or go outside by ourselves, which was for our own safety. Shortly after we arrived we were informed that there were three Rock Machine members who would soon be joining us—Martin "Blue" Blouin, Alain Brunette and Will. I was quite surprised to hear that Alain was in the area and soon found myself anticipating his arrival.

Because I wasn't feeling well and needed to get some sleep I crawled into a small sauna room to relax but wound up playing ace of spades with Johnny all night. This was a game the Swedish Bandido liked to play where Johnny would attempt to catch a brother sleeping and place an ace of spades on the Bandido without waking him up. I had told the Sargento-de-Armas I was a very light sleeper and bet him he couldn't do it—although he tried a few times that night he was ultimately unsuccessful.

The next day we had meetings off and on all morning and afternoon. We would convene for a while, then watch television, then meet again for a while, then eat and repeat. All of the cooking was done by the European Bandidos and supervised by Vice-Presidente Mike, who was also known as "Kok" or "Kokken" which means cook in Danish. Mike had gone to culinary school when he was young and actually was a very good chef. Over the next few days we discussed a myriad of items that were of importance worldwide, none of which were illegal. Everything that was discussed that day is reflected in the minutes I took:

WORLD MEETING NOTES IN DENMARK

November 15, 2000

Old Business:

1. USA to provide Europe & Australia with disc of correct patch design.

2. Call Tudy regarding German MC club about patch—advise German Bandidos

New Business:

1. Canada—someday soon is OK—currently there is peace—RM removed SYLB Patch and HA changed colors on support club as part of the peace—peace is very important to keep.

2. Relationship with Outlaws in Canada, USA, Australia & England—stabbing of Bandido by Outlaw probate in Guernsey. George will talk to Frank and set up meetings worldwide between us and the Outlaws.

3. Consider updating Fat Mexican—drawings to be submitted.

4. Check and see if probationary members in USA are wearing 5 yr. charter patch—if so, remove immediately.

5. Actual color of gold on patches to be determined by patch reps (USA, Europe & Australia) and standardized.

6. The shield is the official 5 yr. patch worldwide.

7. Patch reps (USA, Europe and Australia) to make decisions on officers' patches: President, Vice Pres, Sgt. At Arms, Sec-Treas, Secretary, Treasurer, Road Captain with no periods.

8. Europe—return history books to George via CT Ed.

9. Patch reps (USA, Europe, and Australia) to make decision on Life Member patch.

10. No more mandatory visits to other countries for Europe and Australia members.

11. Whispering Jim and Uncle Mad—giving away ENM patches in Europe.

12. Switzerland HA incident—Munich chapter—Sep'00—rest area.

13. Relationship with HA in USA, Europe, Germany, Scandinavia,& Australia.

14. Outlaws friendship with Black Ghostriders in Germany; Pagans friendship with Bats in Germany

15. Thailand—support club—Diablo MC

16. USA runs are: Birthday Run (1st week of March) & Memorial Day Run (last weekend in May) & Sturgis (1st full week of August) & Labor Day Run (1st weekend in September) & Thanksgiving (last Thursday in November).

17. Australia's triangle international patch is OK to be given to USA and Europe Brothers that have visited Australia—all gift patches given to Australia & Europe Brothers are not to be worn on vest without approval from their national officer.

18. If your death is the result of a suicide, you are not deserving
of a Bandido funeral.

19. If you borrow a bike, ol' lady, or any other Bandido-owned
property while visiting another area, chapter, or country, leave
the property in the same or better condition than what you
received it in when you leave.

During the afternoon dialogue the subject of the Rock
Machine becoming Bandidos was discussed many different times.
At that time the Rock Machine had been a hangaround club for
eighteen months. The European and Australian contingent was
adamant that the Rock Machine should become Bandidos
immediately, but George and Jeff's defiant position was that the
Canadian outlaw bikers should never become Bandidos. I had
already heard a rumor that George had made a deal with the United
States and Canadian Hells Angels that the Rock Machine would
never become Bandidos, and that the El Presidente supposedly had
agreed with their argument that the Bandidos should never patch
over an enemy of the Hells Angels. Whether that rumor was true
or not I didn't know, but the potential assimilation often resulted
in heated discussions.

A compromise was eventually reached after the United
States, European and Australian Bandidos settled their differences.
They agreed that when peace was firmly established between the
Rock Machine and the Hells Angels, then the Rock Machine could

become Bandidos. Early in the evening Alain, Blue and Will arrived. All of us got caught up on our personal situations, ate dinner, and then sat down at a big table to discuss the potential assimilation. The Canadians were told that they would continue to be a hangaround club, but if they could make peace last with the Hells Angels they would be allowed to become Bandidos. Everyone sitting at the table agreed to that, but I think George and Jeff agreed only because they thought peace would never last.

Shortly after the sit-down meeting at the table Alain and I had time to visit for a while. He was in fairly good health in spite of the stress that came from being a member of the Rock Machine. At that time more than one-hundred people had died, the result of the ongoing war between the two organizations. Alain had an awful cold and I must have caught it from him, because a few days later I got real sick and it took me more than two weeks to get rid of it. To this day I still tell him I owe him for that cold—or whatever it was I caught.

I finally escaped from the house that evening and caught a ride into Copenhagen to locate a brother in the club. Kent "Kemo" Sorensen and I had met on an earlier trip to Europe and had stayed in touch regularly since. I spent the night at his home, and the next day he showed me around Copenhagen. While driving around he pointed out a brand-new store run by the Denmark Hells Angels, in which they sold clothes and other items with Hells Angels support logos. It looked very upscale, and since I'd never seen anything like that before I convinced the Danish Bandido to let me go inside. We agreed that Kemo would go downstairs and visit a friend who had a tattoo shop there in order to give me some time to browse the shop.

When I walked in I was quite surprised, although I don't think I showed it. The shop was beautiful, clean and light, and reminded me of an Eddie Bauer clothing store except all of the merchandise for sale was related to the Hells Angels. There were a half-dozen Hells Angels present so I immediately introduced myself as an American Bandido. The Hells Angels first looked at me in shock, then called upstairs to the Angel in charge—his name was Bent "Blondie" Nielsen.

I had heard his name many times, for Blondie was a well-known leader of the Hells Angels in Denmark. He came downstairs, we introduced ourselves, and then chatted for ten minutes about basic world motorcycle club politics and the concept of the store. I told him that I'd never seen anything like it before and complimented him on the quality of the merchandise and decor. After Kemo returned from the tattoo shop downstairs we departed, leaving the Hells Angels with a better understanding of what American Bandidos were all about.

Less than a year later Sargento-de-Armas Kemo was charged with murder for orchestrating the killing of former Bandido president and national officer Claus "Karate Claus" Hansen, who was shot twenty-six times with three handguns and two shotguns in Copenhagen on March 21st of 2001. During Kemo's trial in the spring of 2002 it was disclosed that there had been a meeting between the Hells Angels and Bandidos a few days before the murder, during which the Angels sanctioned the assassination.

The two organizations feared a new biker war because Hansen had been pitting the clubs against each other in revenge for his expulsion from the Bandidos. Jens Christian Thorup was convicted of the murder and sentenced to sixteen years in prison, but Kemo and two other full patch Bandidos were acquitted.

Unknown to most of the United States Bandidos at the time of the world meeting the Rock Machine and Hells Angels had already met in person to discuss peace on September 26th. Quebec City Rock Machine president Frederick "Fred" Faucher and Hells Angels nomad chapter president Maurice (Mom) Boucher had got together in a room at the Quebec City courthouse to discuss a preliminary plan for peace between the two mortal enemies.

Two weeks later with Canadian television and newspaper reporters present, Fred and Mom stood together as they announced the Quebec Biker War was over. I didn't know about the truce so I was quite surprised to learn that less than a week after the world meeting, the European and Australian Bandidos convinced George it was time to patch over the Rock Machine.

On November 22nd George met with the Hells Angels at Peach Arch Park not far from Vancouver and Bellingham. At the meeting the El Presidente confirmed the rumor that the Hells Angels had heard—the Rock Machine would soon become Bandidos. On December 1st the Rock Machine motorcycle club became history and Bandidos Canada was born. A huge party to celebrate the occasion was planned for January 8th in 2001 at the clubhouse in Kingston, Ontario, at which time the Rock Machine would officially patch over to Bandidos.

In December I was notified of the exact date for the patch party and made plans to go to Canada. At that time I contemplated many different scenarios to cross the border. I had been allowed into Canada in recent years, but had also been denied access at times due to my criminal record and affiliation with the club. I truly had no idea if I would be allowed into Canada this time or not, but it was very important for me to be there for I had been designated the task of organizing the new national chapter in Canada—in essence I was assigned to teach them how to be organized and function as a club. I was instructed to open lines of communication, compile and verify phone and email addresses, and establish membership rosters.

Most of the United States Bandidos who had decided to attend the patch party had opted to fly into Toronto's Pearson International Airport. I thought that under those circumstances, with all the publicity, it would be much harder to gain entry through the airport. Immigration Canada was well-known for turning members of motorcycle clubs around at the airport even if they weren't convicted felons. El Presidente George had been deported a few years ago from Canada for being a convicted felon. Since I was a convicted felon, in spite of the fact that it had been almost twenty years since my last conviction, I had little doubt I'd be turned around if I tried to enter the country at Pearson Airport.

Eventually I decided to attempt entry through the Windsor checkpoint just outside Detroit. Someone from Immigration Canada later suggested that I came in through Niagara Falls but that was erroneous and I never bothered to correct them—if you check my immigration case records you will see a multitude of notes regarding my entry at Ft. Erie near Niagara Falls.

I figured that if I wasn't welcome in Canada the officials at the border would simply turn me around when I presented my passport. I also calculated that no one from the club would be expected to come in through Windsor, and therefore my chances of doing so would be much better.

On January 4th of 2001 late in the afternoon on a dreary, cloudy day, I successfully crossed the border into Canada disguised as a construction worker, riding in the back seat of a car with my sister Kitty and one of her friends. I later told the immigration officials that I rode in a van full of construction workers in an effort to protect her.

The Canadian Immigration Officer at the gate didn't ask any of us for identification. I had my passport in hand ready to go, but all he did was talk to my sister for about two seconds and wave us through. I noticed at the time that most of the vehicles alongside of us were going through the entry point as fast as we were, but was informed this was normal procedure at this time of day. This was before the events of 9/11—things are much different today. I traveled with Kitty and her friend to downtown Windsor where they dropped me off at a casino, then found a pay phone and called the Outlaws clubhouse in London, and a member of the chapter was sent to pick me up.

His name was Finn, and he was a full patch member in the Windsor chapter of the Outlaws. He drove me to London the evening of January 4th, and on the trip the Outlaw told me he had joint citizenship in the United States and Canada. As we drove through a light snow storm Finn offered to get any member of the Bandidos across the border at any time for free, which was so disturbing that it made the hair stand up on the back of my neck.

We arrived at the Outlaws clubhouse around 8PM that evening, and then I spent a few hours with Thomas "Holmes" Hughes who was the president of the chapter. After enjoying the hospitality I called the Bandidos clubhouse in Toronto—Bandido Gee from Montreal and Bandido Generator from Toronto were dispatched to pick me up. It was a cold, snowy night, and because of the weather we were forced to spend the night at a London hotel. We got up early on Friday morning January 5th and navigated our way through the snow into Toronto by late morning.

Searching For My Identity: The Chronological Evolution Of A Troubled Adolescent To Outlaw Biker

Just before noon the two Canadians and I arrived at the Toronto clubhouse. After visiting with everyone there for a few hours I asked Gee and Generator to drop me off at the train station. I took a train to Kingston by myself where I had arranged for some Bandidos to meet me when I arrived. From the train station I was taken to the Travelodge Inn hotel, and was assigned to share a room with Bandido Clark from Sweden, who had a personal interest in Bandidos Canada since he had dual citizenship in Sweden and Canada. After visiting Clark and some of the other Bandidos in the hotel, I turned in early to get a good night's sleep. I knew that Saturday would be a major milestone in biker history and I didn't want to miss a minute.

The next morning I started off the day by catching up on all of the newspaper articles from around the world. I always tried to have my laptop with me to monitor the media and keep in touch with friends, family and brothers in the club. One of the first newspaper articles I came across from Canada contained a revelation that shocked me—the story explained how the police had caught a few Bandidos at Pearson Airport in Toronto trying to get into the country for the patch party. It also mentioned that a few Bandidos had actually crossed the border successfully, including an American Bandido from Oklahoma. I was obviously quite concerned for it meant there was a giant leak and the information had been divulged by someone I'd seen in the last two days. I should have realized at the time that this was an indication

258

of worse things to come but I didn't—that oversight turned out to be a colossal blunder.

Saturday was an uneventful day spent hanging out around the hotel visiting new Canadian Bandidos that I didn't know, as well as some I did know. I was meeting so many new faces that I was having trouble remembering most of their names. After consulting numerous brothers I decided not to go to the clubhouse for the actual party due to the police presence, constant media coverage, and publicity. We heard that there were about seventy-five law enforcement officers posted around the clubhouse, and eight American Bandidos had already been detained for possible deportation.

The only thing that saved the American brothers from deportation was that Immigration Canada officials had legally allowed them into the country, and had stamped their passports as proof. Since my passport didn't have a stamp I thought it would in my best interest to skip the party and have a quiet dinner with a new Montreal brother who called himself Tout, which meant beep in the English language.

Robert "Tout" Leger and I had met earlier in the day, and discovered we had much in common. He had a dynamic personality, and like me enjoyed working on Harleys. Tout had what they call in Canada stipulations—in America it's called non-association—so he wasn't able to associate with any member of the Rock Machine due to an ongoing criminal case after being caught with a firearm. In spite of the fact that most Rock Machine were now members of Bandidos Tout felt that there was no need to push the issue, so he was also avoiding the patch party.

After our dinner in the hotel restaurant Tout invited me to visit his home near Montreal to hang out for a few days, and then return to the United States via train through northern Vermont. We planned to leave by 8PM in order to drive to his home and get to bed at a reasonable hour. I left the table and went back upstairs to pack and check my email, which turned out to be a fateful decision for I was arrested in my hotel room for being in the country illegally.

Although I never made it there, the patch party was a huge success for more than sixty new Canadian probationary Bandidos. Everyone had a great time that night except me, as you can see from the newspaper article that appeared in the Kingston Whig-Standard:

Bikers Party In Kingston

By Sarah Crosbie

January 7, 2001

Eight American members of the motorcycle gang, the Bandidos, partied in Kingston Saturday night, after Canadian Immigration officials failed to show up more than two hours after Kingston Police initially detained the men.

Searching For My Identity: The Chronological Evolution
Of A Troubled Adolescent To Outlaw Biker

*One man from Oklahoma was arrested later that night by
Canadian Immigration officials for illegally being in the country,
Kingston police media spokesman Mike Weaver said.*

*Kingston Police Staff Sgt. Brian Cookman said Canadian
Immigration questions bikers to determine if they are members of
a criminal-affiliated group, or if they have a criminal record.*

*The first bikers started showing up at the Burnett Street location
at about 2 p.m. in vans and taxis.*

*The men who were detained by police arrived shortly after 4 p.m.
They were released at 5:40 p.m. to cheers and shouts of "woo-
hoo."*

*Cookman said the police can detain the men to check their
identification and photograph them, but beyond that, it isn't
within their jurisdiction to hold them.*

"This is a federal issue, not a municipal issue," he said.

*Cookman said he was surprised it took Immigration officials
from Lansdowne more than two hours to get to the Kingston site.*

*By 10 p.m. on Saturday, 53 men had arrived at 770 Burnett St.,
for the party called a patchover party, where the motorcycle
group the Rock Machine merged with the Bandidos.*

*The Rock Machine was granted probationary status in the Texas-
based Bandidos last year.*

*"The local eastern chapter are patching over to the southwestern
Bandido chapter in the U.S.," said Neil Finn, a Kingston police*

officer who is a member of a special provincial squad formed to combat biker gangs.

Finn said until the party, Kingston's Rock Machine had seven associates; four members and three probationary members.

He said the merging doesn't mean Kingston will see an increase in bikers.

"What's going on today doesn't mean we're going to have more members," he said.

Throughout the police check system, Bandido members showed their identification and their vests which are decorated with a cartoon Mexican man holding a gun in one hand and a sword in the other.

Some Bandidos were also wearing bulletproof vests.

The men who were not detained drove or walked to 770 Burnett St. When they reached the property, a man inside would unlock the door, walk outside and greet them and then lock the door behind them.

Throughout the day, men would come out and take photographs of the area, including police and the media, but the members themselves didn't want their pictures taken. One man covered his face with a bandanna; another pulled his vest up over his head as they walked to the building.

Although police were braced for possible problems with a heavy presence that included officers from Kingston Emergency Services, a tactical team, the provincial special squad, a joint municipal RCMP-OPP group, as well as Quebec police.

Cookman said there were no problems on Saturday at the largest biker gathering Kingston has seen.

"This is the pinnacle of importance. No one's ever seen this, in this magnitude in a long time," he said.

A detective from the Albuquerque (N.M.) Police Department in the U.S. came to Kingston because of the number of bikers coming to the area.

Gary Georgia, who has studied the Bandidos for 10 years, said that while he can't say what effect the Bandidos will have on Kingston, the new relationship shouldn't go unnoticed.

"Anytime you have a criminal organization coming into your town, it does lead me to be concerned," he said.

"The Bandidos have been known to use intimidation and violence," he said, noting that they are involved in selling narcotics, motorcycle thefts and prostitution.

Georgia said it's significant that the Bandidos decided to meet in Kingston.

"It gives the Bandidos a foothold they haven't had in the past," he said.

"I've tracked them all over the world and now we have them in Canada and in Kingston."

Georgia said on Friday night, before he came to Kingston, he was called to Pearson International Airport to confirm the identities of two Bandidos members who were en route to

Kingston.

They were both sent back to the United States by Immigration on

Friday, he said.

Immigration officials could not be reached for comment

yesterday.

Chapter 22

Bandidos Motorcycle Club Oklahoma
February 2000 To June 2000

On the 5th of February while I was in Denver attending the annual motorcycle parts swap meet with thousands of other bikers I received a phone call. OK Riders Edwin "Sixpack" Collins and James "Cub" Olsen had been arrested for manufacturing a controlled dangerous substance and trafficking in illegal drugs, and were in jail waiting for someone to post their fifty-thousand dollar bonds. They had been caught with a significant quantity of methamphetamine, and to complicate matters their wives had also been arrested and had fifty-thousand dollar bonds. Since I was in charge of legal matters it was my responsibility to handle the situation.

I gave OK Rider president Ray the name of a bail bond agent I knew who had previously agreed to charge anyone involved with the club a ten percent bond fee—the other bond companies required fifteen percent—and would post the bond immediately without requiring money down and allow them to make weekly payments. I advised Ray to let all four of them sit in jail for three more days at which time they would be entitled to apply for a bond reduction—I anticipated the bond amount for each person would then be reduced to ten-thousand dollars during the hearing.

Although the bond reduction would obviously make a major difference in the amount of money they would owe, before I got back Cub decided he and his wife had to get out of jail immediately and would rather pay fifteen percent to a different bondsman than wait three days and pay ten percent to ours. From a financial perspective alone the decision was incredibly stupid, but in the grand scheme of things we should have seen the writing on the wall.

Ray secured the services of a bond company we didn't have any experience with, so by the time I returned Cub and his wife were out of jail and owed fifteen-thousand dollars instead of the two-thousand dollars they would have owed if they'd followed my advice. The OK Rider president had also been coerced into cosigning for the bond fee, so if Cub and his wife failed to make the fifteen-thousand dollar payment Ray would be held responsible. Lee and I were amazed at the idiocy that had transpired in our absence and pissed off that Sixpack and Cub had been arrested on meth charges.

Sixpack and his wife waited another week in jail before their bonds were reduced to ten-thousand dollars each, but instead of bonding out Sixpack remained in jail. Not willing to postpone the inevitable he took the blame for the entire situation and was sentenced to twelve years in the care and custody of the Oklahoma Department of Corrections. His wife posted the bond, paid the one-thousand dollar fee, and all charges against her were eventually dismissed. Cub and his wife ultimately plead guilty and each received a two-year deferred prison sentence.

Lee and I were beginning to wonder what was going on for this was the second time in less than sixty days Sixpack had been busted. In early December of 1999 he had been arrested with another OK Rider, Craig "Shifter" Sherman, in Lincoln County, Oklahoma. Although we had been told that the charges involved knives and guns, we were now wondering if that was true. We had also heard rumors that some OK Riders and Bandidos had been manufacturing meth, and we decided it was time for us to look into it and hopefully put the rumors to rest.

When we eventually learned the truth Lee and I were shocked, for Sixpack and Shifter had been arrested for possession of a precursor substance and possession of a controlled drug with the intent to distribute. They had both lied to all of us about the arrest, and lying was a patch pulling offense. As soon as we had verifiable proof of what had transpired, which took a few months, both were expelled from the OK Riders for drug dealing and lying.

Sixpack again shouldered the responsibility for everything that happened in the Lincoln County case. After pleading guilty to the charges he was sentenced to an additional five years in prison—he now had a total of seventeen years to serve for his Tulsa County and Lincoln County offenses. Shifter eventually plead guilty and received a six-year state prison sentence.

By now we were also hearing rumors that Buddy was manufacturing meth at his home outside Sapulpa, and then selling the finished product to the Outlaws chapter in Oklahoma City. We also learned that Buddy was the driving force behind the arrests of Sixpack, Shifter and Cub—all three had been involved in various aspects of his methamphetamine operation. Doing illegal business with members of another 1%er outlaw motorcycle club was totally against Bandidos national policy and an automatic patch pulling offense.

We had also ascertained that Shifter had bought the red phosphorus, a major ingredient required for the manufacture of meth, from an informant who was part of a law enforcement sting. In addition, Bandido Bill Wolf had been busted in Broken Arrow for possession of meth just after Thanksgiving of 1999. It looked like we had a major meth epidemic on our hands and we had no idea how to nip it in the bud. Like the proverbial children's story of an ostrich that hid his head in the sand Lee and I looked the other way in the spring of 2000 and hoped the situation would resolve itself and make our problems magically disappear.

In spite of all the negativity surrounding some, life was pretty good for the rest of the red and gold world in Oklahoma. Lee sold his Harley and bought himself a brand-new Night Train. I was thankful that I had relinquished my legal liaison position in the Oklahoma Confederation of Clubs in January, but still had too much on my plate.

268

Searching For My Identity: The Chronological Evolution
Of A Troubled Adolescent To Outlaw Biker

In February I started helping a Bandido who had been incarcerated for more than twenty-five years in Louisiana, by selling some of the items he was making. Jimmie "74 Jim" Graves had been in prison so long that when he surfaced it took the club more than a week to find a Bandido who remembered him and the circumstances surrounding his incarceration. I was told the nomad chapter was supposed to have been taking care of him, but 74 Jim wasn't happy with the quality of care he had received. After making initial contact via letters and phone calls I immediately set out marketing his wares worldwide.

74 Jim manufactured beautiful Bandido wooden puzzle plaques, belt buckles, wooden clocks, and other fine-crafted goods from a small prison hobby shop at the Louisiana State Prison in Angola. With a regular crew of inmates assisting him in the manufacturing process, before long he had a pretty good assembly line going. I took orders for his products by sending out emails that included pictures of the particular product we were trying to sell. Over the next sixteen months I sold more than ten-thousand dollars of goods, which was more money than 74 Jim had ever seen in his life. In the process I pissed off more than a few members of the Bandidos nomad chapter.

After repeatedly bitching to the El Presidente and anyone else that would listen, the nomad chapter finally got their way. In spite of all of my protests, as well as the protests of 74 Jim, the responsibility for marketing his products was returned to the nomad chapter. It didn't take long for them to screw everything up, and 74 Jim's life went back to the way it was before I came along.

Probationary Bandido Ree suffered a major heart attack in late February, and by the end of the month we decided that it was in his best interest to let him leave the club in good standings based on his health problems. Shortly thereafter we accepted the transfer of a Texas Bandido from North Houston—Steven "Steve" Buitron had chased his girlfriend to Lawton. Steve was a welcome addition, for we now had brothers living in Tulsa, Oklahoma City and Lawton, but if we had opened our eyes we would have seen Steve for the lying, two-faced coward he really was.

In the middle of March I flew to Mexico, traveling first to Dallas on Southwest Airlines and then catching an American Airlines flight to my final destination in Mexico City. El Presidente George had asked me to attend a Bandidos world meeting with him, and as an added incentive I had been invited to attend the wedding of Martin "Martine" Gonzalez.

Martine was a new Bandido from Washington who had grown up in the Mexico City area, and his family still resided there. He owned and operated a martial arts school in Bellingham, and because of his extraordinary skill in martial arts and proximity to George's home Martine had already been appointed a Sargento-de-Armas in the national chapter.

As soon as I got off the plane I was met at the airport by a member of the Legionaires motorcycle club and Sargento-de-

Armas John "Big John" Lammons, who delivered me to the downtown hotel where we had all agreed to meet. El Presidente George, Presidente Jim and Vice-Presidente Mike from Europe, Presidente Jason and El Secretario Bullets from Australia, and Martine and Jimmie "Jimbo" Garman from Washington had already arrived. We talked a lot about world affairs over the next few days and met officially in one of the hotel rooms to make decisions. As you can see from the notes that I took, our agenda was quite legal:

WORLD MEETING NOTES FROM MEXICO

March 17, 2000

1. New Website Idea:

a. Check on availability of www.freeharley.com or an equal

b. Draft a business plan and distribute to all continents

c. Get contracts between all parties

d. Incorporate in the United States

e. Look for website designer

f. Australia interested – Europe considering – USA interested

2. 5 year patch—anyone can submit a design which will be voted on at a future world meeting.

3. World meetings are for National officers only.

4. Support Gear:

a. No "Bandidos" or "Bandits"

b. Applies to anything you can wear

c. All designs to be approved by national Presidente in each continent.

d. Remove all unapproved support items from the website.

5. Dizzie—webmaster worldwide.

6. All center patches will be identical—one design on a disc to be supplied by USA to Australia & Europe—all El Secretarios responsible for patches will get together as soon as possible via email or phone.

7. All national Vice Presidente rockers will be changed to "Visa Presidente".

8. ENM patch—see appropriate NSA for approval.

9. TCB patch—ok in Europe—not used in, or to be given to USA & Australia.

10. Probationary rockers will be worn in the USA—for all new probationary members.

11. New front patch for hang around clubs in Europe only.

12. USA will check on support patch being worn by USA/Europe club.

13. Asia & Mexico need to be developed.

14. Australia wants visitors from USA & Europe for national run in October.

15. Australia will send USA club by-laws & bike signing agreement.

16. Australia will send 5 Life Member patches to USA & Europe.

17. Addition to Europe's by-laws only—all motorcycles will be rebuilt in winter months only—in season 30 days downtime rule will apply.

18. Australia & Europe will use the same support items.

On the night before Martine got married some of the Legionaires took us out to a local strip joint for an informal, last minute bachelor party. I vividly recall seeing hundreds of orphaned, disparate children begging or selling trivial items on the sidewalks after leaving the bar and being thankful that my daughter didn't have to do that just to survive. Late the next afternoon we set out for a ride across town to see Martine and his wife Whitney get married at a quaint Mexican church with more than fifty of his family and childhood friends, and were surprised to learn the ceremony and reception were going to be implemented in the tradition of a real Mexican Bandido wedding from the nineteenth century.

At the reception dinner all of the Bandidos sat at one table where we were served our drinks and food before anyone else, which was the way real Bandidos had been treated many centuries before. We were told that the original Bandidos were the guardians and the protectors of the town, and in honor of them, as well as to show respect, the old-time Bandidos were always served first.

As soon as I returned to Tulsa from my Mexican siesta Taylor took her first bicycle ride without the training wheels that she had been using for the last two years. For her this was a monumental event—as for me I couldn't have been prouder. With my two projects in Sierra Vista and Rolla now closed out, it was time to move on to the next construction project in McKinney, Texas, completing the Collin County Courthouse in early April. This was a daunting task because the job was way behind schedule and the two-hundred men working there were primarily Hispanic. Ordinarily this wouldn't be a problem, but the foremen for multiple crews were unable to communicate with the employees. This presented an unusual problem—everywhere you looked there were dozens of Hispanic workers standing around doing nothing, in spite of the fact there was a lot to do.

My first day on the job I realized that I needed some help, so I got on the phone and called in two of my Bandido brothers from New Mexico. Bandido Jessie "Chuy" Wicketts and Bandido Keiko were both Hispanic, construction experts, and bilingual. I made airline reservations for them that afternoon, and by noon the next day both Bandidos were in Texas on the jobsite working. By the end of the day we confirmed that the white foremen had no love for the Hispanic workers and we definitely had a major communication problem. The next morning I made the decision that all jobsite orders to the Hispanic workforce would now come from either Chuy or Keiko, bypassing the respective foremen for each crew.

Within two weeks we had gained everyone's respect, and turned the job back around to where it was functioning as normal. One day while putting the finishing touches on the jail holding cells we found some Collin County Sheriff's deputies learning how to operate the jail. Being Bandidos that liked to have fun we decided to play a joke on the deputy in charge. In the process of constructing the actual jail cells, which locked electronically, Chuy had discovered a glitch in the locking mechanism. This bug allowed him to open the lock with a small piece of metal from inside the holding cell while he was locked inside.

After the training officer had locked Chuy in the cell I turned the officer around to face me with his back to the bars. Within thirty seconds the New Mexico Bandido was tapping the training officer on the shoulder, and you can imagine the surprise on the deputy's face when he discovered his million-dollar jail wasn't secure. We never told him how we did it, and for the rest of the time we were there no one ever figured it out. We knew one thing for sure—if Bandido Chuy ever got arrested there was no way they were going to keep him inside one of those cells!

Before I knew it May rolled around and it was Pawhuska Rally time again. El Presidente George and El Secretario William "Bill" Sartelle would be attending with both of their wives, and this year the Pawhuska Rally and Red River Rally were back to back with only five days between them—normally they were two weeks apart.

275

Searching For My Identity: The Chronological Evolution
Of A Troubled Adolescent To Outlaw Biker

Once again the Sons of Silence and the Outlaws were planning on attending, but the Outlaws were having a regional meeting the following weekend in Oklahoma City so Outlaws were coming from as far away as Ohio. The Oklahoma Bandidos relationship with the Outlaws chapter in Oklahoma City, who would be camped right next to us, was strained to its breaking point. The majority of the Oklahoma City Outlaws were heavily involved in the manufacture and distribution of methamphetamine, and they were sampling their product on a daily basis. Trying to reason with a meth addict was like trying to talk to a drunk, and we had no idea what was going to transpire.

In the end everything went as well as could be expected. There were no fistfights and no arguments, probably due to the fact that George was there, although one Oklahoma Outlaw was so obnoxious and arrogant we should have done something about it. Michael J. Roberts was a complete asshole that no one liked, but it took the Outlaws two more years to figure that out.

An interesting aspect regarding the tension with the Outlaws in Oklahoma was that we got along great with Outlaws in every other state. Some of those Outlaws like Patrick "Pudd" Puttrick from Dayton, were old friends of mine from twenty years ago. Others like John "Leadhead" Blackman and Ronald "RT" Taylor from Indianapolis, Indiana, I had met the year before at an Outlaws party in Luther, Oklahoma, and personally liked so much that we all kept in touch on a regular basis.

Searching For My Identity: The Chronological Evolution
Of A Troubled Adolescent To Outlaw Biker

The week after Pawhuska ended we all headed west for Red River where the Bandidos were holding their annual Memorial Day national run. Every Bandido in the United States was required to be there, or they were in trouble and had to pay a five-hundred dollar fine.

Caroline and I drove to New Mexico in a car I rented with more than a hundred shirts we planned to sell, which had the Red River Rally insignia on the sleeve. We had manufactured the shirts with that specific design because we knew the primary reason shirts are bought at biker events, was because the shirt proved someone had been there.

No one else in the chapter felt the same as I did about the importance of raising money for the treasury, so Caroline and I spent the entire weekend on the patio of the *Bull of the Woods* bar selling the shirts. The Oklahoma chapter stayed at two three-story condominiums I rented a few blocks from Main Street. Although expensive, the lodging made for a luxurious vacation and provided a great place to entertain guests.

A few days after I got back to Tulsa we got an emergency call from the Outlaws in Oklahoma City. Mance "Tool" Stephens and RT had been involved in a serious auto accident on I-44 just west of Tulsa. Their pickup truck had been hit hard by another truck that had spun out of control in a thunderstorm, causing Tool's skull to penetrate the windshield—he was hurt bad and headed to the hospital in an ambulance. Although RT wasn't injured, he was seriously shaken up. The Outlaws were busy recovering from their Memorial Day weekend party and asked us to look after RT and Tool.

When Lee and I arrived at the hospital we learned the Outlaw's face had been severely cut from one ear across his forehead to the opposite eyebrow. The female doctor who was going to do the stitching was terrified Tool wasn't going to cooperate while she was repairing the damage, so Lee put on surgical gloves and helped get him ready, then stayed during the surgery to keep the Outlaw calm. While he was being sewed up I took RT to my home for a much-needed shower and something to eat, then returned to the hospital to pick up Tool, who was by now being released. The hospital refused to keep him over night because he had no insurance, and the doctor felt that we were competent enough to provide him with the care he needed.

After we got Tool back to my house we joined forces to give him a bath. His head was a mess, he looked like Frankenstein with stitches across his forehead, and he stunk from not having had a shower for days. To complicate the situation a lot of the blood he had lost hours earlier was now coagulated in his hair and ears, turning his head an eerie shade of black. RT and I did the best we could and eventually got Tool cleaned up, although there was still some dried blood in his hair we couldn't remove. After the bath I was surprised to see the water had turned completely black.

Searching For My Identity: The Chronological Evolution
Of A Troubled Adolescent To Outlaw Biker

After we put Tool to sleep for the night we realized that he was lucky to be alive—as a matter of fact it was almost a miracle he had survived. RT had called Indianapolis and made flight arrangements for their wives, and by 10AM the next morning both of them were in Tulsa. By early afternoon Tool's wife had bathed him again and he was totally cleaned up. By mid-afternoon the Indiana Outlaw was sitting upright in a chair in my living room, and eating a little. Two more days and Tool was well enough to travel back to Indianapolis, where he spent months recovering.

In the middle of June my brothers in Washington and Montana were involved in a violent altercation near Yakima with another motorcycle club which resulted in the death of a Bandido, Frederick "Bulldog" Entzel of Missoula, Montana. When I heard the news I volunteered to represent the Oklahoma chapter at the funeral, for I had known him personally.

The following Friday I flew into Spokane, Washington, and rented a car for the three-hour drive to Missoula where I attended the funeral and after-party for Bulldog. I had just spent a bunch of time with him less than a month ago at Red River standing on the patio of the *Bull of the Woods* bar. He was only forty-eight years old, and it was hard to imagine that he was now dead. I felt really bad for his girlfriend, Angel, as I watched her weeping at the burial site. My only solace was knowing that Bulldog was being buried in the same cemetery as two other

Bandidos who had died many years ago. The next day the local

newspaper did a fine job of reporting on the funeral:

Scores Gather In Memory Of Motorcycle Gang Member

June 25, 2000

By Betsy Cohen and Michael Moore

The mourners wore black leather and yellow and red gang

colors.

They came by the tenfold, many on Harleys, to Garden City

Funeral Home on Saturday to pay tribute to their fallen brother

Bandido, Frederick "Bulldog" Entzel.

Entzel, a Missoula man, was shot to death in a motorcycle gang-

related incident last week in Washington.

While Entzel's family members and Bandido leaders attended the

hour long funeral service, at least 50 other members stood guard

at the door and parking lot.

Across the street, a small contingent of police watched the

funeral gathering using binoculars, telephoto lenses and video

cameras. Watching back, the gang members used their own

supply of surveillance equipment.

After the services, a procession of about 85 motorcyclists and

several dozen vehicles followed the hearse carrying Entzel's

casket to Riverview Cemetery in Stevensville, where he was

buried.

Missoula police kept a close eye on the funeral proceedings, but

not because they expected any problems.

Searching For My Identity: The Chronological Evolution
Of A Troubled Adolescent To Outlaw Biker

*"We're basically interested in seeing who shows up," said Sgt.
Mike Brady.*

*The group approached the police earlier in the week to notify the
department of their route out of Missoula, but didn't ask for a
police escort.*

*The Bandidos, one of the largest motorcycle gangs in the country,
have been relatively quiet in Missoula during the past five years
but, Brady said, police have seen more action in the past six
months.*

*"We haven't had any criminal activity," Brady said. "We've just
seen more of them around on their bikes, wearing the colors.
They're just a little more of a presence."*

*The Bandidos have been out of the Missoula news since 1994,
when club member Joe Cancellare was arrested and sent to
prison for his role in two assaults involving shotguns. Cancellare
reportedly is living in Las Vegas now.*

*Brady said police were aware of Entzel, who ran Attitude Leather
Works on Brooks Street. They had not, however, had any reason
to be in touch with him.*

*The 48-year-old Entzel, a sergeant-at-arms for the Bandidos, was
attending a motorcycle rally in Zillah, Wash., near Yakima when
he was killed. The Bandidos got involved in a dispute with
another club, the Iron Horsemen, last Friday, but walked away
from the trouble.*

Yakima County sheriff's Lt. Dan Garcia said the two gangs set a meeting for the next morning at a park, but the meeting degenerated into a blood bath. By the time authorities arrived, Entzel was close to death, another Bandido had been shot and an Iron Horseman lay bleeding in a van.

The gangs have been less than cooperative as the investigation proceeds, and no one has been charged with Entzel's killing.

Dale Chandler, a Bandido, has been charged with first-degree assault on the wounded Horseman, Darren Patrick Lumsden, who remains hospitalized.

The shooting has heightened concerns Missoula police have about another biker gathering scheduled for late July. As many as 400 members of Hells Angels, the country's largest and most notorious biker gang, are scheduled to roll into Missoula on July 27 for a four-day vacation.

The Angels and Bandidos have been in contact about the visit, and Missoula police Chief Pete Lawrenson has said the gangs have agreed to peacefully co-exist while the Angels are in Missoula. That agreement, however, was reached before the Entzel shooting. The Iron Horsemen aren't directly affiliated with the Angels, but are friendly, Brady said.

"We don't really expect anything to happen because of this, but it's something that concerns us," Brady said. "It concerns us that a member of a local group has been killed. We don't really know what to expect."

Around the same time Bulldog was killed, Bandido Buddy was arrested in Creek County and charged with unlawful possession of a controlled drug with intent to distribute and unlawful possession of a precursor substance, which obviously was the result of Buddy being involved with the manufacture of methamphetamine. Buddy knew that if we found out the true nature of his charges then we would have the proof we needed to kick him out of the club, so Buddy lied about what he had been arrested for. Over the next few months I accumulated the necessary documents to prove that the Tulsa Bandido had been caught with the ingredients for a meth lab at his house, and that he had lied about it. Eventually the lies would catch up to him, it was just a matter of time.

Chapter 23

Bandidos Motorcycle Club Oklahoma

July 2000 To December 2000

On the 4th of July we had an Oklahoma chapter members-only meeting at my home in Owasso. Bill Wolf had finally admitted he had a drug problem and was now scheduled to turn himself in to the Oklahoma Department of Corrections to start serving a five-year prison sentence for simple possession of meth in two days. We all knew that this would be the last time we would be together as a chapter for quite a while. Although it was a somber occasion because of Bill Wolf, the tension in the chapter was almost unbearable due to Buddy's situation.

By the middle of July I was near exhaustion again, emotionally and mentally. I flew my daughter up to Michigan where she was going to spend ten days visiting her cousins and aunt Kitty in Flint. From Detroit I flew back to Dallas where I closed out the construction of the courthouse, and sadly severed my ties with the Grapevine construction company where I had worked for the last two years. It was an amicable separation because the company was being consolidated—both of my supervisors, Mike Crowe and Mike Lewis, were also in the process of terminating their employment.

On the way back to Michigan to pick up Taylor I flew into Indianapolis a few days early and asked the Indianapolis Outlaws pick me up at the airport. I planned to spend some time relaxing with RT, Tool and Leadhead, who had by now become personal friends. I was anxious to see Tool since he had recovered from his accident and looking forward to seeing RT and Leadhead. RT also agreed to let me ride his hotrod stroked Dyna while I was there, for he owned two bikes.

I was so burnt out that RT physically took possession of my cell phone for the next two days and personally screened all my phone calls. If it wasn't the El Presidente, Lee, Caroline or Taylor calling, RT told whoever it was that I was on vacation and suggested they leave a message. After some much-needed peace and quiet I rented a car and drove north out of Indianapolis to Fort Wayne where I spent a wild night running around the town with Leadhead and his crew.

The Fort Wayne Outlaw had a brother who was a member of the Bandidos in Washington, and that connection had been one of the primary reasons we got along well. I also knew Leadhead's girlfriend Anne "Beth" Hombach from when she lived in Tulsa— Beth had a six-year old daughter who was a little younger than Taylor. Eight months later Leadhead showed everyone what he was made of when he rescued Beth's daughter from a house fire by crawling through the flames and smoke to save her life at the last possible moment.

Over the next three years RT, Tool and Leadhead severed their ties to the Outlaws, but didn't escape punishment for what they had done while in the organization. All three were arrested in the spring of 2003 after being indicted with more than fifty other current and former members of the Outlaws in Ohio, Indiana, Kentucky and Oklahoma. After pleading guilty RT, Tool and Leadhead received prison sentences of less than eight years in federal prison.

From Indiana I traveled northeast to Flint where I spent a day with Kitty and her family before driving back to Indianapolis with my daughter, then flying to Tulsa. My thoughts were on Oklahoma during the flight—I needed to get back in time for an IRS auction of a downtown mansion house that was dilapidated and in need of major repair, my brother Dieter was coming to visit for a few days, and I had all sorts of plans for the German biker while he was staying with us.

I won the bid for the old mansion house and was able to take possession the day after Dieter arrived, and immediately put him to work helping me clean out the residence that was going to be my sole construction project for the next three months. As planned it was going to be a massive project for the residence had a total of five-thousand square feet of living space, with six bedrooms, six bathrooms and two kitchens spread out over three floors and basement. I eventually put almost two-hundred thousand dollars of the bank's money into the renovation process, gutting the house to the wooden studs and replacing the electric, plumbing, windows, roof, drywall and HVAC along the way.

Searching For My Identity: The Chronological Evolution
Of A Troubled Adolescent To Outlaw Biker

On July 30th we celebrated Taylor's seventh birthday. Killing two birds with one stone I took Taylor, her mother and Dieter on a whirlwind tour of Branson, Missouri, and spent two days visiting Silver Dollar City. My daughter had already been there so she was quite familiar with the attractions, but for my German friend it was another story—he was like a child in a candy store, and I think he had more fun on the trip than Taylor. It was also interesting to watch Taylor interact with Teresa, for she was now clean, sober, drug free and employed full-time.

My former wife and I had been splitting visitation with Taylor for the majority of the last year, and I wanted to see for myself exactly how she was doing with her sobriety. Having Teresa there also gave me a lot more time to spend with Dieter, while my former wife and Taylor explored the park together by themselves. In spite of the fact that I selfishly ignored Caroline's feelings, I knew I had done the right thing for Taylor, and it turned out to be a great birthday present for her.

While in Branson I learned that a long time Bandido had died and his funeral was going to be held in Arkansas on August 5th. As soon we returned to Tulsa Dieter headed for Kansas to visit a friend while I took off on my bike and headed east to Little Rock to bury Donnie "Deadweight" Nichols. It was a beautiful day, not too hot, and the Pinecrest Memorial Park Cemetery was absolutely a great place to be laid to rest—gentle rolling hills covered with giant shade trees. I watched as Bandidos Earthquake, Beaudreaux,

Sly Willie, DJ, Wiggs, Stubs, Murray and BW carried Deadweight's casket to his grave. After attending the party for him that night I returned to Tulsa on Sunday. The mansion house project was in full swing, and I was going to install the new wood stud framing myself. If the project was going to progress according to its schedule I needed to be there to make it happen.

The following weekend Dieter returned from Kansas and we went to Lake Thunderbird near Norman for a red and gold family picnic put on by the Chandler chapter of the OK Riders. Having borrowed a motorcycle for Dieter to ride just for the trip, he and I soaked up the gorgeous weather for the two hours we were on the road while Caroline and Taylor followed in her pickup truck. As Taylor played with all the other children there I was proud to see that Dieter was being treated like he was part of the red and gold world. When he flew back to Germany the next day I was convinced that his trip had been memorable, but was sad to see him go.

By mid-August the situation with Buddy had come to a head. Everyone knew by now that he had repeatedly lied about everything going on in his life. We even had Oklahoma Outlaws telling us Buddy was selling them meth on a regular basis. When it came time for our weekly meeting I wasn't surprised that he didn't show up. Between the Creek County court docket papers and the mountain of the evidence we had accumulated it was easy for Lee to make a decision, and Buddy was expelled. He was no longer a meth addict riding a motorcycle wearing a Bandido patch, he was now Earl "Buddy" Kirkwood the lying sack of shit that meth had caused him to become. When Joe and Lee went to collect his Bandido property he lied again and told them he had burned it all. We learned months later that the DEA had seized his Bandido colors and his wife's property patch while executing a search warrant on his home in June of 2000.

By the end of August my attention was on attending the mandatory Four Corners Rally in Durango, Colorado, over the Labor Day weekend and simultaneously managing my residential construction project. I needed to be at the Rally or would have to pay the mandatory five-hundred dollar fine, but also needed to maximize the time I spent in Tulsa on the jobsite. I decided to load my bike into Caroline's truck and send her in advance on Thursday to make the ten-hour drive to Albuquerque, New Mexico, where I planned to meet her the next day. On Friday morning bright and early, I caught a Southwest Airlines flight to Albuquerque and met Caroline there before noon. We made the two-hundred mile drive through the mountains in five hours, stopping to visit with the brothers we came across along the way and to admire the fantastic scenery.

The Four Corners Rally produced a significant piece of history. On Saturday afternoon at the Bandidos national campsite we gathered to take a picture of the entire club which hadn't been done since 1970. Many photos were taken that day by many different people, but the nomad chapter eventually settled on one striking photo to be the official one, and mass produced it in the form of a poster which was sold to anyone in the red and gold world. In the photo I can be seen on the left side in one of the first few rows just to the left of Bandido Marshall who was wearing an unusual tan-colored vest.

On the way to Four Corners OK Riders Cub and George "George" Schuppan from the Chandler chapter developed motorcycle trouble and decided to return to Oklahoma City, but had been stopped for a traffic offense by the Oklahoma Highway Patrol in Caddo County. The traffic stop soon turned into a drug search, and George was arrested for possession of a controlled drug and possession of a firearm by a convicted felon. Just as former Bandido Buddy did, OK Rider George lied to my face regarding the circumstances of his arrest, but this time it didn't take as long to learn the truth. We had already heard many rumors that the OK Rider was trafficking meth with former Bandido Buddy, and were also hearing rumors that George was buying and selling meth with Outlaws in Oklahoma City.

Within a few days of the arrest I contacted the Caddo County court clerk's office and ordered copies of George's court docket to discern the truth. As suspected the OK Rider was charged with being in possession of a small amount of meth, but when confronted George was adamant that what was found on him that day wasn't actually methamphetamine. Wanting to give him a chance to prove us wrong we temporarily allowed him to remain an OK Rider, but in hindsight that turned out to be a massive mistake on our part.

At Four Corners we had invited many Bandidos to the Pawhuska Rally in the middle of September. Some of them, like Bandido Fatcat from El Paso, took us up on the offer, and it turned out that he had family living in the Tulsa area. On September 15th, the last night of the party at Pawhuska, we voted in OK Rider Charles "Snake" Rush as the newest member of the chapter. Probationary Bandido Snake became the fifteenth man to wear the Bandido colors in the state of Oklahoma. He was quite surprised because he hadn't asked to be a Bandido—we had just voted him in without asking how he felt—if we waited for Snake to ask it would have never happened.

I was very fortunate to get a bunch of help from the OK Riders in handling all aspects of our campsite and Pawhuska passed by peacefully, but by now I was again running on empty. I was well along on my residential construction project and the end was in sight. Probationary Bandido Hank "CC" Leasure, who was an electrician, volunteered to work as a sub-contractor on the project, and I was thankful the project was running on time and within budget as planned.

On September 21st former Bandido John "Turtle" Fisher was convicted by a federal jury after being indicted earlier in the year for a multitude of drug trafficking crimes. Most of the

Oklahoma Bandidos celebrated the news that he had met his Waterloo, but not me. I still remembered my old friend John Fisher from Michigan, the talented master carpenter I'd known so well. Turtle was sentenced to twenty-seven years in federal prison in early February of 2001.

In late October the construction work on my residential property near downtown Tulsa at 1309 Terrace Drive was finally completed. The project had been exhausting, but I was extremely proud of what I had accomplished. I had even won a zoning dispute brought on by an overzealous, fanatical, next door neighbor who had taken every opportunity she could to cause me trouble.

The newly remodeled home appraised for three-hundred fifty thousand dollars, but I only had about two-hundred twenty-five thousand dollars invested. I had no idea what I was going to do with the residence, but thought it would be easy to sell for three-hundred thousand dollars. That ended up being a serious miscalculation, and over the next six months I did everything I could to sell it with no luck, including drastically lowering the price to two-hundred sixty thousand dollars.

In early November probationary Oklahoma Bandido David "Doc" Mullikin decided to quit the club. He was having major problems complying with requirements that were mandatory for probationary members nationwide. Because Doc had done us no harm we allowed him to leave the club in good standings, which allowed him to socialize with anyone involved in the red and gold world.

In mid-November I flew to Europe again to attend a world meeting in Denmark and the one-year anniversary of the German Bandidos, at which time any member that had been in the club for a year would receive his Germany bottom rocker. Since I'd been present for the actual patch over ceremony of the Ghostriders the year before in Dinslaken, and had visited the Ghostriders for the European national president in the spring of 1998, I wanted to be there when they received their bottom rockers in Aachen. I even brought some of Bandido 74 Jim's wooden puzzle plaques with me to give as gifts to some high-ranking brothers that I considered personal friends.

While I was in Denmark I made time to visit the Bandido that had spent so much of his time taking care of me on my last visit in the spring of 1998. Buller was serving a short prison sentence for driving a car while his license was under suspension. I contacted his wife during the day, and fortunately was able to accompany her that evening to visit. When we arrived at the prison the guard asked me for identification. I was shocked when he took a quick look at my Oklahoma driver's license and let me enter the facility without searching me.

We ended up in a nice private room that had curtains over the windows, and a curtain over the glass in the door that could be closed for privacy. Buller's wife explained to me that the privacy was needed, because it was legal in Denmark to have conjugal visits. Although this wasn't going to be one, she reassured me that this was normal, and that we would probably be undisturbed for the entire visit. I had wondered what she had carried into the prison in a large bag, and now found out that she had brought an entire dinner to eat while we talked. Buller arrived shortly thereafter, and we settled in for a good two-hour visit and wonderful traditional Danish meal. During the visit I was quite surprised to learn the Danish Bandido had his laptop computer in the cell, and could receive and send emails whenever he wanted.

The next afternoon I took a ferry from Elsinore, Denmark, to Helsingborg, Sweden, where I met up with Bandido Clark, who had invited me there while we were both attending the world meeting earlier that week. I only had a few hours to visit, which was just enough time to sit down with him and eat a quick meal. That evening I took the ferry back to Denmark and then caught an overnight ride back to Germany where I planned on spending a day with Nico, the president of the Bandidos Cologne chapter. I planned to attend the one-year anniversary party that night near the Belgium border, but first Nico had promised to give me a tour of downtown Cologne and show me an old church that was supposedly glorious.

I got into Cologne early in the afternoon, and met Nico and his crew on the outside of the city. After a short ride into downtown I was soon standing in the shadow of a church that truly was magnificent. I got a guided tour was told about all of the church's history, and then treated to a great German meal at a downtown restaurant. As soon as dinner was finished Nico drove me to Aachen, which only took about forty-five minutes.

The anniversary party was quite interesting, for it was like old home week. There were lots of Bandidos there from Europe that I knew, as well as El Presidente George, El Vice-Presidente Jeff, and Sargento-de-Armas Martine from the United States. I was also pleased to see Bandido nomad Mick from England there, as he was one of the few that spoke good English. I was surprised to see some members of the Loners motorcycle club from Italy hanging around, who were there as guests of the Bandidos from France. I tried to talk to them but the language barrier was too much to overcome.

At the party I tried very hard to not fall into the same trap as I had the year before. I knew there was going to be another stripper show and I wanted to make sure that I wasn't going to be part of the entertainment. When the dancing girl appeared on the stage I felt sorry for the poor guy who was selected to get up there with her. She had a squeeze bottle of mayonnaise that she squirted down the front of the guy's pants while he had his eyes closed— don't you know that felt good for the rest of the night. The following month I appeared in the *Biker News* magazine again, but this time I was just showing off a wooden puzzle plaque that had been made by Bandido 74 Jim.

Searching For My Identity: The Chronological Evolution
Of A Troubled Adolescent To Outlaw Biker

When I got back to Oklahoma it was time to prepare the annual Christmas cards for the Oklahoma chapter, as well as assemble the United States Christmas card list and make sure that the overseas card lists were received by all United States chapters. For the Oklahoma Christmas card I chose a picture that had been taken at Pawhuska earlier in the year, and although dated was one of the best recent pictures I had access to at the last minute.

I was now working every day for the El Presidente and the national chapter but still was officially a member of the Oklahoma chapter. I had been fired from the national chapter more than any other Bandido in the history of the club, but was still handling a lot of regular time-consuming chores such as coordinating the design of a new worldwide website, producing the monthly United States newsletter, arranging airplane flights, and traveling to promote the club.

In May of 1997 when I became a member of the Bandidos there were less than thirty chapters in the United States and less than fifty chapters worldwide. By the end of December in 2000 there were forty-nine chapters in the United States and ninety-six chapters worldwide. In three and a half years I had helped to double the size of the club. I was very proud of the fact that I was part of the greatest motorcycle club in the world, and what I had contributed to get it to this point.

After more than three years the Bandido chapter in Oklahoma only had seven members, and one of those members was incarcerated. Lee "Lee" McArdle, Joseph "Joe" Kincaid, Hank "CC" Leasure, Steve "Steve" Buitron, Charles "Snake" Rush and me were on the streets—Louis "Bill Wolf" Rackley was getting some much-needed rest and relaxation in the Oklahoma state prison system, and there were almost twenty members of the OK Riders scattered across Oklahoma in the Chandler, Claremore and Comanche chapters.

Christmas was a wonderful time for Caroline, Taylor, and me. Caroline received her PBOL property patch and she gave me a handmade wooden clock that had been made by Bandido 74 Jim that stood almost three-foot tall. Taylor was well-adjusted to life as a seven-year old, growing like a weed, and halfway through the second grade at school. All was well in my world as I made some last-minute plans to go to Canada, where as you already know, my appointment with destiny was waiting.

Chapter 24

Immigration Canada & The Kingpin

January 2001

On Saturday January 6th around 7PM Bandido Tout and I returned to my room after having dinner. We sent a runner to the clubhouse to let everyone know we were leaving town, and sat down for a few minutes to give them time to respond. Since it was only a five-minute ride to the clubhouse we didn't plan to wait long. I checked my email one last time and packed up my clothes.

A brother from the clubhouse called Tout and asked us to wait a few more minutes—he didn't say why, but we assumed it was important. I cracked the door open using the night safety latch as a prop and we waited. It wasn't long before the door came flying open, but it wasn't the Bandidos we expected. It was the Kingston police, the Ontario Provincial Police (OPP) gang squad, and at the back of the pack two agents from Immigration Canada.

The police had first gone to the front desk where the clerk gave them the room numbers of every room the Bandidos had booked. It was standard courtesy in the red and gold world to provide a hotel room for an international guest, and I had been given my room without having to pay—a Canadian Bandido had secured the entire block of rooms using the same credit card for every room. I thought that no one would be able to locate me because I never expected the hotel to give up the room numbers without a warrant. I realized things were much different in Canada when I learned the police had been given a master passkey and opened the door to every room looking for anyone who wasn't at the clubhouse.

It took the cops mere seconds to realize we were Bandidos since Tout and I weren't wearing any disguises and had club logos on our belts and shirts. When asked for our names we told them who we were, for neither one of us had committed a crime and there wasn't anything illegal in the room. At first we didn't notice the immigration agents so Tout and I both thought the police would soon get tired of the game and leave.

When I told them my name was Edward Winterhalder the immigration agents quickly pushed their way to the front. *"You're Connecticut Ed, aren't you, from Oklahoma?"* one inquired. After checking my driver's license to verify my identity I was arrested for violating Canadian immigration law in the corridor and handcuffed. One of the OPP gang squad officers, who wasn't very bright, came running out of the room with Bandido Clark's belt screaming that I was a nomad, like he had made some sort of major find. It was too funny because Clark was twice my size, and it was obvious I could've wrapped Clark's belt around me twice. I denied owning the belt, but the more I denied it the more the OPP officer swore it was mine. I finally figured it wasn't worth arguing with a moron and agreed it was mine. The cops packed the belt in my belongings, and I eventually mailed it back to Clark in Sweden after I returned to the United States.

At the same time I was being arrested in the hall the Kingston police were interrogating Tout inside the room. They rapidly ascertained that the Montreal Bandido was who he said he was, that there was nothing illegal in the room, and that Tout wasn't violating his bond conditions by associating with a Bandido from the United States. One of the Kingston police officers asked me if I owned the laptop computer, and I told them that it belonged to another Bandido who was sharing the room with me so they left it. Tout wasn't allowed to stay in the room, and the last time I saw him that night was in the parking lot as I was loaded into the police car. He was smiling and waved goodbye as I was driven off.

I was transported to a holding facility at Lansdowne forty-five miles from Kingston for my initial booking, which was located less than one-thousand feet across the river from the United States. I could have thrown a rock and hit the American customs office it was so close. I even joked with the agents that I would walk across the river to the United States if they would let me go, and we laughed at the suggestion. One of them later told me that their bosses had requested that I be transferred to Ottawa, the national capital, for a public deportation in front of the media. Immigration Canada was all abuzz claiming I was a big fish and a prize catch, but I had no idea what they were talking about.

Searching For My Identity: The Chronological Evolution
Of A Troubled Adolescent To Outlaw Biker

I've got to admit that the agents assigned to book me were unusually respectful. At one point when the antique digital computer equipment being used to download my photos from the camera to the computer failed, I volunteered to assist them and they allowed me to do so. While waiting in my holding cell another immigration agent asked if there was anything he could get me. I requested the Canadian immigration statutes and he was kind enough to give me the complete manual. He seemed surprised at my request and I'm sure he had no idea of my legal knowledge. At the time I was contemplating waiving my deportation hearing, but by the time I read the entire manual I made the decision to fight. Sometime after midnight I got transferred to a small city jail in a town nearby called Brockville. Once again I was surprised to see how respectful the jail guards were. Being way past my normal bedtime I fell asleep easily in spite of my surroundings.

On Monday January 8th I was transferred to the Ottawa Carleton Detention Center and advised that I had a deportation hearing scheduled for Wednesday, but it was going to be postponed until January 17th. I was placed in the hole for security reasons, and on Tuesday morning January 9th an arraignment hearing was held via telephone. I argued the hearing myself, and over the objections of the Crown attorneys I convinced an immigration adjudicator to grant me bail in the amount of twenty-thousand Canadian dollars. I rapidly calculated the amount of cash I would need to be released at two-thousand dollars, and thought it would be easy to obtain. Imagine my surprise when I found out that in Canada there was no ten percent bond system like there was in the United States. If I was to obtain my release I was going to have to come up with all the money, which was approximately fourteen-thousand US dollars.

I was being held on an administrative charge, not a criminal charge. I hadn't been arrested for committing a crime and wasn't going to be formally charged with any criminal violations. Even if I was found guilty of the administrative charge, incarceration as punishment wasn't an option. The only punishment available was deportation back to the United States which is where I wanted to go. It was ludicrous, but the Immigration Canada attorneys didn't think so. They were serious and proceeding like I had committed murder, and according to the immigration laws I could be held in jail without bail for up to two years pending the deportation hearing. I was extremely lucky to have been granted bail and the first outlaw biker to ever get the opportunity on a deportation matter, more than likely because I had custody of my eight-year old daughter.

I contacted Jean "Charley" Duquaire and convinced him to lend me the money to make the bond. Charley had been selected to be the first Presidente for the Bandidos in Canada. It was imperative that the money came from legal sources and we left an easily recognizable paper trail. The Presidente borrowed the money on his credit card by doing a cash advance at the Bank of

Montreal, converted the money into a bank cashier's check, and then had the twenty-thousand dollar check hand delivered to Immigration Canada in Ottawa. I promised to pay him back as soon as I was released, and did so by sending him a wire transfer from my construction company business line of credit to his account at the bank. After I was released from custody on Wednesday afternoon January 10th the first thing I saw was a newspaper article that shocked me.

Big-Wheel Biker Wins $20G Bail

By John Steinbachs

January 10, 2001

A HIGH-RANKING Bandidos motorcycle gang member is expected to be released on bail today after cooling his wheels in an Ottawa jail.

Edward Winterhalder, 45, appeared before an Ottawa Immigration and Refugee Board adjudicator yesterday for a detention review hearing.

The adjudicator ordered that he be detained but allowed him to be released on a $20,000 bond.

The border-bouncing Bandidos biker was busted after a Kingston patchover Saturday where several local Rock Machine members were inducted into the international club.

The closed event -- attended by an estimated 53 people -- came just one week after the rival Hells Angels patched over dozens of members from smaller Ontario gangs.

The Tulsa biker -- reputed to be one of the most powerful men in the club -- was detained by Citizenship and Immigration Canada on charges that he entered the country illegally.

Winterhalder has been ordered to appear on Jan. 17 for a board inquiry, where an adjudicator will rule if the allegations against him are founded and decide whether or not to issue a removal order.

DIDN'T TELL GUARDS

According to a Citizenship and Immigration report, Winterhalder -- who admitted to being a member of the brazen Bandidos -- told investigators he entered Canada on Jan. 5 through Fort Erie but didn't tell border guards of his gang affiliations.

In 1995, he tried to cross at the same border point but was turned back by immigration officers.

The immigration report also said he has told officials that he has a criminal record, including criminal convictions for concealing stolen property, uttering a forged treasury cheque, possession of a stolen vehicle, carrying a prohibited weapon and carrying a concealed weapon. His last admitted conviction noted in the report was in 1983.

With bikers taking a higher profile in Canada recently, immigration officials have been keeping their eyes peeled for possible spottings at ports, including Pearson International Airport in Toronto.

Officers said the alerts led to the interception of four members of

the Bandidos bike gang arriving here for the opening of the
Kingston chapter.

Police said two members of the group's Denver chapter and one
each from Washington and Amsterdam were turned around at the
airport. A senior member of the Washington chapter did slip into
the country but left on Sunday.

The article noted that I was supposed to be one of the most powerful men in the club, but wasn't. I was beginning to think I'd be railroaded no matter what I did to defend myself. From Ottawa I was driven back to Kingston where I spent a few days at the home of Marc "Garfield" Yakimishan and his family. As a condition of my bail I had been ordered not to leave Canada, to reside at Garfield's home, and to appear at my next hearing. Garfield was scheduled to become the new El Secretario for the Canadian Bandidos, so staying with him for a few days worked out well.

While waiting for my next immigration hearing which was scheduled for January 17th, I went to Toronto one evening with Alain "Alain" Brunette—the Vice-Presidente of the Bandidos in Canada—for a meeting with Pietro "Peter" Barilla from the Loners motorcycle club and to join the new Bandidos chapter for their weekly gathering. The meeting with the Loners took more time than we expected, and by the time we got to the Bandidos clubhouse the meeting was over. To our dismay we discovered the chapter had voted a prospect out of the club for hating the Hells Angels.

Searching For My Identity: The Chronological Evolution
Of A Troubled Adolescent To Outlaw Biker

Eric "Eric the Red" McMillan was a young, tough kid from Oshawa who harbored a deep resentment for some of the bikers who had recently joined the Hells Angels in the Toronto area. Alain and I saw him as one of the brightest stars in the entire chapter, while the rest of the members saw him as too anti-Hells Angels. We left the clubhouse with a bad feeling about the decision and a worse feeling about the chapter, and wondered if some of the members would quit to become Hells Angels in the near future. Alain and I went directly to Oshawa to pick up Eric, and went out to eat breakfast at a local restaurant.

After hearing his side of the story Alain and I decided to reinstate him and transfer the Oshawa outlaw biker to the Kingston chapter where he would be under the direct supervision of the Vice-Presidente. When we called the Toronto chapter and told them what we had done they were pissed. Less than a month later the entire chapter quit the Bandidos—most of them eventually joined the Hells Angels, but some retired from club life and became independent bikers.

One night while I was in Kingston I went out to the Kingston Penitentiary to visit a brother from Montreal. Brett "Lucky" Simmons was serving an eight-year prison sentence for his part in an ill-fated bombing attempt on the Hells Angels in 1995. Lucky had been the only one to survive when the bomb prematurely blew up—the blast killed three other men inside the van with him, which is how he got his club name. All the guard requested before he granted me access for the face-to-face visit was my identification. The time I spent with him was reflected in an email Lucky sent to the Bandidos website not long after:

Name: Lucky

Hometown: Montreal

Sent: 01.52 - 15/1

I would like to send out my respect to BANDIDO ED from Oklahoma for going out of his way to visit a CANADA BROTHER doing time it is always good to have a visit from a bro but it takes a special bro to be in another country and take time out of his trip and visit a bro inside I would like to send all my respect to BANDIDO ED and I will see you soon on the outside also I send my love and respect to all the brothers worldwide

LLR. BANDIDO LUCKY 1%er MONTREAL PROBATE CHAPTER CANADA BFFB

A few months later Lucky sent me a handmade Bandidos belt buckle as a thank you for the visit, but just before his release from prison Lucky had a major change of heart—he quit the Bandidos and joined the Hells Angels.

The highlight of my extended vacation in Canada was a trip to Montreal to first meet with a group of new Montreal Bandidos, and then spend the night with Bandido Tout who I hadn't seen since my arrest. Alain and I traveled by car to Laval, which had been the town where the Hells Angels North charter was located before five of their members had been murdered by their own brothers—the bodies were later dumped in the St. Lawrence River—inside the Hells Angels Sherbrooke clubhouse in 1985. The Montreal Bandidos had rented a room in an upscale hotel there on a high floor with a tremendous view of the surrounding area.

Prior to this meeting it had been decided that Garfield wouldn't make a good El Secretario and that we needed to find another Bandido better qualified for the job. Presidente Charley, Vice-Presidente Alain and I decided that Tout would make an excellent El Secretario. The only problem was he didn't want the job, so we devised a plan to okey-doke him.

We lined up ten men and asked for a volunteer to step forward who wanted to be the next El Secretario. We had previously told nine of them to step backwards three paces when we asked for a volunteer. When Charley asked for a volunteer to step forward, nine men actually stepped back. Tout was left out in front by himself and it looked like he had stepped forward to volunteer. It took him a few seconds to realize what had happened before he said, *"I don't even own a computer."* The Montreal Bandido was now the El Secretario for the Canadian Bandidos.

After the meeting we went to a fancy Italian restaurant in Montreal for dinner. A half-dozen other Montreal Bandidos joined us there and we enjoyed a great meal. I parted ways with the brothers and Alain after dinner and went with Bandido Tout to his home just south of Montreal. I spent two days and nights with Tout and his family and had a blast there.

Searching For My Identity: The Chronological Evolution
Of A Troubled Adolescent To Outlaw Biker

He took me to the local Indian reservation gift shop to make me feel like I was back in Oklahoma, and we talked about going up to his lake house for a few days if I wasn't able to go back to the United States soon. I felt like I had found a long-lost brother and wished I could've stayed there longer. Tout gave me a ride back to the Ontario border the day before my next hearing, and that was the last time I ever saw him.

My immigration deportation hearing was held on Wednesday January 17th. It was surreal for I had originally planned on being in Canada for just a few days and I'd been there almost two weeks. I still wasn't able to return to Oklahoma because the Canadian government wanted me to stay, just so Immigration Canada could deport me. Go figure! Sure made a lot of sense, didn't it?

As soon as I was released from jail, I had hired one of the best criminal defense attorneys in all of Canada, Josh Zambrowsky from Kingston. Josh was well-known for his pro bono work representing people charged with major crimes and had an excellent reputation with the Montreal and Kingston Bandidos. Josh had represented some of them a few years earlier and they thought he was neater than sliced bread.

In addition, Josh was willing to work with me and listen to my opinions since I had some experience with the criminal justice system. As part of our plan to prepare a character defense for the hearing two attorney friends in Oklahoma, Jonathan M. Sutton and

William J. Patterson, each wrote tremendous reference letters on my behalf.

But this wasn't a criminal matter—it was administrative—and we weren't dealing with the criminal justice system, we were dealing with immigration officials who were accustomed to doing things however they wanted with no interference from the justice system. Most of what happened during the hearing was published in a newspaper article the following day.

Bandido's Departure Stalled

Biker Told To Stay In Country Until May

By John Steinbachs

January 18, 2001

Bandido biker Edward Winterhalder is accused of being in the country illegally and Citizenship and Immigration Canada wants him out.

That's why it seemed bizarre yesterday when a lawyer for the government asked for a four-month adjournment during Winterhalder's Immigration and Refugee Board hearing, effectively stranding him on Canadian soil until May.

If he leaves the country and tries to come back, he'll be denied entry by Immigration and forfeit his bail money.

The border-bouncing Bandido -- reputedly one of the highest-ranking men in the organization -- was busted at a Kingston Travelodge after a biker patchover Jan. 7 where several local Rock Machine members were inducted into the international club.

After five days in jail, he was ordered released on $20,000 bail.

Winterhalder, who says he owns a construction company, wants
to go home to take care of his young daughter.

But the adjudicator at the hearing, who admitted his hands were
tied in the matter, ruled for an adjournment and denied
Winterhalder's request that he be allowed to return to Oklahoma
and return for the May hearing.

He ordered Winterhalder to remain on bail and be back in
Ottawa for the May hearing.

Immigration officials say they need more time to put together
their case against him, which includes entering the country
illegally with a criminal record and being a member of the
Bandidos, an alleged criminal organization. Winterhalder
bristled at the suggestion.

"It's certainly not a criminal organization," he said of the
Bandidos after the hearing.

He said he didn't enter the country fraudulently and was waved
through the border stop in Fort Erie before he could identify
himself and describe his criminal record.

At the time I was the secretary of the Oklahoma chapter.
Although I was on another temporary assignment from the United
States national chapter, by no means was I one of the highest-
ranking men in the organization, but everyone in Canada believed
the lie that was being told by the government. To make matters

worse the immigration attorneys had successfully argued that I
needed to stay there for four more months. I was absolutely
amazed at their arrogance and lack of common sense until Josh
explained that this was an attempt to get me to capitulate—they
thought that if I was forced into staying for four more months I
would waive my deportation.

In spite of the fact that it wasn't reported, Josh had argued
that I shouldn't be required to stay in Canada, and that I'd be happy
to return for my next hearing on May 10th. I was extremely
fortunate and finally caught a break when the adjudicator agreed
with Josh. He ordered me to return for the hearing in May but
decreed I could live wherever I wanted in the meantime. The
adjudicator also ruled that if I decided to return to the United States
while waiting for the hearing I should notify Immigration Canada
at the time of my departure. In his own way he had opened a door
and paved the way for me to return home. I could now go back to
my family, the Oklahoma chapter and my construction business.

On January 19th I said goodbye to everyone in Canada that
had helped me and traveled by car from Lansdowne to New York,
then through Watertown to downtown Syracuse. From there I
caught the night train to Cleveland, and from Cleveland I flew back
to Tulsa on a Southwest Airlines flight the next morning.
Oklahoma was a sight to behold—it had never looked so good, and
it was great to finally be back home with my family.

Glossary

Patch

The club colors of a motorcycle club. A patch can be the entire vest with the club colors sewed on or can just refer to the actual club colors by themselves.

Patchover

A patchover is the actual assimilation of a smaller motorcycle club into a larger motorcycle club.

Hangaround Club

A hangaround club is typically an existing motorcycle club that wants to join a larger motorcycle club, and the first stage of the process is for the smaller club to hangaround with the larger club. Being accepted as a hangaround club puts everyone in the biker world on notice—in motorcycle clubs and the rest of the biker world—the smaller club wants to be affiliated with or assimilated by the larger club, and the larger club is considering the change. After a minimum of a year the Bandidos vote to ascertain whether all members of the smaller club are worthy to wear the patch. If the vote is affirmative then the bikers in the smaller club become probationary members.

El Presidente

The United States national president and international president of the Bandidos motorcycle club, is the boss of all members in the Bandidos worldwide, and his corporate equivalent would be the chairman of the board. The El Presidente is the only Bandido that wears an El Presidente bottom rocker on the back of his club colors.

El Vice Presidente

The United States national vice-president of the Bandidos motorcycle club, is the underboss of all members in the Bandidos worldwide, and his corporate equivalent would be the CEO. The El Vice-Presidente is the only Bandido that wears an El Vice-Presidente bottom rocker on the back of his club colors.

Presidente

The Presidente is the boss of all members in the Bandidos in a particular world region, continent, or country, and his corporate equivalent would be the president. The area or country the Presidente is in charge of is signified by the country or area rocker he wears on his side under his arm or by a small ribbon on his chest.

Vice Presidente

The Vice-Presidente is the underboss of all members in the Bandidos in a particular world region, continent, or country, and his corporate equivalent would be the vice-president. The area or country the Vice-Presidente is in charge of is signified by the country or area rocker he wears on his side under his arm or by a small ribbon on his chest.

Sargento-de-Armas

An enforcer in the Bandidos motorcycle club, in charge of enforcing the club's rules and decisions internally and externally. The area or country the Sargento-de-Armas is in charge of is signified by the country or area rocker he wears on his side under his arm or by a small ribbon on his chest.

El Secretario

The Bandido in charge of all other Secretarios in a particular area or country for the Bandidos motorcycle club, and his corporate equivalent would be the CFO. The area or country the El Secretario is in charge of is signified by the country or area rocker he wears on his side under his arm or by a small ribbon on his chest. The El Secretario assigns job assignments for Secretarios and is typically the keeper of the national club treasury.

Secretario

A secretary or treasurer for the Bandidos Motorcycle Club. The area or country the Secretario is in charge of is signified by the country or area rocker he wears on his side under his arm or by a small ribbon on his chest. His corporate equivalent would be the secretary or treasurer.

Searching For My Identity: The Chronological Evolution
Of A Troubled Adolescent To Outlaw Biker

Probationary

When a potential member has previous motorcycle club experience he typically will become a probationary for a minimum of one year while he's retrained in the ways of the Bandidos motorcycle club before becoming a full patch member of the Bandidos. A probationary member wears a bottom rocker that says probationary.

Prospect

When a potential member has no previous motorcycle club experience he typically will become a prospect for a minimum of six months while he undergoes an intensive training period—similar to joining a college fraternity—before becoming a full patch member of the Bandidos. A prospect wears only a top rocker that says prospect.

Hangaround

A potential member will typically hangaround with the Bandidos motorcycle club for a year—or in some cases many years—before becoming a prospect. A hangaround sometimes wears only a ribbon on the front of his vest that says hangaround, but not always.

Appendix A

Hangaround & Prospect Information

The following document has been used over the years by various 1%er outlaw motorcycle clubs as an orientation document to inform the hangaround or prospect of what is in store for them if they choose to join a traditional 1%er outlaw motorcycle club that wears a three-piece patch—a three-piece patch consists of a top rocker, bottom rocker and center piece on their back.

INTRODUCTION

This information has been put together to give you a better understanding of the new world that you are entering and a better understanding of what is expected of you in your new role. Once you understand the scope of the task you are undertaking, you should examine your feelings and question your motives for wanting to become a member of a motorcycle brotherhood. There are many riding clubs that require only casual participation from its members. Others require a total commitment to the MC lifestyle. Your degree of interest will direct you towards an organization that you will fit into.

Be certain that you are both willing and able to commit yourself to the level that will be required. Be certain that your family understands the demands that the club will make of your time, and that those demands will continue to an even greater extent once you become a patch holder. If after reading this packet you should have any reservations about being able to meet any of the requirements, it would be better not to consider moving forward at this time. Instead, either continue your present level of association with the club until you feel that you are ready and are confident of your success or find a different organization that better suits your needs. Such a decision would be respected and would be to your credit.

CLUB

The intent of this section is to give you an overview of the structure and philosophy of the traditional motorcycle club (MC). This does not necessarily express the feelings or priorities of any particular club, as all motorcycle clubs differ on some points. Regardless of the basic philosophy of your club, it is important that you understand the perspectives of other clubs that you may be associating with from time to time. If your lifestyle is influenced by motorcycles, then you are part of the motorcycle community. Of all the types of organizations found within that community, the traditional motorcycle club stands apart and ranks highest in stature.

RESPECT

A serious club commands respect for one or both of two reasons. Those who are correctly informed recognize the deep level of personal commitment and self-discipline that a man has to

318

demonstrate and sustain in order to wear a patch. They understand that it is akin to a religion or vocation to that man. They realize that a club's colors are closely guarded and the membership process is long and difficult. Other factors notwithstanding, they respect patch holders for what they have accomplished by being able to earn and keep the patch they wear. This is respect born out of recognition of dedication and accomplishment.

Those who are less informed see only the surface. They see the vigilance of mutual support. They see the potential danger of invoking a response from a well-organized unit that travels in numbers and is always prepared for confrontation. They know that no one can provoke one club member without being answerable to the whole club, and that such an answer is a point of honor that must come, to the last man. The type of respect that this generates is one born out of fear. We strive for respect for reason #1, not reason #2! This is especially true as it pertains to those persons outside of the motorcycle community. This segment of society is by far the larger, and therefore represents a larger market for any fundraising activities that the club might undertake.

It stands to reason that cultivating a relationship with these people is important, and to be perceived by them as biker scum would not be advantageous to the club. We therefore will conduct ourselves as upstanding citizens in every way—good neighbors so to speak. The goal is to be admired and respected by the general public rather than feared. The serious club, and all of its members and prospects, will always conduct themselves publicly in a highly professional manner. They will not go out of their way to cause trouble or to present themselves as an intimidating force without purpose or provocation.

CLUB COLORS

The general public does not draw a distinction between different club colors. In many cases, they simply can't tell the difference— we're all biker scum to them. If one club causes a problem that touches the public sector, the offending club's identity is either confused or ignored and the heat comes down on all clubs. The clubs tend to police themselves to avoid such incidents.

OFFICERS

Within a club, officers are usually elected to the positions of president, vice-president, secretary, treasurer, and sergeant-at-arms. Other less traditional posts are road captain and enforcer.

PROCESS

In most cases, the patch holder was a hangaround with the club for about a year. Before that he was a long-standing acquaintance and his attitude and overall conduct were well known. He then prospected for the club for one to two years before he got his patch. Of all things in this man's life, his loyalty and commitment to the well-being of the club comes first above all else. There is never any doubt which comes first. Though most things in life can let him down, he knows that his club and his brothers will always be there because he is always committed to being there himself. To be sure that this ideal and attitude continues on with any new members, he participates in teaching, conditioning, and even testing the club's prospects.

The term prospect comes from the phrase prospective member. Before he allows another man to wear his colors, he is sure that the prospect is as dedicated as he is! A patch holder has the attitude that there are only two types of people, those who are brothers and those who are not. For this reason he will not discuss any club business whether it's about membership numbers, club goings on, or any member's personal information with anyone outside of the club. He will keep his voice down when discussing club business and he will be aware of anyone coming within listening distance. He understands that he is a patch holder 24 hours a day whether or not he is wearing his colors. Everything he says or does in public can affect the club or the brothers. He also understands that if he gets out of line, he is subject to be counseled by his brothers for his own good and for that of the club.

Wearing a patch is more than getting together for good times. It also means getting together for the other times, too. It constitutes a lot of work. It's committing yourself to a lifestyle in which you do not look for how your brothers can help you, but for ways that you can be of help to your brothers. You always look to give rather than to receive. All of this may seem very idealistic, and in some cases it's just that. But it is an ideal that all clubs profess and are always striving for in principal and practice. You should be aware of the golden rule of conduct while traveling in club circles—if you give respect, you'll get respect; if you act like an asshole, you'll be treated like one.

PARTICIPATION

It is important that you understand that it is the patch holders that run the club, not the officers. This may seem a moot point to some, but it can't be overstressed. This is not to say that the officers don't deserve respect from the other patch holders. These members have shown leadership qualities and have probably been in the club for quite some time. They are in office to carry out the wishes of the membership in a timely and efficient manner, as it is not always possible to get the members together to make decisions or take action.

Officers are elected to act as spokesmen for the club and perform various responsible tasks, but they don't run the club. When they speak or act on club matters, it is in a manner that they believe that the members of the club would agree upon, if a quick vote were taken. If an officer doesn't understand the membership's feelings about various matters, then he is out of touch with his brothers and should step down. This is a critical point because the strongest and most representative form of rule is one in which the power comes from the bottom up. If things were the other way around and the leaders or officers continually dictated down the chain of command, a sense of apathy and noninvolvement would eventually set in.

If this were to happen, the individual patch holder would have no intuitive sense of his club's direction and would hesitate when he feels that he should act in the best interest of the club. Having little or no say in what is going on destroys a man's motivation to get involved or voice his own opinion. It would also drain his feelings of unity with his club brothers. Without such unity, a brotherhood cannot exist. Remember that the strength of a brotherhood rests with the membership at the bottom of the chain of command and is passed up. This is why aggressive participation is such a prized quality that is expected from the patch holder and is looked for in the prospect.

LEVELS OF COMMITMENT

When a man earns his patch, it does not mean that he has reached the ultimate goal and from that point he can kick back and coast. Moving from hangaround to prospect to patch holder is not climbing from the bottom to the top, but rather more like climbing a constantly ascending slope, and in time becoming a stronger and more committed brother. A man's prospecting rocker and later his patch are merely presented in recognition of what he has demonstrated along the way. In this fashion, the more senior the patch holder is in the club and the more he experiences, the more of a brother he should be to all.

PURPOSE OF PROSPECTING

Prospecting is not an initiation as you would find in a fraternity. It is instead a period of training that is sustained until the prospect, in every sense, conducts himself as a patch holder. It's a time in which the man's attitude is conditioned so that he displays a sense of responsibility and respect toward the patch holders of the club, without which he will not develop a sense of brotherhood. He is educated in basic MC protocol and etiquette.

He is given time to develop the habits that are basic to good security and good communications: to get the man into the habit of participating, to give his family time to adjust to the demands of the club, to experience and learn an essential degree of humility, and to become accustomed to trusting the judgment, at times blindly, of those patch holders who will someday be his brothers. To break the man of habits that are self-centered and self-serving. The list could go on but the point here is to demonstrate that prospecting has definite objectives and that a prospect will go nowhere in the club if he is not aware of this and does not apply himself to those ends. It's not possible to make a check list of what is expected from a prospect in all cases. There isn't any formula for success, but the key is ATTITUDE. Everything else can be learned in time, but a man's attitude comes from the heart.

The testing of a prospect may come in many ways. It may be planned or spontaneous. In any event, when a prospect is given a task, the patch holder is going to be looking for the man's attitude and the spirit in which he carries out the task. The prospect should be alert and always attentive in looking for more to do. If he is ever in doubt of his priorities or he can't find something to do, he should ask.

The patch holders know which of the prospects hustle, and those are the prospects that are spoken of with the greatest pride and respect. It is also the way by which confidence and trust are developed. These are the seeds of brotherhood. Remember that you will be prospecting for the whole club and not just one individual or individual chapter. The patch holders of one chapter are always held accountable for the actions of a patch holder of another chapter. It is therefore only right that the patch holders of all chapters have a hand in developing the prospects on their way to becoming a full patch holder.

SOME DO'S AND DON'TS

As a prospect, strive to conduct yourself as a responsible patch holder at all times. Always display a positive attitude. Participate as much as you think is acceptable; then participate more. If you see a patch holder of your club that you have not met, take the initiative to introduce yourself. Always introduce yourself as 'prospect (your name)'. At all gatherings, make it a point to circulate when you have the time to do so and greet every patch holder who is there. Anticipate the brothers' needs and offer to supply them. Don't wait to be told what to do and don't get overly friendly with someone that is not a regular acquaintance of the club.

If someone outside the club has questions, refer him to a patch holder. Never give out a patch holder's name, phone number, address, or any personal information to anyone outside the club. Never give out any information about the club itself to outsiders. This includes, but is not limited to, where the club is based, how many members are in the club, etc. Always be security minded, look around and see what's going on around you in public places and report anything that seems suspicious. While in public places, always conduct yourself with your association with the club in mind. Remember that what you do people will remember, good or bad.

Never let a patch holder walk off alone in an unsecured area. If he is going out to his car, his bike, or even just out to get some fresh air, go with him. Watch his back at all times. If you are at an open function and pick up on some negative attitudes, especially if from another club, quietly alert a patch holder immediately. Keep your ears and eyes open and feed any information that you may pick up on to a patch holder, especially information regarding another club. Remember that you are a prospect 24 hours a day. Your association doesn't go on and off with your colors.

Searching For My Identity: The Chronological Evolution
Of A Troubled Adolescent To Outlaw Biker

Remember that you are every patch holder's prospect, not just your sponsor's or just your chapter's. Never wear your colors out of your area without your sponsor's approval and never out of state unless you are with a patch holder. If two or more patch holders are having a private conversation, don't approach them within earshot, especially if they are talking with a patch holder of another club. If you need to interrupt, put yourself in a place of visibility and wait to be acknowledged. If it is important that you interrupt, ask another patch holder to break in for you.

Never use the term outlaw club when speaking to a member of another club. Never lie to a member of another club. If you are in a situation where you are asked about the club or its membership, it is acceptable to say *"That seems like club business and I really can't talk about it."* If this doesn't put the subject to rest, offer to put him in touch with a patch holder for him to speak with. Always show respect to a patch holder of another club. Even though he's with another club, he's earned his patch, you haven't.

Always carry a pen and a paper, a watch, and a calendar. Frequently ask the patch holders how you are doing and if there's anything you should be doing differently. Never ask when you may be getting your patch. Never call a patch holder brother—he's not your brother. Never call a patch holder of another club brother— he's not your brother either. Remember, your patch is earned, it's not given to you.

Never bring a personal friend or a stranger into the presence of patch holders without asking permission to do so first. At an open function, never turn your back to a patch holder of another club. This is not so much for safety reasons, but as a show of respect. Always show respect and courtesy to patch holders of other clubs. Don't come across like you want to be best friends. Be professional in such encounters—keep it short, then move on. Keep away from women associating with other clubs.

Never be quick to walk up to a patch holder of another club in a public setting, even if you know him well and the clubs are on friendly terms. If you want to greet him, walk up slowly and wait for him to indicate that he wants such a public display to take place. He may be on some club business and may not want to give the general public the impression that the clubs are on such friendly terms. If he looks like he's going to ignore you, accept it and keep your distance. The best approach is always to wait for them to come to you, and to let everyone else see that.

Learn what different parts of our patch represent and what the different color combination of yours and other clubs represent. As you can see there's a lot to think about. This decision is probably one of the biggest you'll ever make. Be absolutely sure this is for you, and GO FOR IT!

Appendix B

Bandidos Motorcycle Club By-laws

June 2002

1: Requirements for a chapter:

Five (5) member minimum – One (1) "Charter Member".

Charter Member = 10 years.

Keep pictures and information on all members.

Hold weekly meetings.

$25.00 per month per member to national treasury by the 1st of each month.

Probationary chapters (new) will pay a one-time donation of $1,000.00 to national treasury.

Probationary chapter member's bikes and titles will be pledged to national chapter for the first year.

2: Patches:

Only a top and bottom rocker, Fat Mexican, 1% diamond and MC patch should be on the back of your cut-off. It should be visible from 150 feet.

A 1%er diamond will be worn over the heart.

Anything else is up to the individual.

Year patches & buckles are not to be given early.

National can grant a "Lifer" patch or membership on a person to person basis.

One property patch per member. If she rides her own bike it is NOT to be worn while riding with or around patch holders or prospects. It shouldn't be worn in public without her old man in view. There is no limit on property belts.

3: Do's:

Labor Day and Memorial Day are MANDATORY RUNS.

A chapter may leave one (1) member behind from a mandatory run. A member on medical leave or a Life Member is that member. This is for security reasons; that person should have access to a phone as much as possible.

When you are traveling, you should attend your host chapter's meetings.

You must abide by those chapters' by-laws and policies.

4: Don'ts:

Things that will cost you your patch:

You don't lie.

You don't steal.

This includes ol' ladies as well.

Needle use will not be tolerated.

Neither will smoking of any chemicals - coke, speed or Mandrax - if it didn't grow don't smoke it!

5: Motorcycles:

Each member will OWN at least one (1) Harley-Davidson or

facsimile of at least 750cc.

No more than 30 days a year down time.

After 30 days that member's chapter will pay national $500.00.

Have a good reason? Ask for more time.

Road Captains should inspect all bikes regularly.

If you are visiting another area, chapter, state or country and you borrow another brother's property (bike, tools, money, etc.), you are responsible for the return of that property. It will be returned in as good or better condition than when you borrowed it.

6: Membership:

Hangaround period to be determined by chapter President.

Harley-Davidson Motorcycle or facsimile capable of meeting the demands of pledge period.

Members must be at least 21 years of age.

Sponsor may be individual (preferably charter member) or may be sponsored by entire chapter.

Sponsor—do not turn your Pledge loose without help. If you think enough of him to sponsor him into this club, it's up to you to teach him the right way, the BANDIDO WAY. If you're not ready to sacrifice your time and share your knowledge, don't do it. The simple things – Who's the neatest MFer in the world? Or don't wear your patch in a vehicle. Trivial things that will get a prospective BROTHER run off.

Pay $275.00 to national treasury.

Pledge bike and title.

Be voted in as pledge by chapter (100% vote).

Receive your patch or rocker.

DO YOUR TIME.

Prospect: 6 months MINIMUM.

Probationary: 1 year MINIMUM.

This man is pledged to the whole BANDIDO NATION, not just one chapter or area, city or state. He will attend every meeting, party, bike event or gathering of any kind in his area where Bandido patch holders will be present.

He will not miss any national or regional runs, especially funerals.

This club is about sacrifice. Get used to it! His motorcycle should be in up and running condition his whole pledge period, ready to go anywhere. In other words, NO DOWN TIME.

Pledge is not eligible for vote if there are any outstanding debts, chapter, national or private (inside club). He should start into this club on a level playing field.

After the mandatory time period has passed, and the sponsor feels the pledge is ready, a meeting should be called. All surrounding chapter secretaries should also be notified in advance.

The pledge should be voted in by a 100% chapter vote. Club members outside the chapter should have a chance to voice their opinions. The pledge's sponsor should base his decision on these things, for he is the one who will have to fade it if things go foul.

It is a lifelong commitment, DON'T RUSH IT.

Charter member is 10 years of unbroken service.

National may grant leave of absence – this is not automatic.

Two (2) year members are eligible for transfer, only if both presidents involved have agreed and a $50.00 fee is paid to national treasury.

Any brother who commits suicide WILL NOT be allowed to have a BANDIDO funeral.

Other national fees:

New Patch Fee	$275.00
Transfers	$50.00
New Charter	$1,000.00
30 Day Downtime Rule	$500.00

Appendix C

El Secretario Projects & Job Assignments

March 2001

01. Money

02. Commissary program & inmate affairs

03. USA website

04. USA website – graveyard

05. USA website – history of the club

06. T-shirts

07. All other merchandise (except t-shirts)

08. Life insurance

09. Support clubs – members list & email list & phone list &
club list/cities

10. Patches & stickers

11. Newsletter

12. Travel arrangements for the national chapter

13. World email list

14. USA secretary list

15. USA phone list

16. Time in club – members & chapters – actual date of entry into
club

17. Legal issues & oversight of all criminal cases

18. Public relations issues

19. Club tattoos – uniform rules & regulations worldwide

20. Dress shirts - uniform rules & regulations worldwide

21. PBOL guidelines – merchandise & patch

22. List of deceased brothers – each chapter – grave sites for same

23. Business – incorporation & trademark administration

24. Funeral guidelines – one guy from every chapter (however you can get him there) for any funeral; two guys from each chapter within 500 miles on bikes; every chapter sends flowers or money for each funeral.

Appendix D

CT Ed's Projects & Job Assignments

For National Chapter

March 2003

01. Keeper of the USA Phone List & USA email list & USA 15-year member list & USA support club chapter/member list

02. Keep tabs on the Fat Mexican trademark

03. Monitor most internal federal criminal cases for Bandidos members & some state criminal cases

04. Provide occasional internal travel arrangements worldwide

05. Provide occasional national public relations services

06. Provide suggestions for forms of communication between the national chapter and the national chapter members

07. Provide suggestions for forms of communication between national chapter & all United States chapters

08. Provide suggestions for design changes to the USA website

09. Provide suggestions for legally structuring the club's financial affairs

10. Provide emergency backup for publishing the USA newsletter

Appendix E

Bandidos Support Club Chapters

August 2003

Name of Club/State	City	Members
ALABAMA		
Pistoleros	Auburn	5
Pistoleros	Birmingham	6
CMA	Birmingham	2
Soldiers of the Cross	Birmingham	3
Wayward Wind	Birmingham	5
Pistoleros	Dothan	2
Pistoleros	Huntsville	
Pistoleros	Jasper	5
Iron Hawgs	Jasper	5
Pistoleros	Mobile	4
Soldiers of the Cross	Mobile	12
CMA	Mobile	2
Alabama Riders	Montgomery	5
Pistoleros	Montgomery	5
ARKANSAS		
Ozark Riders	Eureka Springs	7
Ozark Riders	Rogers	6
COLORADO		
Peligrosos	Denver	16
No Names	Grand Junction	5

Los Bravos	Denver	11
John's Guys	Pueblo	12

LOUISIANA

West Bank	Baton Rouge West	5
Louisiana Riders	Baton Rouge	6
Louisiana Riders	Bogalusa	4
West Bank	Point Coupee	7
Hole in the Wall	Lafayette	5
Road Shakers	Acadiana	7
Rat Pack	Lake Charles	12
Grey Ghosts	Minden	3
Grey Ghosts	Natchitoches	4
Louisiana Riders	New Orleans	6
Grey Ghosts	Shreveport	14

MISSISSIPPI

Asgards	Biloxi	6
Asgards	Gulfport	6
Pistoleros	Hattiesburg	5
CMA	Jackson	10
Pistoleros	Jackson	2
Asgards	Kiln	6
Asgards	Pascagoula	6
Mississippi Riders	Tupelo	5

MISSOURI

Hermanos	Jamesland	11

Searching For My Identity: The Chronological Evolution Of A Troubled Adolescent To Outlaw Biker

MONTANA

Hermanos	Kallispell	5
Hermanos	Missoula	4
Amigos	Ronan	1

NEW MEXICO

Native Thunder	Acoma	3
German MC	Alamogordo	9
Black Berets	Albuquerque	9
Native Thunder	Albuquerque	4
Bandoleros	Albuquerque	4
Pacoteros	Artesia	4
Native Thunder	Dine Nation	2
US Vets	Hobbs	10
Regulaters	Roswell	7
Bandoleros	Santa Fe	6
Bandoleros	Truth/Consequences	3
US Vets	Tucumcari	7
Native Thunder	Zuni	3

OKLAHOMA

OK Riders	Tulsa	9
OK Riders	Shawnee	8
OK Riders	Comanche	9
CMA	OKC	2

SOUTH DAKOTA

Hermanos	Sioux River	5

Ghost Dance	Pine Ridge	6

TEXAS

Iron Riders	Amarillo	28
Companeros	Austin	10
Iron Riders	Borger	29
Southern Pride	Beaumont	3
Border Brothers	Brownsville	20
Rebeldes	Corpus Christi	10
Macheteros	El Paso	4
Del Fuego	El Paso	5
Coyoteros	El Paso	6
Amigos	Estralla Sola	3
Rebel Riders	Fort Worth	14
Aces & Eights	Fredericksburg	12
Amigos	Galveston County	8
Macheteros	Hill Country	5
Los Dorados	Hill Country	5
Soldiers of Jesus	Houston	10
Amigos	Houston State	5
Amigos	Houston East	5
Amigos	Houston North	8
Amigos	Houston West	4
Southern Raiders	Houston West	5
Los Malos	Jefferson County	
Renegades	Laredo	4

Aces & Eights	Levelland	37
Desperados	Longview	8
Los Cabboleros	Killeen	5
Amigos	Montgomery County	13
Los Riders	Plainview	39
Macheteros	San Antonio NW	14
Southsiders	San Antonio SW	12
Westsiders	San Antonio	9
Campesinos	San Antonio	9
Malditos (Bad Lance)	San Antonio SW	9
Texas Wheels	Waco	80
Equestrians	Waco	12

WASHINGTON

Warriors	Everett	7
Destralos	King County	5
Amigos	King County	8
Hermanos	King County	4
Hombres	La Costa	4
Hombres	Olympia	4
Amigos	Pierce County	10
Hombres	Seattle	6
Amigos	Snohomish County	9
Hombres	Snow Valley	4
Hombres	Tacoma	6
Hermanos	Tacoma	5

Destralos	Thurston County	5
Hombres	Wenatchee	4
Canyon Riders	Whatcom County	11
Unforgiven	Yakima	6
WYOMING		
Hermanos	Gillette	5
47 Support Clubs	**Total Members**	929

Appendix F

Credit For Newspaper Articles

Page 260   Reprinted by permission. Copyright © Kingston Whig-Standard, Kingston, Ontario. All rights reserved.

Page 280   Reprinted by permission. Copyright © The Missoulian, Missoula, Montana. All rights reserved.

Page 303   Reprinted by permission. Copyright © Ottawa Sun, Ottawa, Ontario. All rights reserved.

Page 310   Reprinted by permission. Copyright © Ottawa Sun, Ottawa, Ontario. All rights reserved.

ABOUT THE AUTHOR

Edward Winterhalder is an American television producer who has created programs about motorcycle clubs and the outlaw biker lifestyle for networks and broadcasters worldwide; an author who has written fifteen books about motorcycle clubs and outlaw biker culture that are published in the Dutch, English, French, German, Japanese and Spanish languages; a singer, songwriter, musician and record producer; a screenwriter; and former outlaw biker.

Winterhalder has produced documentaries, episodes and segments for television shows such as *Living On The Edge*, *Gangland*, *Outlaw Bikers*, *Gang World*, *Iron Horses*, *Marked*, *One Percenters*, *Biker Chicz* and *Recon Commando: Vietnam*; and is the creator and executive producer of the *Quebec Biker War*, *Steel Horse Cowboys*, *Real American Bikers* and *Biker Chicz* TV series.

A prominent member of the Bandidos motorcycle club from 1997 to 2003 and associate from 1979 to 1996, he was instrumental in expanding the organization worldwide and was assigned to coordinate the assimilation of the Rock Machine into the Bandidos during the Quebec Biker War—a conflict that cost more than one-hundred and sixty people their lives.

Associated with motorcycle clubs and outlaw bikers for almost thirty years, Winterhalder has been seen on Fox News (O'Reilly Factor with Bill O'Reilly & America's Newsroom), CNN, Bravo, Al Jazeera, BBC, ABC Nightline, MSNBC News Nation, Good Morning America, History Channel, Global, National Geographic, History Television, AB Groupe, and CBC.

www.ingramcontent.com/pod-product-compliance
Lightning Source LLC
Chambersburg PA
CBHW062113020426
42335CB00013B/951